The Intentional Makerspace: Operations

Dale Grover and Tom Root

Copyright © 2020 by Makerworx, LLC.

All rights reserved. Printed in the United States of America. Except as permitted under the United States Copyright Act of 1976, no part of this publication may be reproduced or distributed in any form or by any means, or stored in a database or retrieval system, without the prior written permission of the publisher.

1st printing, September 2020. Document version 1.11.0

ISBN 978-1-953439-00-0

Library of Congress Control Number: 2020915866

Cover design by Beth Johnson, http://bethjohnsonorigami.com.

The pewter coin on the cover was designed and cast at Maker Works by Marty Hedler using Inkscape, a mold made from laser-engraved 1/8" Baltic Birch, R98 pewter, and enamel paint.

Published by Makerworx, LLC, Ann Arbor, Michigan.

Maker Works is a registered trademark of Makerworx, LLC. All other trademarks and copyrights are the property of their respective owners.

Disclaimer

First, while it is our hope that using the principles in this book will help you create a safer makerspace, we do not assume responsibility for what happens in your makerspace. You alone are responsible for evaluating and, if you decide, implementing the information we present, and should do so thoughtfully, with the help of experts as appropriate, and with the safety of your staff and members foremost in mind.

Second, there are many legal issues that businesses in general, and makerspaces specifically, must attend to. Everything from zoning, property taxes, trademarks, rights of renters, waivers, limitations around non-profits, labor laws, etc. We're not lawyers, and every country, state, and locality will have their own set of laws, regulations, etc. So consult with experts. We do not accept liability for any legal issues that come up.

Fourth, there is no third item.

Fifth, while we do mention various third-party software or other products and services, it is in the context of what we have used or has worked (or perhaps not) for us. It may or may not be good for your situation. In addition, physical and software offerings can change radically over time, so the current offerings under that name may be very different in feature or policy from when we have used it.

Sixth and lastly[1], our discussion of such broad topics as Lean, the Toyota Production System, open-book management, and the like, are limited by our format and context. We hope the brief details we share, filtered (some would say distorted?) by our fixation on operating a makerspace, will inspire you to learn more—we are just scratching the surface of rich and useful tools.

---

[1] As Dogberry would say.

Contents

1 Introduction 11
   1.1 What's a Makerspace? 14
   1.2 A Meta Toolbox 15
      1.2.1 "Freedom From" vs "Freedom To" 15
      1.2.2 Don't Take Our Word For It 16
      1.2.3 Training Compact 16
      1.2.4 Baking vs. Cooking 17
      1.2.5 Make It Easy To Do The Right Thing, And Hard To Do The Wrong Thing . . . 17
      1.2.6 Learning vs. Systems 18
      1.2.7 The Tragedy of the Commons 19
      1.2.8 Be Intentional and Consistent 20
      1.2.9 Connection with Zingerman's Community of Businesses 20
      1.2.10 The 80/20 Rule 20
      1.2.11 Fix What Bugs You—15-Minute Improvements 21
      1.2.12 Help, I'm Trapped in a Local Minima . . 22
      1.2.13 Your Enemy 23
   1.3 Liked Best, Next Time 23

2 Using Recipes in your Makerspace: SOPs — 25
- 2.1 Why Use SOPs? — 26
- 2.2 Objections to SOPs — 27
- 2.3 What Does an SOP Look Like? — 29
- 2.4 Forms "Standard Work" Can Take — 31
- 2.5 How to Write an SOP — 37
- 2.6 An Exercise in SOP Writing — 40
- 2.7 Your SOP Guidelines — 42
- 2.8 Checklists Augmenting SOPs: The War Against Hubris — 42
  - 2.8.1 Mnemonic Devices — 43
  - 2.8.2 Checklists for Project Planning — 44
- 2.9 Improving SOPs — 44
- 2.10 How Many SOPs Does Maker Works Have? — 45
- 2.11 Summary — 45
- 2.12 Resources — 46

3 Organizing Workspaces Using 5S — 47
- 3.1 Why 5S? — 50
- 3.2 The 5 S's (in English) — 51
- 3.3 Maker Works' 5S SOP and Standards — 52
  - 3.3.1 Overview — 52
  - 3.3.2 Deadly Wastes and 5S — 52
  - 3.3.3 Resources for 5S-ing — 55
  - 3.3.4 5S SOP — 55
- 3.4 Tool Address SOP — 61
  - 3.4.1 Overview — 61

		3.4.2 Addresses 61

- 3.5 Home Tag SOP 64
  - 3.5.1 Creating Part Outlines 66
  - 3.5.2 Mounting Home Tags 66
- 3.6 Process Tool SOP 70
  - 3.6.1 Marking Tools SOP 70
- 3.7 Area Labeling SOP 74

4 An SOP for Business: The Business Perspective Chart 77
- 4.1 Flying to San Francisco Using the Business Perspective Chart 78

5 Mission: The North Star 81
- 5.1 Characteristics of a Useful Mission 82
- 5.2 Creating a Mission Statement 85
- 5.3 How to Use the Mission 86

6 Measuring Success: The Bottom Line(s) 87
- 6.1 For-Profit or Nonprofit, You're Still a Business 88

7 Vision: A Key Document for Leadership 91
- 7.1 Why is Vision Important? 93
- 7.2 What Should You Create a Vision For? 94
- 7.3 What is in a Vision? 95
- 7.4 SOP for Writing a Vision (Solo) 96
- 7.5 SOP for Writing a Vision (Group) 99
- 7.6 What to Do With Your Vision 102
- 7.7 Creating an Updated Vision 102
- 7.8 Example 102

8 Values/Guiding Principles   105

8.1 Values of the Maker Movement 105
8.2 Discovering Your Guiding Principles 107
8.3 Writing the Guiding Principles 107
8.4 Integrating Values 107

9 Instruction and Learning   109

9.1 How to Instruct 109
9.1.1 TWI and How to Instruct 109
9.1.2 Should You Be Instructing in the First Place? 109
9.1.3 Back to How to Instruct 110
9.1.4 The 5-Step Plan 111
9.1.5 Summary of HTI 116
9.2 The 4 Levels of Competency 117
9.3 4 Levels of Learning 117
9.4 The Training Compact 118
9.5 "If the Worker Hasn't Learned, the Instructor Hasn't Taught"—The Out 120

10 Other Systems   123

10.1 43 Folders—Expensive, But Worth It 123
10.2 Effective Meetings 125
10.3 Improving a Process with How To Improve . . 127
10.4 A Scientific Approach to Improvement: The Improvement Kata 130
10.5 K-Base (Knowledge-Base) 133

10.6 Creating and Organizing SOP and Other Documents 134

10.7 Membership 134

    10.7.1 Machine and Access Control 135

10.8 Classes, Tools, and Other Resources 136

11 Culture 137

11.1 Who Do You Serve? Who is Helping You Do That? 138

11.2 Mind the Gap! 140

12 Value-Add 143

13 Giving Great Service 147

13.1 Why Give Great Service? 147

13.2 Why is Great Service Hard to Find? 149

13.3 Zingerman's 3 Steps to Giving Great Service . 150

13.4 The 5 Steps to Handling a Complaint 151

13.5 Steps to Handling a Compliment 154

13.6 10-4 154

14 Learnings from TWI for Makerspaces 155

15 Learnings from Lean for Makerspaces 159

15.1 A System of Systems 161

15.2 The Benefits of the Toyota Production System (TPS) 162

15.3 The 8 Deadly Wastes 162

15.4 Look Familiar? 165

15.5 Error Proofing / Mistake Proofing 166

16 Safety — 167
16.1 Maker Works Principles of Safety — 167

17 Management Tools — 171
17.1 Servant Leadership — 171
17.2 Open Book Management — 172
17.2.1 The SOP for Open Book Management — 173
17.2.2 The 10 Rules — 175
17.3 Bottom Line Change — 176
17.3.1 The Effective Change Formula — 176
17.3.2 Zingerman's Bottom Line Change (BLC) Recipe — 177
17.4 Appreciation — 180
17.5 Decision-Making — 181

18 On-Boarding Members and Staff — 183
18.1 Members — 183
18.2 Staff — 186
18.2.1 No Surprises — 186
18.3 "Outside" Instructors — 186

19 Challenges — 189
19.1 Checkout Classes — 189
19.2 From Checkout Class to On Their Own — 190

20 Floobydust — 191

Chapter 1

Introduction

As you step through the front door of our makerspace, you hear a cheery "Welcome! What brings you in today?"

Josh—irresistibly optimistic, a big smile, with "hair by Cuisinart"—waves from behind the front desk.

"I heard about this place from a friend and wanted to see what you have here."

"AWESOME![1] Do you have time for a tour?"

And off you go. You may have just found your long-lost tribe, or maybe just the right tool for your next project. But you're going to see some pretty cool people and stuff for the next 45 minutes or so. And maybe you'll be back.

It turns out that "Why are you here?" is a very useful question in a lot of situations. ("What brings you in today?" is our current favorite phrasing.) We ask it when people come in the door. We ask at the start of each class. We ask (in one form or another) when a member comes up to the front desk. It's not just a useful question, but is necessary if we want to deliver GREAT CUSTOMER SERVICE—but, that's a few chapters from here...

So, *why are you here*, reading this book? Hopefully because you are looking for ways to improve the way your makerspace runs. And if we ask "why" to that, you might respond along the lines of "because my makerspace is important to me." If we ask yet another "why", and another, eventually we're likely to end up with a response about your makerspace providing value to someone. Maybe it's students in your school, entrepreneurs in your city, or hobby roboticists in your area. For some folks, the primary mission may be to deliver monetary returns[2] to the makerspace owners. But the makerspace is delivering something of value to someone. Otherwise there's no reason to do it.

What value might a makerspace provide?

Some values that almost all makerspaces will provide include:

- Access to tools

---

[1] Nearly everything is "excellent" or "awesome" with Josh. You could come up to the front desk and tell him you broke the plasma cutter, and his response would literally be "AWESOME—let's get that fixed for you." No, you may not steal him from us.

[2] Mmmmm, filthy lucre!

- Access to space
- Development of the members and staff (learning new things, gaining confidence)

Other values could include:

- Providing employment opportunities (e.g., gigs for members, jobs for staff)
- Providing business development examples and support
- Formal(-ish) instruction for school-age children (e.g., STEAM)
- Resources to support research
- Support for hobbyists to pursue their passions
- Return on investment to investors
- Economic development in a community via support of prototyping and small-scale production
- Recreation
- Skunk works for a business
- Promotion of makerspaces in other communities

A makerspace can deliver these values as a standalone entity whose entire purpose is providing these values, or the makerspace could be part of a larger organization in education (schools, universities), community (recreation center, library), business, etc.

This book is about how our makerspaces can:

- deliver more value,
- to more people,
- continuously improving,
- using less resources (time, money, energy, materials),
- in a safe way,
- and economically, environmentally, and socially sustainably.

These last three are critical. Anyone can deliver a particular value, at least for a short time, given unlimited resources and a lack of concern for how safe or sustainable the enterprise is. In the real world, we do need to think about resources, safety, and sustainability—or our makerspace isn't going to be around very long.

This is a book of techniques for operating a makerspace. It's going to be very useful when you are starting one up, but we're not going to go into the details of what tools to buy, what shop areas to set up, where to get insurance—that kind of stuff. We've only started one makerspace, so we're going to put those issues to the side for now. (Maybe a later book.) But we've operated a makerspace—and other businesses—for quite a while now using these techniques, and we think they will be helpful to you, too.

We're going to start with the two most useful techniques: using recipes ("standard operating procedures" or SOPs), and organizing workspaces ("5S"). These are the low-hanging fruit, and if you read nothing else, we think your makerspace will still benefit a lot.

Seriously, if you're on a deadline, just jump to Chapters 2 and 3 and go for it. It is not going to hurt our feelings! Come back later when you have more time.

SOPs and 5S-ing are great tools. And after seeing those, you might ask if there are more techniques where those came from. Yes, in this book we'll discuss tools for instructing, for improving, for changing cultures, for giving great customer service, and so on. But we'll first provide a framework—a picture of how the various elements in any organization go together, so we can talk about not just isolated techniques, but how they all work together to deliver value, reduce waste, increase safety, and do so sustainably.

We'll often say "there's nothing virtual about a makerspace" as a way of saying that our members make physical things here. Every day our members walk out the door carrying a chair they built, a prototype for an invention they made, a t-shirt they customized. But, fair warning—we believe very strongly that your makerspace will need to have a clear and shared mission, vision, bottom lines, guiding principles, and values, and that these and other organizational tools of the makerspace are every bit as necessary as the very physical wood planer, drill press, or laser cutter. We'll explain how each of these fits into the organizational framework, how to create them, and how to use them. Again, all in the service of delivering value efficiently, safely, and sustainably.

(By the way, we're not saying that you don't have some or all of these elements already, and if you do, hopefully we can provide a framework that will make it easier to share, use, and improve these elements.)

We'll go into more detail as we go along, but you may be curious now about where these different tools come from. A major thread comes from a system developed during WWII called TRAINING WITHIN INDUSTRY (this is how Rosie the Riveter built bombers), which in turn was arguably a major influence on the TOYOTA PRODUCTION SYSTEM now widely used across many major industries (or more generically, LEAN manufacturing). From Training Within Industry and Lean we get techniques like SOPs, 5S, and so on.

Another thread comes from a business that one of our founders is in, ZINGERMAN'S, quite well-known in the US for both its food and its corporate training. Here we find the business perspective chart (our framework), recipes for giving great service, and a proving ground for most of the techniques we describe.

Some other sources: Some decades ago the successful changes at a struggling engine rebuilding plant gave rise to a movement engaging employees in the financial well-being of the business, now known as OPEN BOOK MANAGEMENT. And an approach created to improve leadership in religious organizations turns out to be a powerful leadership approach for all types of businesses, and an excellent match for makerspaces, and is known as SERVANT LEADERSHIP.

So we're not trying to sell you some stuff we just made up. These are the heart and soul of some pretty big organizations. And while we're not building airplanes or cars, these techniques can work at all scales—personally, in your family, etc., as well as in your local makerspace.

This book is also about the intentional choices that the leaders of the makerspace must make. Just to be clear, we're not saying this is the only way you can run a makerspace, but we are saying that it is worthwhile—even necessary—to be informed about the options and to make an intentional decision.

1.1 What's a Makerspace?

It's unlikely you've opened this book without having your own image or definition of a makerspace. But we think it is probably useful for us to define what we mean by a makerspace (as well as what we don't), so you know where we're coming from.

For us, a makerspace involves the following key points:

A physical space. This doesn't have to be a persistent, dedicated space. It could be a mobile makerspace in a bus. But a physical space is necessary for shared, physical tools, and important for "in real life" interactions. We could also say the space is not just physical, but psychological—someplace other than your own home, more akin to the so-called "third place" that is neither home nor work such as the neighborhood coffeeshop you can hang out in. A makerspace is also a place where noise, sawdust, and even questionable smells or the bright flash of welding are tolerated or even welcomed.

Tools. One of the biggest draws of a makerspace, in our mind, is the shared accessibility to tools. They could be modest tools (even 3D printers are now, at the low end, nearly impulse-buy items for some households), or could include high-capital equipment and/or equipment with substantial infrastructure and support requirements. For example, a charcoal blacksmith's forge might be very low in cost, but require ventilation, fire-proof flooring, etc. We'd also suggest that the variety of tools spanning multiple areas of making (wood, metal, plastic, textile, etc.) is a prime characteristic of a makerspace, allowing a project to incorporate a variety of types of parts and processes.

User-defined projects. The makerspace user defines their work, not the makerspace (or parent organization). Which is not to say that some users aren't making money or producing items for sale—they are—but they or their business define the work, and the user is driven in their skill acquisition by their interests.

Values/Guiding Principles. We're going to have more to say about this later, but we're going to argue that a makerspace will generally promote the sharing of information, especially informally. This openness multiplies the value of the makerspace to the user, since especially with more sophisticated equipment, a great deal of knowledge may be necessary to get good results. Risk and exploration is welcomed and supported.

Every makerspace is going to be a reflection of the community that creates and uses it. For us, we expect a wide range for each of the following aspects:

Size: Two people can have a makerspace. A makerspace could serve a single classroom. Or an entire county.

Nonprofit/For-profit: There is no requirement that a makerspace be nonprofit, for-profit, etc. The business type and governance can range from being nearly irrelevant (for example, it may be part of a larger organization, and all the business stuff happens "magically") to benevolent dictator. However, we will claim that some types of business structures and governance will present a bigger or smaller challenge to align with the other values of the organization.

Mission: To what end is the organization focused? Whom does it serve and how? Makerspaces can advance the mission of many organizations (churches, prisons, universities, libraries, economic development units, community centers, corporations, neighborhoods, etc.), and even standalone makerspaces could address a wide range of missions.

Vision: We'll define what we mean by "vision" in much greater detail shortly and why it is so important, but take this for the moment as a "preferred future". Again, this can and must vary as much as the organization's mission.

Membership: Membership (and the somewhat wider question of "who is being served") could include limitations or emphases based on affiliations (e.g., members of a university department, prisoners at a specific facility) or other aspects—again, perhaps, tied to the mission. And the reality is that the wider culture may formally or informally place restrictions on membership (e.g, by gender).

Capabilities: There is no requirement that your makerspace has tool X or Y. It may not have a woodshop at all, and may have a commercial kitchen or biochemistry lab. In fact, we feel it's likely that sustainable makerspaces will always vary in their capabilities depending on the community in which they're located. (Contrast with "FabLabs", which appear to have a specific definition of required tools.)

1.2 A Meta Toolbox

Here are some brief "meta" topics that might be useful to keep in mind as you read.

1.2.1 "Freedom From" vs "Freedom To"

So what if you read the SOP section and you're just not feeling it? Or maybe 5S is sounding like a complete waste of time? It's certainly possible that we continue to suck at describing how really useful these things are (and your feedback would help us to improve), but it could also be something that we've noticed about differences in the guiding principles of makerspaces that we might summarize as FREEDOM FROM vs. FREEDOM TO.[3]

If the vision for your makerspace has an emphasis on eliminating constraints (i.e., freedom from rules imposed by "the man"), SOPs and 5S may feel counter to the feeling or experience that you want to create. In that case, a lot of what's in this book may not be a good fit, though we hope you'll make an intentional decision about trying it out or not. You certainly don't need our permission or blessing, but a "freedom from" makerspace is a completely valid and wonderful thing. (Though there may be some challenges with operating such a space on a sustainable and/or safe footing—just saying.)

In contrast, the "Freedom To" mindset accepts constraints we may place on ourselves as useful and even necessary to reach particular goals. For example, we may agree to always install a router bit with 20 foot-pounds of torque as a way to eliminate tool breakage or damage to our work, saving us a lot of time and money. (This may sound needlessly technical, but it may help knowing that 1) using less torque could mean the tool slips out and breaks, and 2) it's easy to set a special wrench to click at the correct torque, so it is fast to

---
[3]This idea of "positive" and "negative" liberty goes back at least as far as the philosopher Kant. Which is probably not what you want to lead off with when you're explaining why we use the guard on the wood lathe.

tighten to the correct setting. In fact, we're going to say that you should make it so easy to tighten the collet properly that it takes more effort to do it wrong!) This second outlook is going to be an easier fit with what we're going to discuss in this book.

Again, people and organizations will be in different places at different times. We want to point it out here since the "freedom from" vs. "freedom to" distinction may be useful in creating or examining your organization's guiding documents and making sure everything is consistent. If your makerspace has a core "freedom from" value, that needs to be right there in your guiding principles and elsewhere, so that when there's a question "why don't we do X?", you can point out the intentional decision to, for example, have a minimum number of constraints *with the acknowledged possibilities of additional costs*. Likewise, a "freedom to" makerspace needs to make sure everyone is clear about that, so members don't have to guess how to behave or what the overall guiding principles of the makerspace are.

1.2.2 Don't Take Our Word For It

If we've done our job in this book, some of these topics should feel unsettling. You might feel we're taking all the inventiveness and creativity out of makerspaces with procedures, organized workspaces, and the like. Or conversely, that all our talk of developing people and having bottom lines besides profit smells distinctly of herb-enhanced aging hippies. (We've been accused of both. Go figure.)

Some of the things we're going to suggest are probably outside the usual examples of how businesses or organizations are run. But after many years of using these ideas, we're pretty confident that there's some real value here, particularly in the running of a makerspace.

Here's the thing—you're not going to have to take our word that these approaches bring value. In fact, baked into the very fabric[4] of Lean, for example, is the idea that we have to be able to demonstrate the improvement in any process. *We are after improvement, not change for change's sake.*

At the end of the day, SOPs, 5S, Visioning, and all the rest better be worth the time you put into it, measured in real day-to-day effects. So if you're feeling a bit uncomfortable with some of these ideas, bear in the mind that these have produced real-world results for other people, and that it is at least possible, if not probable, that they can produce those measurable results for you in your makerspace. We hope we can provide a compelling argument to try them out.

1.2.3 Training Compact

Here's our agreement with you, the reader. It's the first part of the Zingerman's Training Compact[5] we'll discuss later.

The trainees (readers) agree to:

Take responsibility for the effectiveness of their training. In this case, actively reading, doing some of the exercises, even digging deeper into interesting topics in recommended books or online.

---

[4] Yes, you don't bake fabric, but hear us out.

[5] The last two parts of the training compact describe the recognition and reward associated with the training, things that are more difficult to do via the medium of a book.

The trainers (writers) agree to:

Document clear performance expectations. For this book, this means by the end of this book you'll have a framework and a set of tools to continuously improve the efficient, safe, sustainable delivery of value to members and others of a makerspace.

Provide training resources. This book, and the resources we list in it.

Why mention this? We think it's valuable to both reader and writer to know what's being covered and what the expectations are. These become critical when applied to the classes covering safety and basic operation that we'll argue should form the core of your makerspace. We'll have more to say about this in our discussion of How to Instruct.

1.2.4 Baking vs. Cooking

We like to use the concepts of baking vs. cooking as short cuts for the following distinction:

Cooking: Here's a recipe, and if you follow it, you'll get consistent results, but you can vary the ingredient amounts (and even omit or add new ingredients) and it's going to turn out reasonable. Think soup. Whatever you do, within reason, it will be more or less some kind of soup.

Baking: This recipe is more about chemistry, and the right ingredients and amounts do matter. If you don't use enough baking powder, it's not going to turn out like a cookie, but more like a brick.

These labels allow us to flag recipes in this book that fall into the "this works for us, use this as a rough guide until you have your own" vs. "this is probably not a recipe to change a lot, at least not on a whim or to avoid hard work—as best we know it, each of these steps and ingredients is important".

1.2.5 Make It Easy To Do The Right Thing, And Hard To Do The Wrong Thing

Dale's dad often says "You can't push a rope". (Usually preceded by "if there's one thing I learned in engineering school...") In a makerspace, you can waste a lot of time and energy working against people's natural inclination. (This includes our staff and ourselves!) What can we do, since most people tend to want to do less work to accomplish their goal rather than more? (Okay, that's a polite way of saying most folks, including us, are lazy.)

Make it easy to do the right thing, and make it hard to do the wrong thing.

For example, the right thing may be to return a tool to its home when you're done with it. We could certainly try posters, stern looks, cajoling, electric shock collars[6], and so on. But

---

[6]For some reason, we had several years of staff immediately suggesting shock collars for nearly every problem. Members not turning on the dust collector? Shock collar. Dirty dishes in the kitchen sink? Shock collar. It turns out, though, that decent shock collars chew through the batteries, so there's an ongoing cost. We'd have to stock several different sizes. Do we need allergen-free ones? And so on. In the end, they're just not a good, sustainable solution.

if that tool's home is nearby to where it is usually used and is clearly labeled, we've made it easier to do the right thing.

Many (though not all) of our members will even feel good about bringing order to disorder, so we've not only made things more organized, we've created an environment that the member likes.

For another example, the "wrong thing" might be leaving a chuck key in the chuck of a drill press. You can buy chuck keys with a spring loaded tip, so if you're not actively holding it in the chuck, it pops out. Now it's very hard to do the wrong thing. (*Please do not, however, underestimate the ability of a motivated member to do the wrong thing* if that's what they set their mind to.)

No matter what you paid for this book[7], this sentence should be more than worth it, so we'll repeat it:

Make it easy to do the right thing, and make it hard to do the wrong thing.

1.2.6 Learning vs. Systems

When something bad happens in a makerspace, it's often common to see it as a learning problem. The darned member didn't learn how to do that operation properly. The staff didn't learn the correct way to change the dust filter—or, didn't even learn the need to change it frequently.

Very early automobiles required that drivers learn how to make many engine adjustments on the fly, such as setting the choke just so depending on the temperature and so on. Not so long ago, manual transmissions were still fairly common. Learning these things was just part of the driving experience. Many people certainly did learn (perhaps not all, or as well as they might think), and automobiles were driven. But that knowledge wasn't central to driving (we would argue it did not add any value), and we replaced that knowledge with systems—the automatic choke, automatic transmission, and so on. In the bigger picture, the problem that cars were difficult to operate properly was solved not by more education/training, but by using systems. Yes, there are exceptions—it can be a blast to master some complicated task like driving a historic car, but let's be clear that in this case you'd be excited about and valuing the skill you mastered, and not the fact that you're getting from point A to point B in the most efficient way.

When a problem comes up, a useful lens to use is to first ask if this is a problem that could be solved by changing or adding a system, rather than starting with the idea that every problem is due to the members not learning well.

For example, when your members constantly forget to turn on the dust collector, you could argue they just haven't learned properly. "Those darned members—perhaps if I glared more often at them..." But if you instead ask "what system is failing to help the member?", you might end up automating your dust collector so it turns on when the machine is running.

When we take the time to modify our systems to make it easier for our members to do the right thing, we are hopefully better able to provide them with the value they are expecting, such as functional machines, tools they can find and use, and so on. It also makes it easier on the staff—fewer machines to repair, fewer tools to track down, etc. However, when we make it hard to do the wrong thing, in some cases we may be forcing the member to do

---

[7] Well, at least up to about $3.95.

more work than they would normally, so we had better make sure that members feel deep down that our policies are, in the long term, in alignment with their own interests as well as our own. For example, if we purposefully do not have a compressed air hose that reaches the milling machine, we've made it hard to "clean" the milling machine by just blasting off the chips. Now, we happen to know that blowing chips off a machine is bad for safety and bad for the machine (it blows chips in places they shouldn't be, which eventually gums up the works), but if we fail to convey that to the member, it just seems like we're placing an artificial and arbitrary constraint on them.

What's the alternative to using systems? We could instead rely almost exclusively on educating our members. For example, we could have a year-long apprenticeship program where we teach everything there is to learn about the shop. Realistically, that's not something most of our members would want or could really do. Rosie the Riveter and her colleagues didn't have time for years of apprenticeship—they needed to be quickly competent so that bombers (correctly assembled!) would roll off the lines right now. Systems like what we'll discuss made that possible, and make possible the operation of makerspaces without an insurmountable burden of instruction.

1.2.7 The Tragedy of the Commons

Economists have long had the concept of how common elements can be problematic to share if the benefit to an individual for abusing the common elements is less than their share of the damage—as a shorthand it's known as "the tragedy of the commons." The shared use of tools in a makerspace brings this into very sharp focus, such as in the following scenarios[8]:

- someone runs a board through the planer with a nail in it, chipping the expensive-to-sharpen blades

- someone leaves their dirty mug in the sink

- someone doesn't clean up the epoxy spill on the floor where it hardens into a new permanent feature

- someone leaves a tool where they used it, rather than return it to its home

In each case the individual benefits (usually by not having to do something), while "someone else" has to do extra work and/or the group as a whole bears an additional cost.

This is nothing new to you—unless you're on a deserted island, you're potentially on one end or the other in most any situation with another person, even if you haven't heard the specific name for it. Beyond that, though, the tools and concepts in this book should go a long way towards minimizing this type of behavior via systems, culture, and guiding principles. Just "making it easy to do the right thing" is a strong start, but we strongly believe the sum of all these tools and concepts will also shift our members' (and staff's!) division between what is "someone else's problem" and what is their problem. We're never going to have perfect alignment between the organization and the individual, but we're not going to let that stop us from trying to improve the situation.

---

[8]You, gentle reader, will not be surprised that we could extend this list to several pages without breaking a sweat.

1.2.8 Be Intentional and Consistent

We realize there's a lot of potentially new and perhaps unconventional perspectives in this book. Do you have to do everything, to buy all of what we're saying?

Not at all. But we do ask that you make an intentional decision. Servant leadership not your thing? Excellent. But please make that an informed and intentional decision. Make sure people know—"Here's why we are doing things the way we are." And then be consistent.

Making an intentional decision, especially one that is communicated, will help everyone be consistent. And that consistency is necessary for continuous improvement, which is what is going to lead to a bright, sustainable future for your makerspace.

1.2.9 Connection with Zingerman's Community of Businesses

From time to time we're going to use examples from much larger businesses than our own makerspace—ranging from Toyota to a local deli.

While we don't have any connection to Toyota, one of our owners is in fact also an owner in Zingerman's, a collection of businesses here in Ann Arbor, Michigan. Zingerman's began as a small deli downtown, and has grown to include some restaurants, mail order, bakery, coffee roasting, corporate training, events center, and so on.

Zingerman's factors into our story for two reasons. First, they are masters at defining what they call "organizational recipes". At Zingerman's there are recipes for how to provide great customer service, how to build and maintain culture, even how to achieve financial success. This has been a big inspiration to us in how we've approached our makerspace. Second, Zingerman's Mail Order was the laboratory where, for years, Tom and others tested and refined the approach to Lean, training, systems, and service that we'll be sharing here.

1.2.10 The 80/20 Rule

The 80/20 Rule (also known as the PARETO PRINCIPLE) is a useful rule of thumb that says in many circumstances, 80% of the effects comes from just 20% of the causes. There are mathematical reasons why this is the case for certain situations, but it is applicable in a surprising number of situations. It's particularly helpful to us as makerspace operators since it suggests that we can often concentrate our efforts on just a few (20%) of the causes and expect to see much or most (80%) of the effects changed.

For example, if you keep track of the questions your staff answers from members, you might find that the laser cutter and the CNC wood router, while only two out of many machines in the space, account for most of the questions. If you have time to improve SOPs, you can spend your time on this shorter list of tools, rather than working your way through the list of tools alphabetically.

Usage of tools? 20% of your members probably account for 80% of tool usage. (What are the implications of that?)

So, don't be overwhelmed by your to-do list for the makerspace. 20% of the items will get you a lot of the way there.

We sometimes use the phrase "let the pain prioritize" when we're faced—as we almost always are—by the need to prioritize our tasks. What is costing you time or money right

1.2. A META TOOLBOX 21

now? Just be sure to balance that approach, since the loudest voices are not always the most important (you might not be working on your 20%), and to some extent letting pain prioritize is a reactive mode. Constantly reacting can be a strange mix of tension and relief—tension that we never get to stop and look at the big picture, and relief that each new crisis provides a clear top priority. Use pain to save time when prioritizing short-term tasks.

1.2.11 Fix What Bugs You—15-Minute Improvements

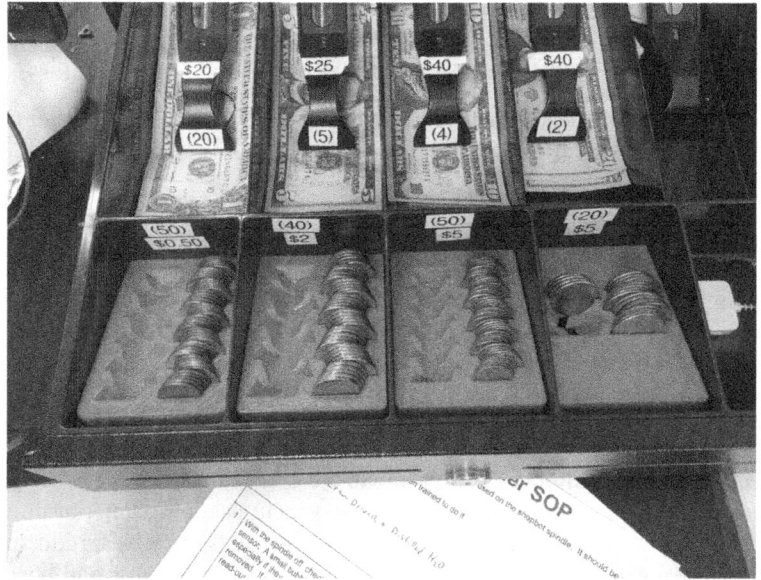

Figure 1.1: A simple 3D printed coin organizer saves time at closing.

One of the themes we'll talk a lot about in this book is the idea of continuous improvement. What to improve? Sometimes it will be clear to everyone what needs improvement, but one thing we can do is ask everyone to "fix what bugs you". One of Dale's favorite "fixes" had to do with counting change in the register at the end of the day. Whenever he closed the register, it took him forever to count all the coins. So he designed and 3D printed plastic counting trays that fit into the change drawer. The coins stay "counted" by default. Now it's very quick to see how much is in the register.

We can systematize these improvements as daily "15 minute improvements". Everyone can be asked to devote up to 5 minutes to document an existing problem, 5 minutes to improve it, and 5 minutes to document the solution. Half the value of this kind of activity may be in the change in attitude we get when we put on our improvement-seeking (or waste-seeking) glasses. And of course many problems won't be solved in 15 minutes, but if we don't see them in the first place, we don't have a chance.

There is a flip side to these small, incremental improvements, though. Which leads us to the next topic.

1.2.12 Help, I'm Trapped in a Local Minima

Let's say you are in a desert, full of sand dunes, and your goal is to go to the lowest point. (I'm not sure why you want to do that, but you've been out in the sun a while, maybe you're a little dehydrated, so we won't look too deeply into your thought processes.) One strategy would be to drop a beach ball where you're standing and see which way it rolls—then follow it downhill. This strategy is guaranteed to direct you to a place lower than where you currently are or, if the ball doesn't move, tell you that there's no path that goes downward from here.

What this strategy doesn't do is find the lowest point in the desert. It finds the lowest point that is found by always moving lower from where you are right now. If the lowest point happens to be in the depression on the other side of this dune, we can't get there because our strategy doesn't look over there—we can't go uphill to get to a better place.

So why are you carrying a beach ball in the desert, and why should this matter to us? We're trying to run a makerspace (probably not in a desert).

Just like the beach ball, our seeking to improve a process can lead us to what are called "local minima"—the new situation is indeed a minima (the lowest point in terms of the fastest delivery time, the lowest cost per transaction, etc.), but only on a local scale. It's not necessarily the overall or "global" minima, and if we don't think about the bigger picture, we can mistakenly believe we've reached our goal when in fact the lowest or highest or whatever place is somewhere else.

Here's an example: We used to use a standard router motor in our CNC wood router. They cost us about $250 a piece, but on a regular basis we were wearing out bearings and burning out the speed controller built into the motor.[9] So we made improvements—we got a second motor so we could repair one while the other one was in use, reducing our downtime. We learned how to replace the speed controller and the bearings ourselves, reducing our costs and downtime. We installed a timer that recorded how long a motor had been on, so we could proactively replace bearings. So we improved—we were reducing the wastes around this situation.

We probably could have gone further—making up special jigs to reduce the rebuild time, that kind of thing. But we were in a local minima—we were optimizing a situation that even in the best case was worse than some other solutions. In this case, we decided to replace the router motor with a high-speed, water-cooled spindle. Now we go much, much longer before changing the spindle, and the spindles themselves are a little cheaper. As a side effect, though, we had to install a red safety light—the new spindle was so quiet that, with the dust collector running, you might not notice that the spindle was running.[10]

Our cash register was another—we worked on and refined our documents (SOPs) for how to operate the register, improving a bit at a time. But a better solution was moving to a credit card processing service that integrated the cash and credit sales in an app we ran on a tablet. Now there's just the change drawer and a receipt printer.[11]

---

[9]These were decent, brand-name router motors, but they just weren't designed to be run for hours on end in a CNC router.

[10]As Paul Saginaw, co-founder of Zingerman's, often says, you never run out of problems, but as you improve you get more interesting problems.

[11]Dale does not know what the deal is with cash registers and their miserable user interface. If there's one piece of technology he could wipe out from the face of the earth, it might not be cash registers, but they should be pretty darn nervous. Just saying.

Like so many of the tools we share in this book, we're not saying that you're always going to be in a local minima, or that shock collars are always bad.[12] What we are saying is that here are some ways of looking at the business, and that as leaders we are responsible for making intentional choices after gathering all the relevant facts. And sometimes it is just fine being in a local minima—the global minima just isn't that much better, and we've made an informed choice. Excellent—move on to the next item in your to-do list.

1.2.13 Your Enemy

There's a reasonable chance that your worst enemy will be perfection. Please don't read this book and imagine Maker Works or any other makerspace in the world is perfectly organized, 5S-ed and SOP'ed to the hilt. They are not. There is not enough time to write the perfect SOP. The moment the wood shop tool board is completed, the claw hammer will go walkabout and its replacement will not hang the same way. Perfection is a dream that can lead us far from our path.

The best is the enemy of good.[13]

A tool board that is 90% done is infinitely better than the perfect tool board that never makes it off the drawing board (or CAD program). By all means, do a great job, go home happy with the work you've done, but beware of the disproportionate time and resources you'll need for the 100% solution.

1.3 Liked Best, Next Time

"Liked Best, Next Time" is a short-hand for evaluation. We ask it at the end of each huddle—what did you like best about the meeting, and what should we change next time. We ask at the end of classes. It's one way of soliciting feedback to improve a system, and we like that it's framed in the positive—we don't ask what you hated, but in what way we can improve.

We'd appreciate hearing from you about what you liked about this book, and what we could change (improve!) for the next version. Email us at membership@maker-works.com with your thoughts.

We keep a page at the www.maker-works.com website titled "Makerspace Resources," which we try to keep updated with useful resources for makerspace operators. This book will also have a page at our website with errata and other information.

---

[12]Wait, I think we *would* like to say that shock collars for members in fact are always bad.
[13]Voltaire.

Chapter 2

Using Recipes in your Makerspace: SOPs

Figure 2.1: An SOP binder in its native environment

Standard Operating Procedures (SOPs) are recipes for anything that you need to do more than once.[1] Makerspace members use SOPs to operate machines safely and efficiently. Staff use SOPs to maintain machines, process membership transactions, and teach classes. You can even use an SOP to write an SOP.

SOPs are exactly like a recipe for a cake or soup. There's a list of required ingredients (1/2 cup flour, or a 1/2" end mill). There's a sequence of steps (make a roux, or set the spindle speed). Usually we'll find the required time listed, often a photo of the finished item, and even an indication of the skill level required.

---

[1] Or something like a rocket launch that you want to get right the first time.

SOPs in business are known under a number of different names like "operations manual" and "standard work". Rosie the Riveter used them in WWII making bombers at Willow Run just a few miles from our shop; odds are your car was built using hundreds, if not thousands, of SOPs. International standards like ISO-9000 require the use of SOPs. As you read further in this book, you'll see that SOPs are a core element of much of what we're advocating.

But there's a downside: good SOPs can take a long time to write. At Maker Works, we spent three months writing SOPs before opening to the public. We are still writing SOPs for new tools, classes, membership transactions, and so on, and constantly updating the SOPs we've already written to reflect tool changes, errors we made, or improvements we've found.

SOPs take a really long time to write.

Sorry. That's the way it is.

If that's the case, there better be some really compelling reasons to use them.

2.1 Why Use SOPs?

- SOPs codify the best practices for an operation. Everyone can use the safest, most efficient procedure, instead of what they think they remember from training, or even what they remember accurately from a trainer who perhaps wasn't teaching the best method. SOPs make it easy to do the right thing!

- SOPs don't require the member to remember anything. In fact, we want to see the SOP open in front of a member as they work.

- Even when a member may perform the operation often, people are not good at consistently doing every step[2]. SOPs (and checklists, which are related but not the same) address the fallibility of our memory and attention, especially for tasks that feel mundane.

- SOPs make the member more independent, and require less staff time. When someone comes up to us with a question, often the first thing we will say is "What step of the SOP are you on?" This works, by the way, even if the staff person doesn't know the machine at all—just reading the SOP along with the member solves most problems.[3] It's amazing how many questions go away when the SOPs are used!

- Conversely, in the absence of SOPs, *all your staff time will be taken up with member questions*. All of it, and then some. We are not kidding about this one.

- SOPs give us consistent results. Each time our members use the plasma cutter, we want them to have good—even great!—and repeatable results.

- SOPs preserve the investment we make in the tools by reducing misuse and accidents. They improve everyone's experience by making it less likely that a user will make an adjustment or change to a setting that isn't helpful. (SOPs can define what actions are and are not acceptable, like changing configurations.)

---

[2] Ask a pilot how easy it is to skip even very important steps.

[3] Early on, Dale was not very familiar with the ShopBot CNC wood router operation, but when a member came up to the front desk with a question, he'd head back to the machine with the user. Walking through the SOP, it was usually the case that the user, while describing the steps they'd done and reading the SOP, would suddenly realize they had skipped a step. Problem solved! The user gets more proof that the SOP is useful, and the staff person gets to feel helpful, even if they aren't yet skilled on the machine.

- Because SOPs give us consistent results, we can improve on the SOP and expect to be able to tell if we've made an improvement. If each time we do a procedure we do it a little different, it could be very difficult to identify potential improvements or evaluate their results.

- SOPs carry the member through the stage we call "unconsciously incompetent"—that is, the member doesn't know that they don't know. (Further stages are consciously incompetent, consciously competent, and unconsciously competent.) Don't count on members knowing things they might not actually know. We never want to hear "but I didn't know that operation was important".

- SOPs are necessary for good instruction. Another TWI[4] tool we'll call "How to Instruct"[5] requires that the job being taught have an SOP.

- Our SOPs are the basis of our safety and basic operation classes (or as one of us sometimes calls them, the "How Not to Kill Yourself" classes).

- Training new staff is made much easier with SOPs documenting each step of handling member transactions and so on.

- Just like teaching, writing an SOP is a learning opportunity.

Honestly, there are very few circumstances when writing an SOP will not save you time and expense. Most of the time, it will save many, many times the initial time spent. Even if it's just break-even, time spent writing an SOP is creating an asset, and as Josh put recently, is probably more interesting than the alternative—"How many times do you want to repeat the same thing over and over and over?"

Some years back, we visited a makerspace that shared the following sad tale which illustrates a few of these points. They had a nice wood lathe in their woodshop, and someone came along who professed great skill and knowledge around the lathe and was interested in teaching a class on how to operate it. Sounds great, they thought, so they set him up with some classes, and it sounds like all was well, at least for a bit. Then the lathe died. Apparently in a non-trivial, expensive-to-repair way. It turned out the expert was—well, not so expert. The manner in which the instructor operated the lathe and had taught some number of other members was destructive to the machine. They ended up with a broken machine plus a bunch of people who were incorrectly trained. (Fortunately in this case, the bad information wasn't safety related. It could have been much worse!) How were the staff to know that the content being taught was destructive? There wasn't a defined, vetted process—i.e., an SOP—for teaching the class, so the class was whatever that person thought.

And do note that your SOPs do not have to be perfect to be better than nothing. Start with something and have a way (i.e., a system) and an interest (i.e., guiding principle) in making it better.

2.2 Objections to SOPs

One objection we hear from time to time is that SOPs sound restricting, that they take the creativity out of making. ("Freedom From"[6], anyone?) We're going to argue exactly the

---
[4]Training Within Industry.
[5]Officially called "Job Instruction".
[6]See section 1.2.1

opposite—SOPs let us get our work done faster and better, and let us continually improve. They free us from making easily preventable mistakes. (You may argue that it's your time, and hence your business if you want to waste it, but on shared equipment damage to a machine affects everyone.) SOPs give us more time to be creative where creativity is needed and valuable, but as we say, there's not a lot of room for creativity in how you install a router bit on the router. Use the time you save with SOPs to be even more creative in what you make.

Another objection is that SOPs turn our staff and members into robots, mindlessly following an SOP. Yes, one could force SOPs on people and stand over them with metaphorical whips[7], making sure they do everything exactly the same each time, but that's not a pleasant situation for anyone. Instead, SOPs must be provided in the context of giving our members and staff the tools and attitude to be process engineers, and asking them to always be on the lookout for improving SOPs or writing new SOPs when needed. Far from asking for a mindless, robotic presence, we want everyone to be thinking about how to make things better—that is, delivering better value. Performing operations that add value are necessary, so let's make those easier, faster, even more fun if we can. Operations that are not "value-added"—let's eliminate those.

SOPs are just tools, and they need sharpening and improvement just like a wood plane. (Later on, we'll see that improving SOPs is value-added for the staff.)

An SOP that no one is allowed to improve is about as useful as a knife that no one is allowed to sharpen.

There's another objection to SOPs that you may run across, and it hinges on how people feel valued in their work. Creating SOPs will feel threatening to someone if they feel that their job or self-worth is dependent on knowledge that only they have. If they write it down, what value do they have? And they're right—SOPs and other Lean practices only work if the introduction of these practices are not threatening people's jobs, but improving them. Otherwise, we're asking people to act against their own best interest. What would happen if respect and compensation were related to the ability to teach, to share, to document, to improve processes? Rewarding someone (even only with continued employment) only because of knowledge they're hoarding is not a productive place to be.

---

[7]Or shock collars.

2.3 What Does an SOP Look Like?

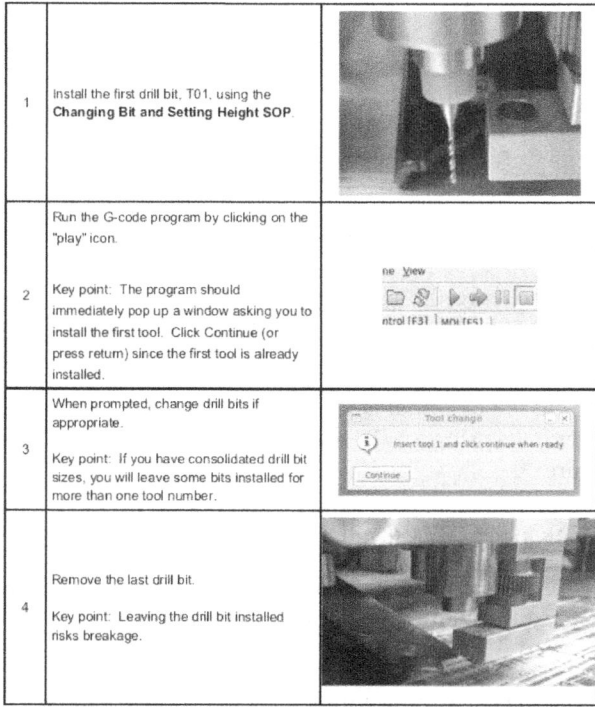

Figure 2.2: Some steps from a printed circuit board engraver SOP for drilling holes.

What's an SOP look like? Figure 2.2 has some sample steps from our printed circuit board engraver "learner" or operating SOP. This is the SOP that members will use each time they operate the machine, and the one that forms the basis of our checkout class. (We'll discuss other types of SOPs shortly.) Physically, our operating SOPs live in white 3-ring binders by each machine. It should be easy for a member to find and refer to the SOP. (*Make it easy to do the right thing.*) All the operating SOPs for a machine are in one binder, often with tabs, and sometimes a table of contents for really big collections of SOPs.

An SOP describes the sequence of steps to accomplish a task. The number of steps is however many are needed—some SOPs will be very brief, others will be multiple pages. Often these SOPs will be executed as part of a larger sequence. For example, after using the "Mount a Tool" SOP on the ShopBot, a member then might use the "Touching off Z" SOP, followed by several more SOPs to finish creating their project. A very simple tool (say a laminator) might have just a single SOP.

Just like a food recipe, a Maker Works SOP has some front material:

- a title
- the result (hmmm, perhaps a photo?)
- when the SOP should be used (and what other SOPs might be appropriate for other circumstances)

- who should use the SOP (e.g., anyone; anyone who has taken the check out class; staff only; or even staff that have been through specific training)
- safety issues specific to the operation (which are in addition to the overall shop safety rules and perhaps a reminder of those for the machine)
- tools required
- time to complete the operation
- materials required

Then for each step, there are several items: *step number* (if needed), *step description*, *key point(s)*, *reason*, and *photo or diagram*.

Step numbers allow you to have the user repeat past steps or skip ahead—for example, "Remove the remaining 3 bolts by repeating steps 6-8" or "If the tool is already installed, skip to step 17."

The step description spells out first *what* is accomplished and then *how* to do it. For example, "Remove the four cover bolts using a 5/8" socket", or "Turn the controller on using the red toggle switch." Steps are:

Atomic: they can not be logically broken down into smaller steps.

Bite-sized: the operator can remember the step and any key points during the step. If a step involves too many details, the operator may have to interrupt the step to consult the SOP.

Logically grouped: a step may group a number of related sub-steps. For example, several screws of the same type and in the same location may be used to install a vise. They are all similar and perform the same function, so a single step could be to tighten all four screws. If several screws are associated with more than one function (e.g., one setting motor speed, another setting motor acceleration), then two steps should be used.

The *key point* is a separate element of the step description located right below it (or in a separate column) that provides additional information necessary for the safe, efficient completion of the step such as cautions, locations, alternatives, clarifications, or other useful details. For example:

Turn the power to the router off using the control panel power switch.

Key point: Rotate the red switch counter-clockwise so the pointer is to the "0".

The key point does not provide more steps, it augments the existing step, and experienced users will generally know that information after using the SOP a few times.

SOPs may benefit from a separate *reason* for some steps. Normally it will be pretty clear why some step is called for, but if it is not, a reason (or key point) should be included so the user is aware of the function and importance of the step. For example, the order of steps may be very important to avoid damage to the tool—e.g., disengaging a brake before turning a spindle on. (You could combine this with the Key Point.)

Finally, having a *photo or diagram* is so important that we recommend assuming that each step will have one—you should have to make the case that a particular step doesn't need a photo. Photos are usually very quick, but diagrams can often simplify or emphasize a particular aspect of an operation. Often a good compromise can be a photo modified with arrows or other graphics for emphasis or clarity.

iFixit.com has a long list of SOPs they call "repair guides" that step you through even complicated repairs like completely disassembling an Apple laptop to clean the keyboard. (Do not ask Dale why he is familiar with this particular guide.) They're well worth looking at for a form an SOP can take.

2.4 Forms "Standard Work" Can Take

The full-blown SOP we just described will fulfill all our needs, and is by far the most common type we use. It is easy to update (you can even write changes to the page directly in the moment), but does require reading skill.

As long as we make sure we are creating a stable, consistent process, the SOP or "SOP-helper" might take other forms, depending on the context. For example:

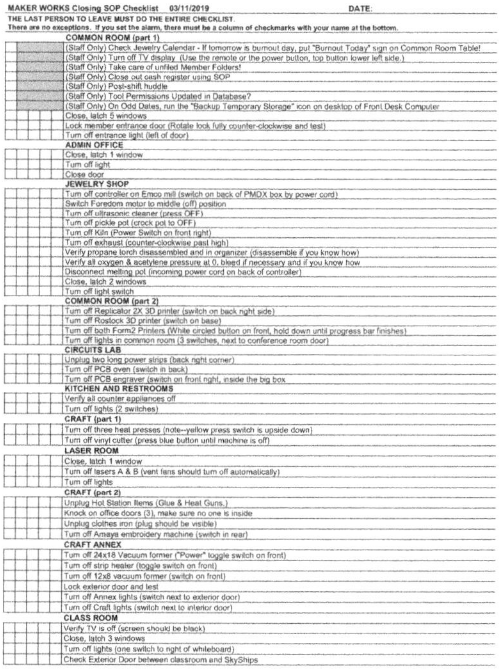

MAKER WORKS Closing SOP Checklist 03/11/2019 DATE:

THE LAST PERSON TO LEAVE MUST DO THE ENTIRE CHECKLIST.

There are no exceptions. If you set the alarm, there must be a column of checkmarks with your name at the bottom.

COMMON ROOM (part 1)
(Staff Only) Check Jewelry Calendar - If tomorrow is burnout day, put "Burnout Today" sign on Common Room Table!
(Staff Only) Turn off TV display (Use the remote or the power button, top button lower left side.)
(Staff Only) Take care of unfiled Member Folders!
(Staff Only) Close out cash register using SOP
(Staff Only) Post-shift huddle
(Staff Only) Tool Permissions Updated in Database?
(Staff Only) On Odd Dates, run the "Backup Temporary Storage" icon on desktop of Front Desk Computer
Close, latch 5 windows
Lock member entrance door (Rotate lock fully counter-clockwise and test)
Turn off entrance light (left of door)

ADMIN OFFICE
Close, latch 1 window
Turn off light
Close door

JEWELRY SHOP
Turn off controller on Emco mill (switch on back of PMDX box by power cord)
Switch Foredom motor to middle (off) position
Turn off ultrasonic cleaner (press OFF)
Turn off pickle pot (crock pot to OFF)
Turn off Kiln (Power Switch on front right)
Turn off exhaust (counter-clockwise past high)
Verify propane torch disassembled and in organizer (disassemble if you know how)
Verify all oxygen & acetylene pressure at 0, bleed if necessary and if you know how
Disconnect melting pot (incoming power cord on back of controller)
Close, latch 2 windows
Turn off light switch

COMMON ROOM (part 2)
Turn off Replicator 2X 3D printer (switch on back right side)
Turn off Rostock 3D printer (switch on base)
Turn off both Form2 Printers (White circled button on front, hold down until progress bar finishes)
Turn off lights in common room (3 switches, next to conference room door)

CIRCUITS LAB
Unplug two long power strips (back right corner)
Turn off PCB oven (switch in back)
Turn off PCB engraver (switch on front right, inside the big box

KITCHEN AND RESTROOMS
Verify all counter appliances off
Turn off lights (2 switches)

CRAFT (part 1)
Turn off three heat presses (note--yellow press switch is upside down)
Turn off vinyl cutter (press blue button until machine is off)

LASER ROOM
Close, latch 1 window
Turn off lasers A & B (vent fans should turn off automatically)
Turn off lights

CRAFT (part 2)
Unplug Hot Station Items (Glue & Heat Guns.)
Knock on office doors (3), make sure no one is inside
Unplug clothes iron (plug should be visible)
Turn off Amaya embroidery machine (switch in rear)

CRAFT ANNEX
Turn off 24x18 Vacuum former ("Power" toggle switch on front)
Turn off strip heater (toggle switch on front)
Turn off 12x8 vacuum former (switch on front)
Lock exterior door and test
Turn off Annex lights (switch next to exterior door)
Turn off Craft lights (switch next to interior door)

CLASS ROOM
Verify TV is off (screen should be black)
Close, latch 3 windows
Turn off lights (one switch to right of whiteboard)
Check Exterior Door between classroom and SkyShips

Figure 2.3: Part of the closing checklist.

Checklist SOP: In some cases, SOPs can be very useful when expressed as a list or checklist. For example, if a process has a number of steps, if the steps can be expressed succinctly and fully, and if you want to emphasize the importance of completing each step by requiring an explicit acknowledgement that the step is done, the checklist may be your ticket. Pictorial or text, a checklist can optionally have one or more columns to record the completion of the step (and perhaps who and when). There's an implied order to the items, which you can emphasize with numbering. We use a checklist for the SOP for closing up Maker Works at night—the last person checks each item off and signs the checklist (Figure 2.3). Note that in the example checklist in Figure 2.3, we have to note where things like light and power switches are located, since they're not always obvious.

Later we'll discuss the checklist when used to augment an SOP, as well as some other uses for checklists.

Hint: Use an erasable material (e.g., laminated paper) to make a reusable checklist.

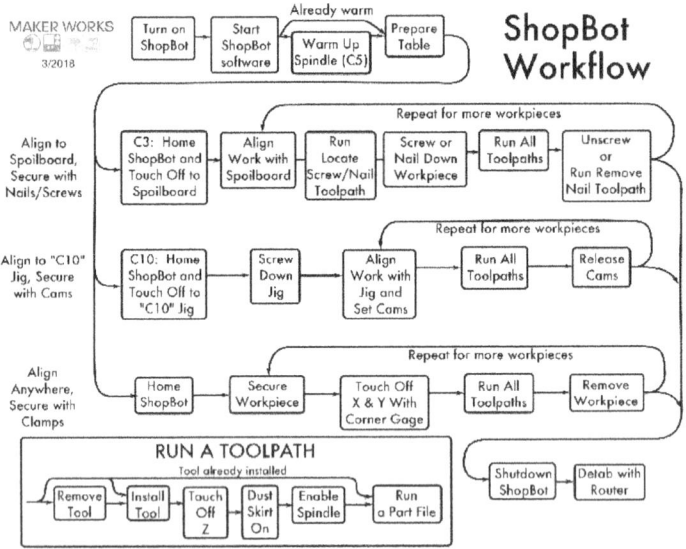

Figure 2.4: Example Flowchart (for ShopBot).

Flowchart: Some processes are not a single, linear sequence. (Check out some of our front desk processes sometime!) A flowchart can capture a multitude of decision points and alternative steps in a compact form. The steps can be steps of an SOP, or could refer to a separate SOP, as in Figure 2.4 which shows the different flows possible with the ShopBot CNC router. A flowchart might take a little longer to create and update than text. It is very similar to a checklist in its value in reminding people of the steps, rather than necessarily forming the entire SOP.

2.4. FORMS "STANDARD WORK" CAN TAKE

Figure 2.5: A custom metal jig for making up *Learn to Solder* kits. Slide one item (or two for LEDs) from each slot into the bag.

Template or Jig: Instead of a visual guide, sometimes you can create a physical template or jig that guides, forces, or facilitates the operation, as in Figure 2.5. Place object A here, B there, and so on. You can go further and make it hard to do the wrong thing by, for example, requiring every space be filled before the next step can be completed, using mechanical or electrical means. Such jigs could range from fairly fast to create to very involved. Needless to say, Murphy's Law suggests that the harder a template is to change or modify, the more likely it is that you'll need to.

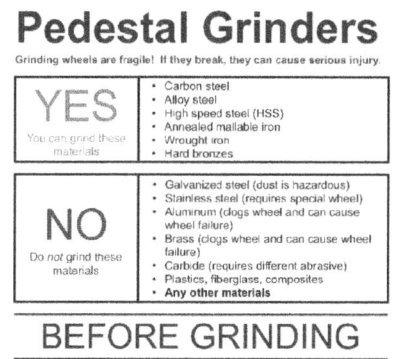

Figure 2.6: Example of an SOP as a poster.

Poster: The SOP doesn't have to be on multiple, small sheets of paper in a binder. We've experimented with posters for some processes, like our SOPs for grinder use, as in Figure 2.6. Here there were not as many step-by-step processes to convey as much as there were acceptable and unacceptable materials, etc. Having the information easily visible and hands-free may increase its use.

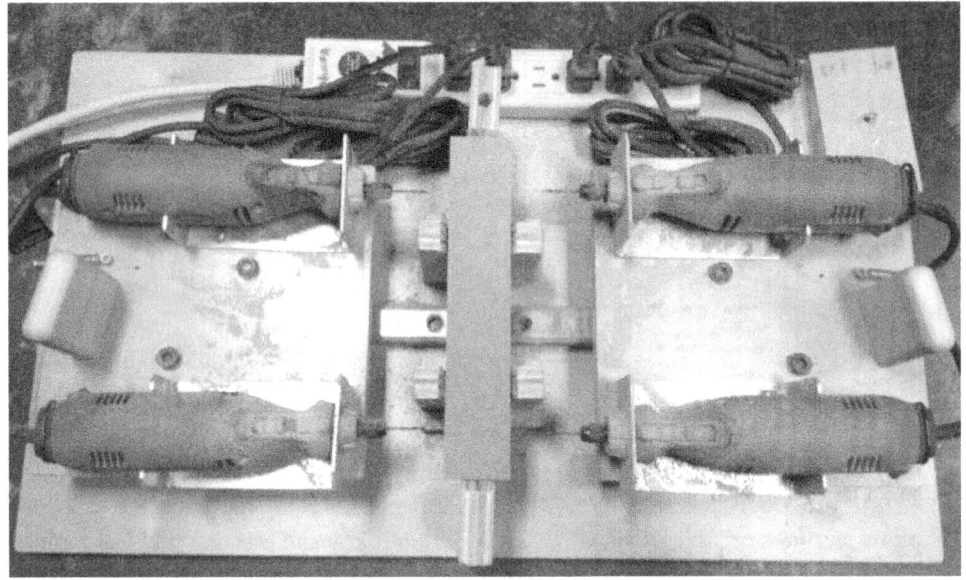

Figure 2.7: The *Drillinator 4000*, an example of a special-purpose machine.

Machine: Make it easy to do the right thing by creating a special-purpose machine. For example, we created a machine to drill four holes in a block of wood at one time, each to the correct depth, with a jig to hold the wood block in an exact location (Figure 2.7). The work, and the SOP, is now radically simplified from the earlier multi-step process. Hopefully you can find these opportunities before you get to the SOP stage, but if you find your SOP doesn't seem realistic, maybe there's an opportunity to change the work itself.[8]

Audio or Video: If someone's eyes or hands will be occupied with the task, perhaps audio or video can convey the process. However, beware—such forms may be more time-consuming or otherwise difficult to improve. SOPs don't serve us if we can't improve them, and we always want to make it easy to do the right thing. Having a printed SOP means that staff can quickly slide a sheet out of a protective sleeve, write in a correction or clarification, slide it back in, and be done. (Well, at some point we want to update the SOP in our files.)

Audio and video are also linear, and not "random-access". It is relatively harder to skip ahead or back in an audio or video stream, and content is delivered at a (usually) fixed rate, which may be too fast or slow for the member. If the method of delivery doesn't work well for the member, we've made it less likely they'll want to use it.

---

[8]Toyota encourages workers on their assembly line to create machines to make their work more efficient—search for the term "karakuri kaizen" for more details.

2.4. FORMS "STANDARD WORK" CAN TAKE

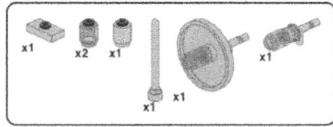

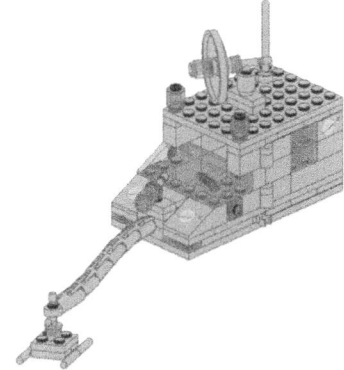

Figure 2.8: Example of a wordless assembly diagram (from LEGO Instruction Creator, aka Web Lic).

Wordless diagrams: Lego makes excellent wordless assembly manuals. (Figure 2.8 was not done by Lego, but is the same style.) You might find inspiration there, perhaps substituting photos for line drawings.

As Tom says, the non-negotiable part is that we'll have an SOP; the negotiable part is what form it takes. As long as we have some kind of SOP, we can improve on it. Having a uniform format for your SOPs will make it easier to write and update them.

What else is in the SOP binder besides the SOP?

Figure 2.9: What's new? This SOP got a major rewrite, but most of the time we'll note the specific areas that have changed.

- On the cover we often list recent changes we've made to the SOPs (Figure 2.9). Handy when you add new accessories or make improvements.

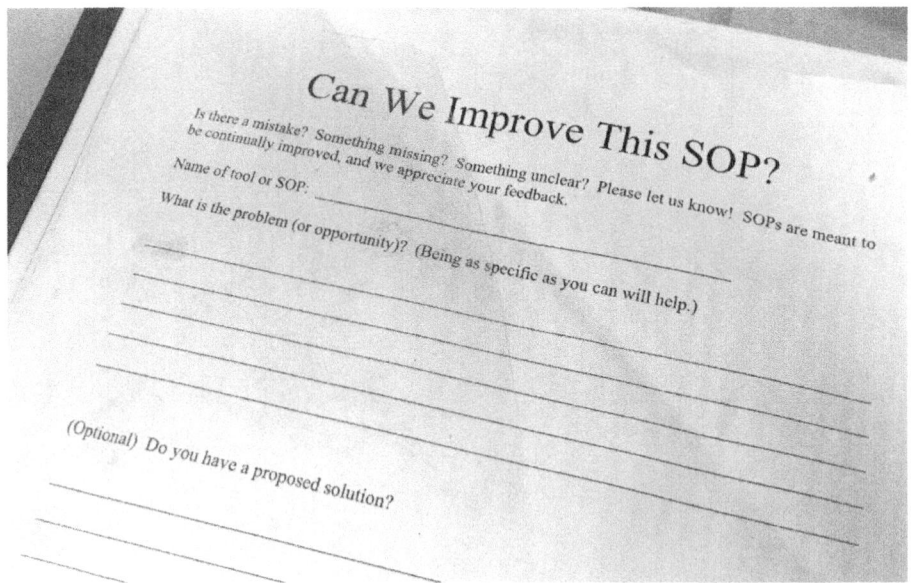

Figure 2.10: Example of seeking improvement for an SOP.

- Inside the front cover is a form "How Can We Improve This SOP?" (Figure 2.10) It provides an opportunity for any user to make suggestions. (Is this the easiest way for a user to tell us? If we really want improvements, we should make it really easy for someone to offer that feedback. Which, by the way, you don't have to take!) It also makes it clearer that we don't want users to make changes to the SOPs—that we'll leave to staff (properly vetted—not every staff person is qualified to make SOP changes on every machine).

- Overview/introduction to the tool: What it does, when used, specifications, capabilities. This is also a good place to list other resources, such as online manuals, user groups, forums, books, online documents, etc., that may be useful to the member.

- General Maker Works safety policies.

- Tool-specific safety: These are elements of safety that are specific to the tool, but can and should also emphasize all appropriate safety issues even if mentioned in the general Maker Works safety guidelines.

- Workflow for tool: When appropriate, an overall flow of the SOPs may be useful to lay out the order of operations when using the tool. A graphical flowchart can be employed if clearer.

- SOPs in order they are typically used. It is often helpful to add tabs to the SOPs so it is easier to locate a given SOP.

- Reference material: Example: tables for feeds & speeds; material charts; settings charts. (These are often located with the specific SOP where they'd be used.)

- You could also have the manufacturer's operator's and service manual, your maintenance SOPs, any machine logs, and other resource material in the SOP binder. We typically keep these other things in a separate filing cabinet up front, but that does mean working on a machine often involves a trip to the front desk.

Figure 2.11: You have to pick up the SOP to use this machine.

Where should you place the SOPs? You might consider the following guideline: make it easy to do the right thing—and hard to do the wrong thing. Make it hard to ignore the SOP. For example, to reinforce the expectation that SOPs will be used, we put the closing SOP hanging in front of the alarm panel. You can't get to the alarm panel to set the alarm without having to handle the SOP. The milling machine SOP is hung in front of the controls (Figure 2.11). You have to physically remove the SOP to operate the machine.

Make sure there's a place to have the SOP open so it can be consulted when using the machine—*make it easy to do the right thing!*

By the way, you'll notice the SOP binder in the Figure 2.11 is scuffed and dirty. We love it when we see covers like that. *Beware the SOP in a clean binder!*

A Cautionary Tale

"In September 2018, the USC team launched Traveler III, which may have been the first collegiate rocket to make it to space. The team expected it to reach about 370,000 feet, but the USC team failed to activate the avionics payload, so none of its flight data got recorded. Prior to the launch of Traveler IV, Tewksbury says, the team overhauled its operational procedures to avoid a similar gaffe."[9] See our discussion below on using checklists to combat just this kind of situation.

2.5 How to Write an SOP

We'll call this a "cooking" recipe—but before you make big changes, try it once or twice following the recipe so you have a baseline for comparison.

---

[9]"A Rocket Built by Students Reached Space for the First Time", https://www.wired.com/story/a-rocket-built-by-students-reached-space-for-the-first-time/, posted 5/22/2019, accessed 5/25/2019

Ingredients:

- Existing documentation (manuals, books, etc.) and/or SOPs
- A partner
- Uninterrupted time
- Vision of success and/or specific outcomes
- Scope of the SOP with start and end points
- Knowledge of when SOP should be applied
- Pencils and note cards
- Domain expert (may be optional)

#	Step Description	Illustration/Diagram/Photo
1	Review the existing processes by reading documentation and/or SOPs. Key point: You may wish to highlight important points in the manual and later review to make sure they made it into your SOP.	
2	Perform the operation several times using the documentation and the domain expert to become familiar with the task, space, and materials.	

2.5. HOW TO WRITE AN SOP

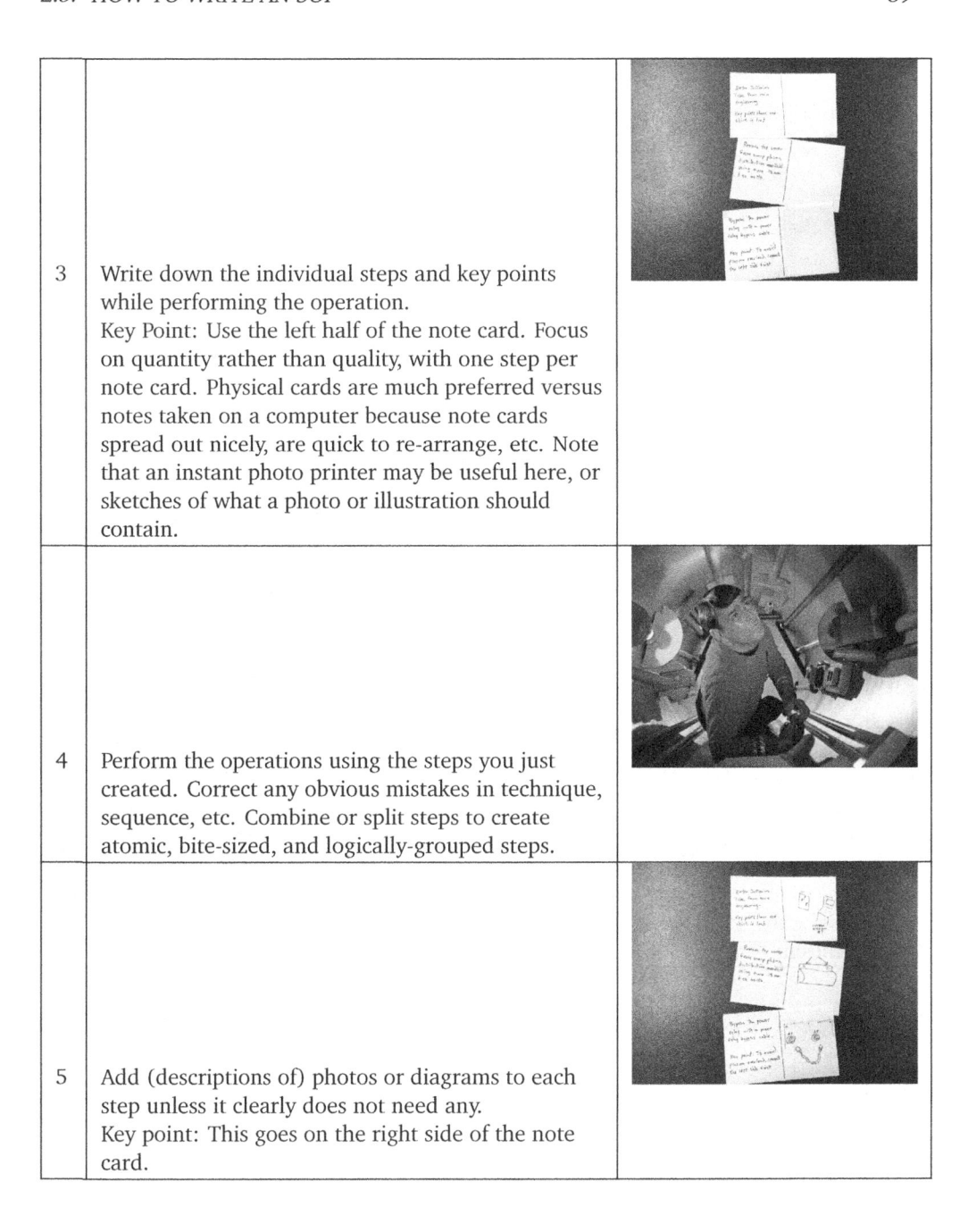

3	Write down the individual steps and key points while performing the operation. Key Point: Use the left half of the note card. Focus on quantity rather than quality, with one step per note card. Physical cards are much preferred versus notes taken on a computer because note cards spread out nicely, are quick to re-arrange, etc. Note that an instant photo printer may be useful here, or sketches of what a photo or illustration should contain.	
4	Perform the operations using the steps you just created. Correct any obvious mistakes in technique, sequence, etc. Combine or split steps to create atomic, bite-sized, and logically-grouped steps.	
5	Add (descriptions of) photos or diagrams to each step unless it clearly does not need any. Key point: This goes on the right side of the note card.	

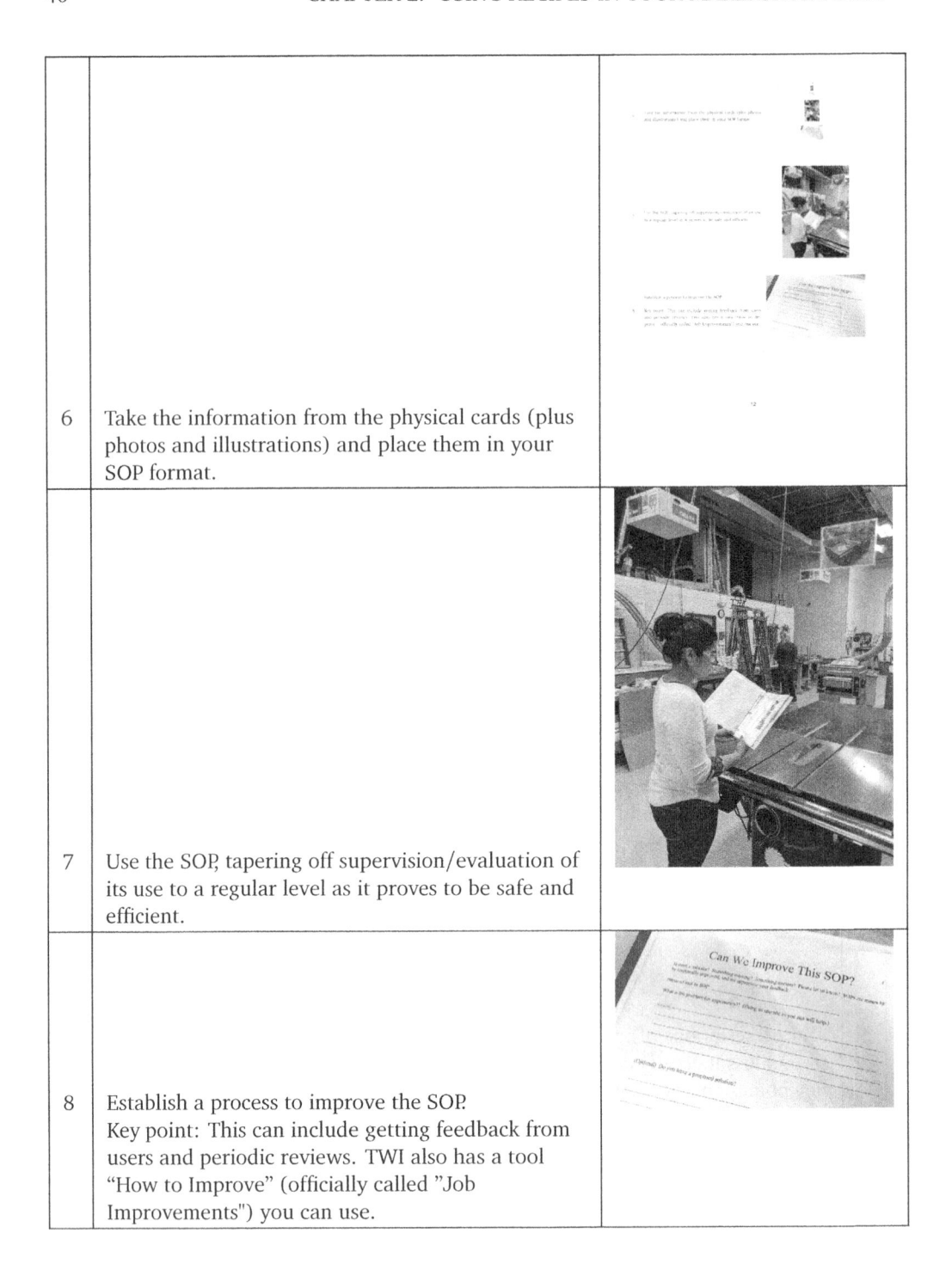

6	Take the information from the physical cards (plus photos and illustrations) and place them in your SOP format.	
7	Use the SOP, tapering off supervision/evaluation of its use to a regular level as it proves to be safe and efficient.	
8	Establish a process to improve the SOP. Key point: This can include getting feedback from users and periodic reviews. TWI also has a tool "How to Improve" (officially called "Job Improvements") you can use.	

2.6 An Exercise in SOP Writing

We highly recommend you try the following experiment in writing SOPs. We can just about guarantee that until you try writing an SOP, you won't have an appreciation of the process.

2.6. AN EXERCISE IN SOP WRITING

You can also use this exercise during your staff training.

Grab a box or something box-shaped (we often use 4x4x4 blocks of wood), some wrapping paper (or newsprint), scissors, tape, and a straight edge.

Your job is to write an SOP for wrapping a present.

Set aside a good 45 minutes or so, grab a partner, and follow the "How to Write an SOP" SOP.

Yes, 45 minutes or more.

Come back here when you're done.

Figure 2.12: Yes, it's Minions Christmas paper. Don't judge.

So, was it an interesting experience?

Here are some questions to ask yourself and your SOP partner:

- Did you both agree at the start on what the outcome should be? For example, is it permissible to tape to the object? (In some families—Tom isn't saying whose, you understand—a person could be ostracized for this Yuletide faux pas. In other families, merely the attempt to wrap a gift, versus using a gift bag, would be a Christmas miracle of the highest order.)

- Did you have a common set of words for the operations and results? Talk to an origamist sometime—they have a well-developed vocabulary for paper manipulation, though that's not something we would expect of our average user. It can sometimes be helpful to teach a special vocabulary at the start of an SOP so we then can use it.

- Will the directions work for a left or right-handed person?

- How did you deal with directions and orientations?

- Does your SOP cover oblong or round objects? (Did you intend it to?)

- Did your SOP align the patterns on the wrapping paper? (Once again, it's not entirely clear you're going to be invited to next year's Christmas.)

- How did you deal with steps where you needed an illustration or photo? (Does it make sense that the default is to have an illustration or diagram for each step?)

We highly recommend you find someone else to use your SOP to perform the task. One memorable time one of our groups had omitted the step where the paper is cut off from the roll—it didn't even occur to them that after measuring the paper that the user wouldn't then cut off the paper. A second group, following their instructions to the letter, ended up with a wrapped box, but with the remaining roll of paper hanging off one end, still attached. Wish we had taken a picture.

2.7 Your SOP Guidelines

Many people in your makerspace may create SOPs. It will help a lot if everyone creates SOPs using the same guidelines. Pick a software tool that everyone has access to (LibreOffice, Google Docs[10], Word, etc.). Elements to specify or provide in your guidelines:

- Template for cover
- Where to store photos
- Front matter for SOPs (shop safety, etc.)
- Font face, size for titles and regular text
- Size of photos (e.g., specify the width in pixels, but with a maximum height)
- Page numbering
- Footer information (such as file name, date of last update, etc.)

2.8 Checklists Augmenting SOPs: The War Against Hubris

Earlier we discussed checklists when used as a form of SOP, especially when we want to document the fact that a process was executed. However, checklists have another strong role to play in makerspaces, surgeries, airplane cockpits, SCUBA diving, etc., where they're used not as much as standalone SOPs but as memory aids.

The situation is this: our member, our surgeon, our pilot, etc., has used some form of instruction (hopefully including SOPs!) to learn the process they're executing, be it a cut on a table saw or sewing up an artery in someone. Over time, with practice and repetition, they have mastered it—that is, they no longer need the SOP when they perform the operation.

---

[10]Google Docs, at least at the time of this writing, is a nice solution since multiple people can collaborate, and it can produce nicely formatted output. Just be sure that documents and folders are "owned" by a central figure or entity, rather than individuals who may come and go.

2.8. CHECKLISTS AUGMENTING SOPS: THE WAR AGAINST HUBRIS

Except humans are fallible, and also susceptible to excessive self-confidence. See surgeon Atul Gawande's book "The Checklist Manifesto: How to Get Things Right" for many examples of highly skilled people, such as surgeons, forgetting to do very basic things like washing hands or asking for basic information. Pilots and astronauts have checklists and run through them for each and every flight—it is just too easy to forget to set just one switch. A painful example is that of the B-17 Flying Fortress, the result of a competition in 1935 to design a new long-range bomber. The prototype crashed almost immediately on take-off during evaluations, not because of any defects in the plane, but because the pilot had failed to disengage a single locking mechanism on this complex plane. Two died in the crash, and Boeing lost that competiton. The military apparently realized the inherent value of the design, but how to deal with the complexity of the new plane? The response wasn't to train the pilots more, as might be expected, but to provide them with a checklist of the operations needed. Armed with the checklist, the B-17 went on to be one of the most-produced aircraft of all time—over 12,000 were produced.[11]

The checklist in this case is not a basis for instruction, conveying information to the user, but a succinct summary of the steps that ensures no step is omitted. It is quick to use, increasing the odds that it will in fact be used. If a member is not going to use the full SOP, then in many cases they should at least use a checklist.

We think there's a very strong argument that a makerspace culture should include the use of SOPs as the basis for instruction and operation until the SOP is fully mastered. Then, if it is likely in practice that a member will tend to not use the SOP, a checklist should be front and center, particularly where the sequence of steps has a safety component (e.g., we have a checklist for the oxy-acetylene torch in our jewelry studio). The danger is that the checklist is used before the SOP is mastered, but with a solid checklist we're probably ahead of the situation where neither SOP nor checklist is used at all.

2.8.1 Mnemonic Devices

Say the phrase "blue whales really are fat" to a scuba diver and you may get a nod of acknowledgement. (Or they'll look at you strangely until you say "you know, BWRAF". At this point it's either a smile of recognition, or a slow backing away to a safe distance.) It's a mnemonic device to remember the pre-dive checklist that most scuba divers go through each time they get in the water[12]. The "B" is for checking their buoyancy; "W" is weights; "R" is releases; and so on. A lot of divers, including experienced divers, are alive today because of those 5 simple letters.

There's no arguing that a mnemonic you've memorized is handy—it's never going to get lost (forgotten, perhaps), smudged, etc. If there's a real obvious mnemonic for your processes, it could be useful. But in practice in a makerspace, we'd suggest physically writing things down is the better approach, and having an explicit (check)list is better than just a mnemonic. Among other things, you can update a poster; it's a little harder to update someone's mind. It's another tool to be aware of.

---

[11] https://blog.nuclino.com/the-simple-genius-of-checklists-from-b-17-to-the-apollo-missions

[12] Note that this "buddy check" as well as the dive is done with a buddy for safety. You actually are expected to demonstrate or verify each of the steps with your buddy. That makes it even harder to skip a step; you're also taking some responsibility for another person's safety, which you might take a little more seriously than your own.

2.8.2 Checklists for Project Planning

Just as an aside, some folks will talk about project planning tools like Gantt charts or to-do lists when discussing checklists. While these are very important tools, project planning and to-do lists differ from the SOPs we're discussing in that they're typically specific to a particular project, are usually executed once with no expectation of re-use or improvement, and rarely discuss the "how", instead emphasizing the "what" and "when".[13] If you don't know what a Gantt chart is, it's well worth learning about—it's a pretty handy tool that provides a graphical picture of the tasks, dependencies, and timing of a project. GanttProject is an open-source program that works nicely to create Gantt charts and more. For a discussion of checklists as practical project planning aid, check out chapter 3 of Adam Savage's[14] book "Every Tool's a Hammer".

2.9 Improving SOPs

Your SOPs are out in the shop. Ideally, the covers are looking well used, and there are smudges[15] on some of the pages. You're not done yet, though.

Make it easy for anyone who is using the SOP to provide feedback. Will you always act on that feedback? Not every time, but the harder it is to provide feedback, the less you'll get. We provide a form in the front of each SOP binder that asks for suggestions for improvements:

- Name of tool or SOP
- What is the problem or opportunity (as specific as they can be)?
- Optionally, do they have a proposed solution?
- Optionally, their name and contact information so we can follow up.

Monitor what questions or problems members are having. Ideally, each time someone comes up to a staff person with a question, we should ask ourselves if a system (for example, the SOP, or perhaps the way we've set up the machine) has failed.[16] Now, many times it's some unique situation that's unlikely to come up again (our members will tend to be very creative, after all). But if this is an issue that isn't in the SOP but seems likely to come up again, then it probably should go into the SOP (or perhaps a knowledge-base). This approach, letting the pain guide our response, works if the "pain" is minor. We don't want to always be in a reactive mode, and we don't want injuries to members or damage to machines to be our notification that we have an SOP or other system to improve.

We have a staff huddle every Wednesday afternoon, and a regular agenda item is "Items of Significance (IOS) from the daily huddles". A tool broke. A member was unhappy with

---

[13]However, our SOP for lost-wax investment casting has a real project-planning vibe to it. It turns out that you have a very specific window to mix, de-gas, pour, de-gas, then store the investment. Something like 10 minutes, plus or minus 2. Take too long or short and you won't get a good, detailed mold. So the SOP includes a stop-watch time as a guide.

[14]Co-host with Jamie Hyneman of the TV show *Mythbusters*.

[15]Dale has a wonderful old book of activities for kids from about 100 years ago. The pages that describe how to make cotton candy are a bit sticky.

[16]Note that we typically don't start from the viewpoint that the member failed to learn, for reasons we'll go into in other sections of this book.

a policy.[17] We ran out of gas for the welder. In a surprising number of instances, we end up asking ourselves, do we need to change our SOP or other systems to prevent this from happening again?

You can also institute a formal SOP review on a regular basis. Having an outside "domain expert" may be helpful, though having an outside person with absolutely no experience may be even more informative since they will easily pick up on issues that the expert will forget are not common knowledge. Get both if you can.

2.10 How Many SOPs Does Maker Works Have?

We recently counted how many SOPs we have:

- Craft (Plastics & Textiles): 17
- Electronics: 5
- Jewelry: 11
- Maintenance: 16
- Metal: 27
- Software: 5
- Checkout classes: 26
- Wood: 23

In addition, we have around 100 administrative SOPs (start of the day, taking payment for an invoice, dealing with a power outage, etc.), and all told we figure right now we have about 240 or so SOPs in the shop with a total page count of around 2,100. The longest SOP is for the ShopBot CNC router at 78 pages (9,400 words).

That sounds like a lot of work, and it has been, but it's the end result of almost 10 years of work. Also recall that 20% of the SOPs will account for 80% of the usage. We'd say you definitely need SOPs for tools before you let anyone use them, but you don't have to have the "what to do if the power goes out" SOP done on day 1.

2.11 Summary

SOPs are nothing but recipes, and they let us deliver value consistently and sustainably. They're absolutely necessary for instruction, and the basis for continuous improvement.

Before you use them, they may feel constraining, a straightjacket on our creativity. But SOPs are shortcuts in the best possible sense, delivering us to our destination without getting stuck in swamps or deserts. If you want to spend time in the swamp, that's excellent. More power to you. But if you really wanted to get to that nice hill in the distance, SOPs get you there faster, so you can spend your time on what is valuable to you.

---

[17] I know—seems unlikely, doesn't it?

SOPs tell us how, but what's the reality of the workspace that we will try to execute these SOPs in? It's one thing to know you need a 5/8" wrench to tighten the bolts, but if there's no telling where it's hiding, are you closer to your goal? In the next section, on 5S, we provide—what else?—an SOP for creating organized workspaces that support our SOPs and all the other activity in our shops.

2.12 Resources

Most of this chapter is available as a free PDF on the www.maker-works.com website.

Chapter 3

Organizing Workspaces Using 5S

When we "5S" an area, we create an organized workspace that delivers better value to the user by reducing waste. There's actually a very useful definition of waste we'll get to in a later section—the 8 DEADLY WASTES—but for the moment, waste includes things like time wasted looking for tools, movement wasted in walking a long distance to get a tool, and so on. When we 5S, it's assumed that the area and operations are worthwhile—that is, they're "value-add"[1] or at least necessary. *We don't get credit for reducing the waste of an operation that isn't value-add or necessary*—as we'll see later, our response should be to *eliminate* that operation.

The term "5S" comes from 5 Japanese words, all beginning with "S" in Japanese, that map roughly to English as follows:

- Sort

- Set in Order

- Shine

- Standardize

- Sustain

The end result: "A visual workplace is a work environment that is self-ordering, self-explaining, self-regulating and self-improving—where what is supposed to happen does happen, on time, every time, because of visual solutions."[2] Figure 3.1 shows a part of a pegboard of tools for our jewelry area as an example.

---

[1] See section 12.
[2] "Visual Workplace, Visual Thinking" by Dr. Gwendolyn Galsworth, www.visualworkplace.com

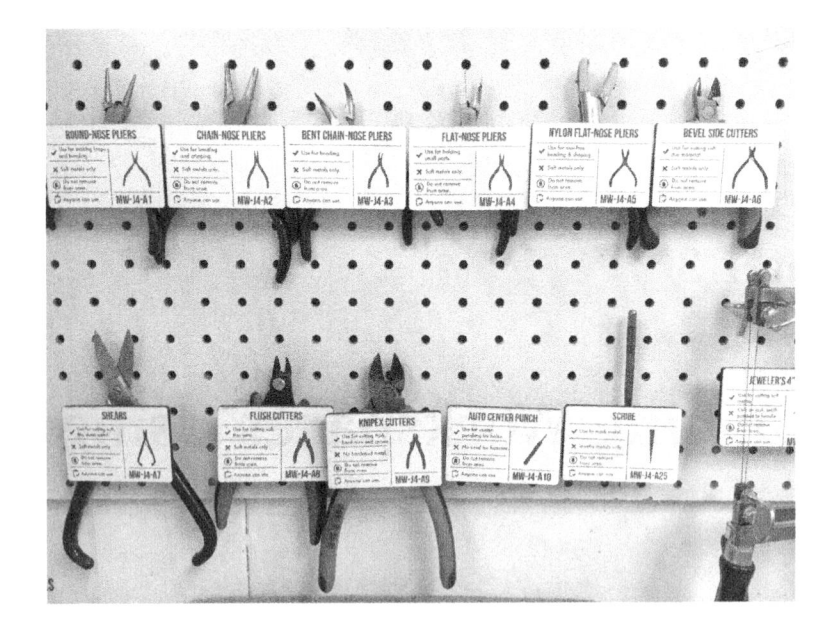

Figure 3.1: Pegboard of jewelry tools.

Are there any tools missing?

Can you locate the bent chain-nose pliers?

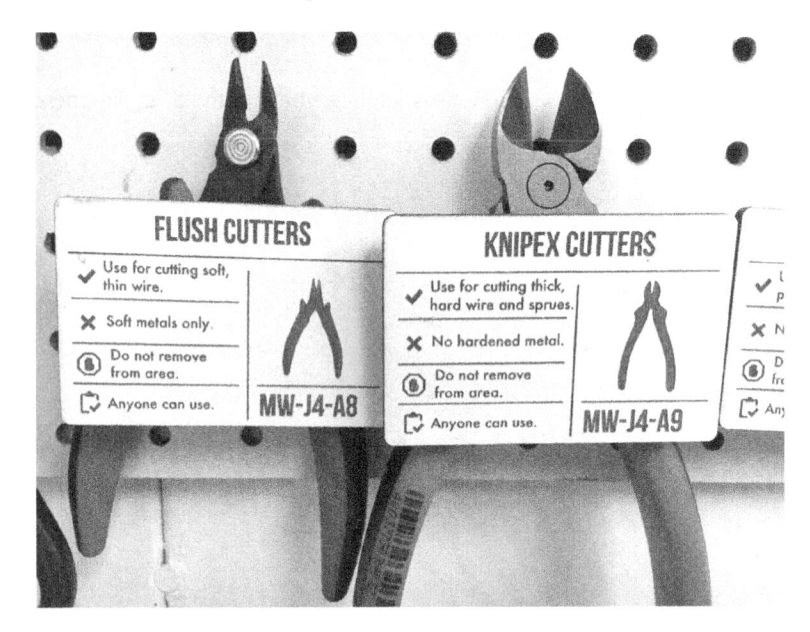

Figure 3.2: Two jewelry tool *home tags*.

Figure 3.2 is a close up of two of the labels. Should you use the flush cutters to cut hard wire?

Compare at least the ideal of the above with trying to work at a friend's workbench. Where do they keep the precision screwdrivers? If they're in a drawer, you'll have to open each drawer to find them. Can you use their Knipex brand cutters to cut hardened wire? (For some models of Knipex cutters the answer is yes, but are you sure the one your friend has is that type?) Where should you put the wire strippers so your friend can find them?

If you're not into electronics, a more relatable analogy may be to think about going into someone else's kitchen to try to cook—same idea. It's even better as an example in some ways because private kitchens are often designed to hide a lot of the variation or disorder in contents behind a lot of doors and drawers. Where are the drinking glasses? Behind one of the cabinet doors no doubt, but good luck guessing which. Where's the whisk? Probably a drawer. More problematic, which of the three drawers with cooking utensils in them does the whisk go into if you don't know or forgot where it came from?

Note that in this situation, when we're looking for something, we succeed when we find it. When we want to put it back, we can't be sure we succeeded. 5S in the makerspace needs to address both situations.

In a recent video, Adam Savage put it this way: "If you can't see it, you don't have it."[3]

This feeling of confusion and frustration—not to speak of the major waste of time all around—would be a constant in our makerspace if we don't intentionally work to avoid it. 5S is our major tool to do that.

A 5S-ed area will look like this:

- The workspace will emphasize safety.
- Personal protective equipment, guards, notices, etc. are available.
- The correct tool and accessories will be available and ready for use for common operations (think area around a tool like the drill press or laser).
- Tools are located near their area of use.
- Extraneous tools and "stuff" are removed and do not clutter up the area.
- The area is clean.
- Tools are not half-hidden by sawdust or swarf.[4]
- Tools and accessories are labeled so the function is clear and the correct tools can be picked (e.g., called out in an SOP).
- SOPs for the tool are available and prominent, demonstrating our commitment to their use.
- Tools labeled for ownership and "address", making it easy to identify and return tools to their home.
- The workspace can be modified over time to improve.
- Tools can be located visually and quickly.
- Doors and drawers are avoided as much as possible since they make it harder to see what is inside.

---

[3] "Adam Savage's One Day Builds: Machinist Tool Drawers!", YouTube, retrieved 8/16/2020, around the 16:55 mark.

[4] And, they are not *fully*-hidden by sawdust or swarf, either. And that comment alone should convince you that we really do spend our time in a makerspace.

In general, we will try to "make it easy to do the right thing, and hard to do the wrong thing" around tool use in our 5S-ing.

If you haven't read Adam Savage's book "Every Tool's a Hammer"[5], you should. It has a ton of great messages for the maker community. In it (Chapter 10, "See Everything, Reach Everything"), Adam describes his organization method, which you might say amounts to "5S for one"—that is, a workspace and tool organization strategy tuned for use by one particular person. His goals are to minimize wasted time by making it visually clear where everything is, make it easy to identify missing tools, and fast to get at anything. (As a measure of how serious he is, Adam has a full page photo of his tape storage, along with half a page of text describing it.) He does this by locating tools near where they're used (duplicating if necessary), visually displaying tools (see his tool rack on page 232), avoiding drawers, and always looking for ways of improving.

3.1 Why 5S?

When we 5S, we send a message to our members that we care about their experience using the tools, and we care about the tools. This message seems to translate into better use and care of the tools on the part of members.

5S-ing increases the value of the makerspace to our members. They can be more efficient, instead of wasting time looking for a tool. Labels can provide guidance on how to use hand tools, for example, in ways that are appropriate and avoids damaging the tools. They also make it easier for the member to keep the space looking good—members are not all lazy, and many will really appreciate not just coming into an organized area, but being able to keep it organized.

5S-ing reduces wastes on the part of the member and staff—wasted time hunting down tools, movement as staff returns far-flung tools to their homes, and so on. (See the Maker Works 5S SOP below for a longer discussion of waste in the context of 5S.)

5S-ing makes it readily apparent when a tool is missing, so we can replace it or track it down.

Just like SOPs, though, 5S-ing takes some time. While everyone here is excited when we go through and 5S a new area or revisit an old one, it's really easy to try to get by without taking that time. All we can say is that it's very unlikely you're going to regret 5S-ing. The impact on member experience, staff time, tool damage, and so on is always worth it.

Anecdotally, 5S can have a huge impact in tool-heavy areas. In our Electronics area, tools would often go "walk-about", and it always took time to collect the handful of tools—snips, strippers, pliers, etc.—for a project. After we 5S-ed, "borrowing" and misplacing went way down, and it was readily apparent when we needed to replace tools. Members seemed much happier working at the bench.

Pamela, one of our staff, notes that 5S-ing really helped with our COVID-19 response. Hand tools were collected after member use in plastic tubs, then brought to an ozone cabinet for sanitizing. 5S—in particular, tool addresses—made it possible to efficiently return tools so members could find them. This was not one of the benefits we anticipated in 5S-ing the shop, but was much appreciated in a trying time.

---

[5]Mentioned earlier in the discussion of checklists in Chapter 2.

Please note that the last "S" isn't "*Stroll away*, content in the knowledge that you have permanently and for all time 5S-ed the heck out of that workspace." Instead, the reality is that 5S-ing will require us to make a *S*ustained effort, pushing gently back against entropy or even, dare we say, continuously improving.

3.2 The 5 S's (in English)

Sort

Sort through the items in the workspace to eliminate everything that shouldn't be there. Identify what should be there that isn't already (or has been lost/broken). Use the "red tag" process (described later).

Set in Order

Arrange tools so they are easily accessible and in a logical order.

Avoid doors and drawers—items should be easy to visually locate.

It must be easy to find the tools, and easy to return them to their correct home once done with them.

Create labels to provide additional information or context when appropriate.

Provide SOPs when needed.

Shine

Clean the workspace on a regular basis.

Make it easy to keep the workspace clean—keep cleaning supplies nearby.

Reduce the need for cleaning—e.g., fill in corners where dust collects.

Standardize

Have a procedure in place so the first 3 S's are regularly performed.

Sustain

Make sure all the business elements support 5S-ing. Share the 5S concepts with staff and members. Actively look for improvements. Like an SOP, a 5S-ed workspace that cannot be modified is as useful as a knife that can't be sharpened.

3.3 Maker Works' 5S SOP and Standards

What follows is our SOP for 5S-ing at Maker Works. (There's a little bit repeated from what we've already said.) Your makerspace will have its own SOP and standards. Maybe you try things without using addresses, for example. But from as early as you can, your makerspace should have a documented process that anyone on your staff (or perhaps members!) can follow so your 5S-ing is uniform, and serves as the basis for a better process.

3.3.1 Overview

This document describes how we're going to organize our makerspace. Anyone can use this to improve an area—either 5S-ing for the first time, or improving the existing organization.

3.3.2 Deadly Wastes and 5S

The end result of 5S-ing is an organized arrangement of a workspace that reduces *waste*. Waste is anything that doesn't increase value from the perspective of the customer (our members). (For our purposes, we will treat safety as a defect form of waste.) In particular, we are talking about the *8 Deadly Wastes*[6] from Lean. (We'll order them using the "DOWN-TIME" mnemonic.) 5S is an element of Lean manufacturing, which has as a central tenet making obvious what adds value by reducing everything else.

Defects. We reduce defects by

- Maximizing safety! This means physically (via choice and outfitting of tool), environment (clean, well-lit, etc.), behavior (of user and others), and culture

- Having the correct tool (and accessories) available and ready for use (e.g., sharp, or easily sharpened) for common operations, reducing the chances of a poor result

- Labeling tools so function (operations and materials allowed) are clear and the correct tool can be picked

- Having SOPs easily at hand for the tool or station so correct operation is more likely

- Making it easy to do the right thing

- Making it more difficult to do the wrong thing (unsafe operations, incorrect tool use, inappropriate tool application)

Overproduction. We reduce the amount or desire for overproduction (producing more than the customer wants right now) by

- Reducing setup time for an operation
- Reducing operation time
- Reducing wait time

---

[6]We'll have more to say about the 8 DEADLY WASTES later on. We included it here in our internal SOP as a way to provide some context to our staff for why we're 5S-ing.

3.3. MAKER WORKS' 5S SOP AND STANDARDS

- Increasing the actual and perceived ease for operations
- Educating ourselves and our members about the downside to overproduction/batching

Waiting. We reduce time wasted waiting by

- Having multiple tools when it makes sense (relieve bottlenecks)
- Making it easy to return tools when done
- Making it easy to locate tools when needed (less need to hold onto them)
- Reducing time to set up tools
- Having tools that are efficient at common operations (versus using tools that can do the job, but take a longer time)
- Having accessories that improve efficiency (e.g., jigs)
- Minimizing the time members have to wait before being allowed to use a tool (i.e., checkout classes)

Not Utilizing Talent. We use members' and staff's talents by

- Making it easy to provide improvements to processes (e.g., feedback forms)
- Creating and sustaining a knowledge-base of information generated from everyday interactions (e.g., common answers to problems outside the SOP)

Transportation. We minimize transportation waste by

- Reducing the distance that materials must be moved in the course of work (e.g., lots of work surfaces handy to machines, member storage fairly close to shops)

Inventory. We reduce inventory waste by

- Not needlessly duplicating tools (but sometimes we need multiples in different locations to minimize other waste)
- Eliminating tools or materials not carrying their weight
- Making it easy and fast to identify items actually in need of replacing (vs. temporarily misplaced)
- Actively managing short term, medium term, and long term storage for members and the organization

Motion Waste. We reduce motion waste by

- Locating tools close to point of use
- Making it easy to locate tools

- Making it easy to return tools

Excess Processing. We reduce excessive processing by

- Minimizing the administrative burden on members and staff (e.g., collect data in the most efficient manner, treat the burden or time of processing as a service we provide, etc.)

- Minimize the overhead required to use a tool

Other wastes. (Not part of the deadly wastes)

- Better use of floor space

- Reduced use of staff time locating tools for members or returning tools

- Better use/maintenance of tools

The solution to some of these deadly wastes is a visual management system for organizing work areas which can summarized as the following 5S process:

Sort: Go through all items in the area and keep only the essential. All else is moved off site for redistribution ("red tagging") or is discarded. Communicate clearly with everyone affected.

Shine: Clean appearance and fully operational. This includes an initial effort to clean (appearance) and inspect all items (function). Look for ways to reduce on-going clutter and sources of dirt and debris (e.g., install dust collection, choose fixtures that don't collect dirt, etc.). Include lighting, floor, ceiling, fixtures, shelves, drawers, tables, counters, chairs, data/power, HVAC.

Set in Order: Organize—a home for everything, everything has an address. SOPs or tool information (e.g., labels) are available. Safety warnings and equipment in place. Gauges/indicators easy to interpret. Inventory processes in place (e.g., kanbans[7]).

Standardize: Create standardized procedures to maintain the operations/workspace. This includes procedures for keeping things clean, inspected, repaired, maintained. SOPs (or other usage information) may be needed for tool use.

Sustain: Have processes such as "43 Folders" (see page 123) to make sure procedures are used. Practice continuous improvement!

The end result: "A visual workplace is a work environment that is self-ordering, self-explaining, self-regulating and self-improving—where what is supposed to happen does happen, on time, every time, because of visual solutions."[8]

---

[7] In this context a kanban is an indicator, often a physical tag, that signals the need to replenish inventory.
[8] "Visual Workplace, Visual Thinking" by Dr. Gwendolyn Galsworth, www.visualworkplace.com

3.3. MAKER WORKS' 5S SOP AND STANDARDS

3.3.3 Resources for 5S-ing

When 5S-ing an area, you may need some of the following resources:

- Marking tools
    - Fine tip sharpie (misc colors for various areas)
    - Fine metallic sharpie (silver and gold)
    - Vibrating engraver
    - Paints: Testors enamel, 3–4 small cheap paint brushes, jar w/cleaner or acetone
    - White heat shrink tubing, various sizes
    - Clear heat shrink tubing, various sizes
    - Heat gun (or space for)
- Tags, etc.
    - Laser engravable dog tags[9] (black, red)
    - Laser engravable luggage tags (black, red) (larger versions of above)
    - Whiteboard[10] pieces (24" x 12", to fit smallest laser)
    - Laser-cut pegboard inserts (1/8" baltic birch)
    - 6", 12" zip-ties
    - Ball-chains w/connectors (keychain type)
    - Template files on Google drive
- Kaizen foam[11]
    - Knife
    - Marker (long-neck)
- Other material:
    - Thermark/Cermark[12]

3.3.4 5S SOP

Use this SOP as an overall guide to 5S-ing an area. Consult other SOPs for Tool Addresses, Home Tags, Processing Tools, Marking Tools, and Area Labeling.

---

[9]Anodized aluminum tags and other materials are available from, for example, Johnson Plastics at https://www.jpplus.com/laserbits

[10]Big box hardware stores—Lowes, Home Depot, etc.—sell smooth white hardboard sheets for under $15 a piece. These laser engrave very nicely, as seen in Figure 3.2.

[11]A multi-layer closed-cell foam often used for 5Sing. Sold by FastCap.

[12]Paint or spray-on material that allows you to mark metal using a laser engraver.

Determine the scope of the workspace to be 5S-ed. Key point: Coordinate with others to make sure the area makes sense and fits in with other 5S-ing to be done. (May want to think about 5S-ing an area in the context of Bottom Line Change[13].)	
Document the "before" status with photos and any metrics available. Key point: Can you measure how long it takes to complete a task? Are there existing records, like Code Reds[14], that you can refer to?	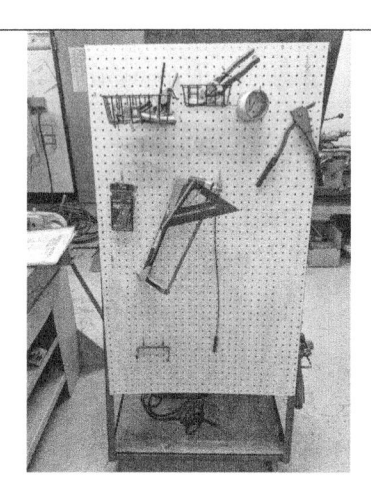
Communicate with affected people. Key point: This communication may be an opportunity to also exercise Bottom Line Change.	

---

[13] Bottom Line Change is discussed at 17.3.
[14] Code Reds document instances where a member has a problem—see page 153.

3.3. MAKER WORKS' 5S SOP AND STANDARDS

	Sort: Meet with area experts to identify tools to be added, retained, red-tagged, or discarded. Key point: Look for any tools we should have and are missing, issues with existing tools, accessories or consumables (e.g., blades for knives), tools we should have, and tools that we have but are not used or useful. Don't forget tools for maintaining the area, like cleaning supplies and tools. Also include SOPs! "Red Tagged" items have a red tag affixed with the current date, and are moved to a special area. This "purgatory" is used to figure out if an item should be in the shop. If someone then uses the item, the tag is removed. If after a certain time the item hasn't been used or retrieved, the item can be discarded.	
	Move red-tagged items to the red-tag holding area. If needed, post a notice telling where red-tagged items have been moved too.	
	Discard items to be discarded. Key point: See if the items can be used as is by someone else (staff, licensees, members), broken down and parts reused, or recycled. Follow appropriate procedures for disposing of hazardous materials.	
	Order or create additional items required (tools, SOPs, etc.).	
	Shine: Clean remaining tools and items, and the space itself. Make any needed repairs and do any maintenance.	

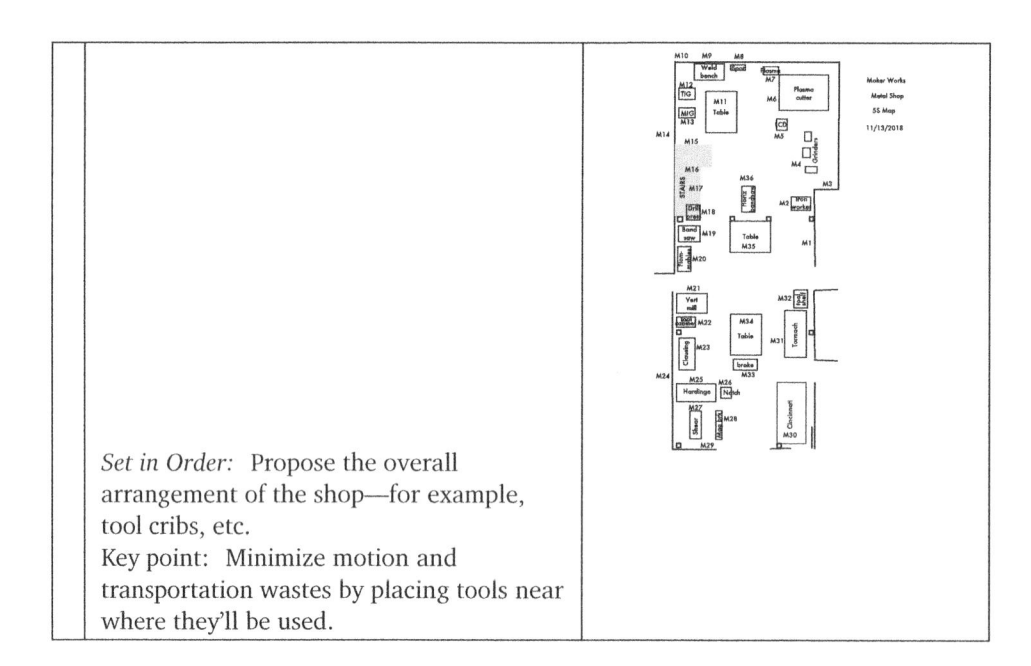

Set in Order: Propose the overall arrangement of the shop—for example, tool cribs, etc.
Key point: Minimize motion and transportation wastes by placing tools near where they'll be used.

3.3. MAKER WORKS' 5S SOP AND STANDARDS

For each tool crib or workstation, propose a method for visual management—i.e., Kaizen foam, pegboard, custom cabinets, etc. Include a time/money budget.
Key points:

- Reduce obstacles to getting tools.

- Tools are easily found, removed, and replaced (visual management)

- Prevent accumulation of unnecessary objects or dirt/debris/dust.

- Make it easy to find a tool's home.

- Make it obvious when a tool is missing and what tool it was.

- Make it easy to add/change for changes in tools, materials, or operators.

- Allow space for Home Tags or other information like tool addresses.

- "No doors, no drawers."

- Use area experts or people who will be fabricating any solutions to assist with design.

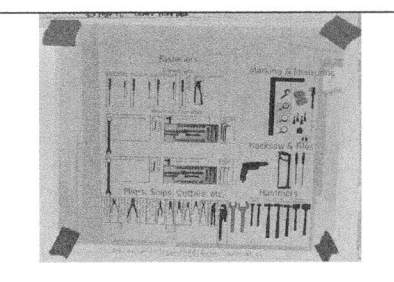

Review the proposed visual management method with manager or owners.

Implement the visual management method within the time/money budget.

Determine the addresses for tool locations using the Tool Address SOP.

Label the locations for tools using the Home Tag SOP. Key point: It is preferable to use a method of labeling locations that can be modified as tools are changed—for example, not engraving directly in a shelf, but using labels that are screwed down.	
Process each tool with the Process Tool SOP. Key point: At a minimum, this is attaching the address to the tool.	
Standardize: Create any new SOPs and review existing SOPs, including • Tool operation SOP • Tool maintenance SOP • SOP for maintaining the 5S-ed area	
Sustain: Use methods like 43-folders to make sure the area receives periodic attention to not just maintain the existing 5S but continuously improve. Evaluate the status of the area to make sure things are working. Make sure 5S is part of the culture for both members and staff. (Periodic audits.)	
Document the "after" with photos! Measure any changes from earlier.	

3.4 Tool Address SOP

Use this SOP to create and assign tool addresses to aid in 5S-ing an area. Tool (or asset) ID numbers and home/tool tags are discussed shortly.

3.4.1 Overview

Tool addresses perform two tasks:

- Associate a tool with where it lives: This is 90% of the value of tool addresses.
- Indicate ownership: At Maker Works, we're indicating ownership to prevent accidental "tool displacement"; it's unlikely to deter outright theft.

Alternatives to tool addresses:

- Captive tool (example: chuck key on a retractable chain, can't be removed physically), especially if it is a small tool.
- Stationary tool (example: Bridgeport Mill), fixed or too large to move.

Even in these cases where tools can wander far, the tool will show up in an inventory list, and there should be an address where one could locate the tool. With large items, the tool itself may be the location for other tools.

3.4.2 Addresses

Tool addresses at Maker Works are in the following format:

MW — <letter><number> — <letter><number>

- "MW" stands for Maker Works (who owns the tools)
- The first group of letter-number is the area (letter) and tool crib within that area. So W2 is wood, tool crib 2. (See Figure 3.3 and Table 3.2.)
- The second group of letter-number is the location within the tool crib—for example, B row, 7th column for B7.

There is only one tool (or type of tool) at any given address. Put another way, there may be three identical tools at the same address, and even three identical tools at three different addresses, but not three different tools at one address. (If you have tools that "go together", maybe append "a", "b", and "c" after the address.)

To aid in quickly identifying Maker Works' tools, each tool should also be prominently marked with a solid white[15] circle (say, 3/4" diameter) with a colored dot in the middle indicating the major area. For example:

A hammer that lives at MW_W2_B7 would have a white circle with green dot for Wood.

A pair of pliers that lives at MW_E1_C2 would have a white circle with red dot for Electronics.

---

[15]Your makerspace should have a different color scheme.

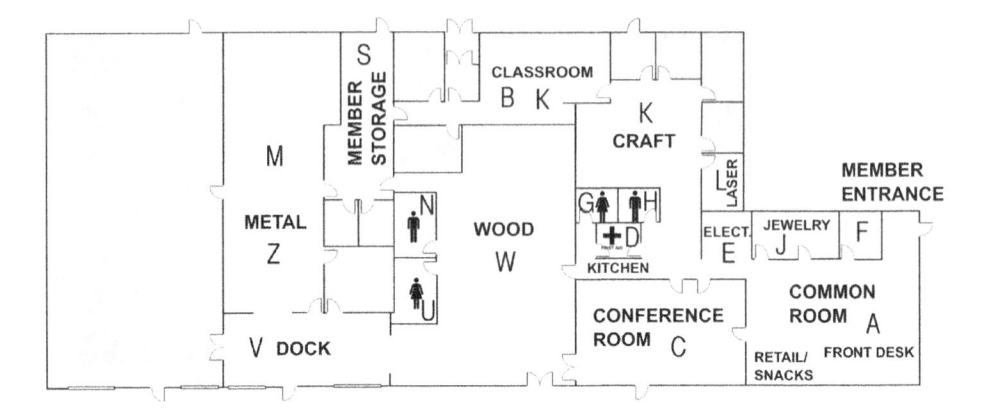

Figure 3.3: Example of a map with area letters.

Area	Letter	Dot Color
(Maker Works)	MW	(white)
Metal	M	blue
Metal Mezzanine	Z	gray
Wood	W	green
Electronics	E	red
Craft	C	orange
Jewelry	J	light green/blue
Computer Lab	B	
Laser	L	
Common Room	A	violet
Member Storage	S	
Front Office	F	
Loading Dock	V	
Kitchen	D	
1st Front Restroom	H	
2nd Front Restroom	G	
Women's Restroom Wood	U	
Men's Restroom Wood	N	

Table 3.2: Example assignments of letters and colors to areas.

(Notes: Avoid giving the letters that can be confused with other letters or numbers—for example, capitals I and O.)

Within an area like Wood or Metal, there will be various tool cribs or places that tools hang out. Some will be stand-alone tool cribs (portable or stationary), others will be larger tools like the Bridgeport mill. Assign numbers starting at 1, keeping in mind that it must be fast and easy to locate a particular tool crib. It must be possible to clearly mark each tool crib such that a person in another part of that shop can easily identify it.

Examples: E1 is the area around one cabinet in Electronics—it is tool location 1 in area (shop) E for Electronics. E4 is the entire opposite wall.

3.4. TOOL ADDRESS SOP

The second letter-number group locates a tool within a tool crib. The letter should indicate some kind of region—for example

- A shelf
- A pegboard
- A row of items
- Under a bench
- A cabinet

The number leads to a specific location.

For example, in Electronics, one entire wall is E4. The top shelf is A, the next shelf is B, the first pegboard area is C, the next pegboard area is D, the last pegboard area is E, the counter is F, and below the counter on the floor is G.

Within the E4-D pegboard area, each position has a number from left to right, top to bottom.

If needed, a new address can be created by appending a letter, like MW-E4-D23a, or a decimal point and number, like MW-E4-D23.5, both of which would be in between D23 and D24.

See Figure 3.4 for an example map of Electronics. See the Area Marking SOP for how to label shops. (Create pictures like below in Inkscape by importing a photo, increasing the transparency, then adding a layer on top for labels.)

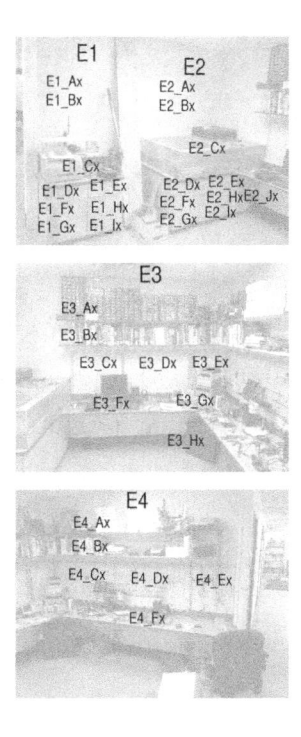

Figure 3.4: Example of a photo labeled with tool areas.

3.5 Home Tag SOP

Use this SOP to create Home Tags, as in Figure 3.5. Home Tags are labels at the tool location that

- Show the address of this location
- Indicate (by name, outline, photo/drawing) what tool goes here
- Provides usage information
- Notes any restrictions (most commonly, not removing the tool from this area)
- Notes any requirements such as using an SOP, taking a class, being staff, etc.

They are important in that they make it easy to do the right thing

- Use tools properly
- Return tools to the right place
- Locate the right tool

Figure 3.5: Example of an area with Home Tags for each tool.

Home Tags can be part of the tool crib itself (e.g., laser engraved into the wood), but making them individually positioned makes it "easier to do the right thing", which is continuously improving the tool crib by changing tools, improving labels, and so on.

3.5. HOME TAG SOP

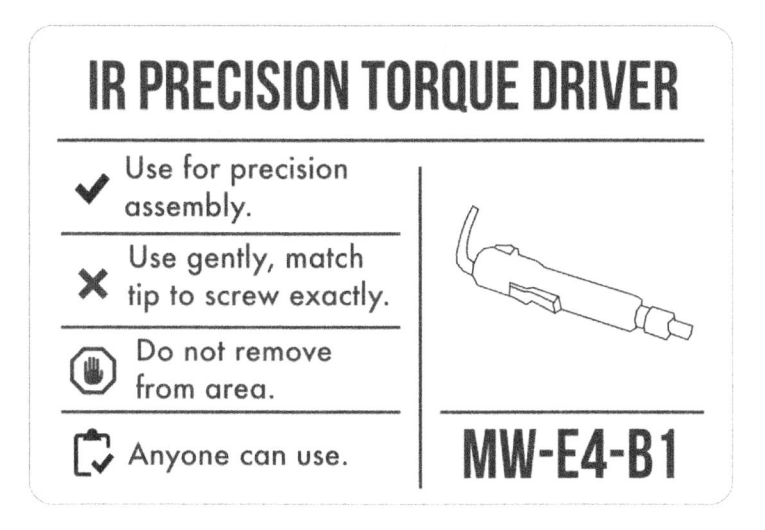

![Example Home Tag showing IR PRECISION TORQUE DRIVER with checkmark "Use for precision assembly", X mark "Use gently, match tip to screw exactly", stop-hand "Do not remove from area", clipboard-check "Anyone can use", and location code MW-E4-B1]

Figure 3.6: Example Home Tag.

Our home tags should follow the example in Figure 3.6, specifically:

- Show the name and alternative names of the tool. Examples: "Allen or Hex Wrench", "Bridgeport Milling Machine".

- The name should be in 20 pt Bebas Neue font.

- Give the address of the tool location in the form MW — <letter><number> — <letter><number> in the lower right corner in 20 pt Bebas Neue font (same as name).

- State allowed operations and materials in the form of "Use for doing X on Y". Example: "Use for cutting component leads and thin copper wires." Precede with a checkmark icon. Use 10 pt Futura font for this and remaining text.

- State disallowed operations and materials in the form of "Do not use for X on Y". Example: "Do not cut thick wires or other materials." Precede with a X icon.

- Note any restrictions (outside of operation and materials) such as "Do not remove from area." Precede with a stop-hand icon.

- State usage policy for the tool. Precede with clipboard-check icon. One of the following:

    o Anyone can use. (No class is required. No SOP is required—i.e., it is fairly clear how to use it.)

    o Use the SOP. (No class is required, but use of the SOP is required.)

    o Checkout Class Required. (SOP is required.)

    o Staff Only. (No member use. Will be rare.)

- If the tool location does not otherwise give the shape or photo of the tool, then include a drawing, photo, outline, silhouette or other visual guide for identifying what tool lives here. (See info shortly.) If the color of the tool is useful for identification and you are using a monochrome method (like laser engraving) to make the label, you can label the color next to the tool outline.

- The outline of the tag is a rectangle, 2" x 3", with 0.08" radius corners.

Templates in Inkscape format for a 2" x 3" Home Tag and other 5S resources are in the 5S Google folder. Laser settings: 400 dpi, 65/80, 13/100/500 Cutting hangers out of 1/8" baltic plywood: 16/90/3500.[16]

3.5.1 Creating Part Outlines

To create a very high contrast photo for creating a silhouette, place the tool on top of a diffused photo light (pointing upwards) as in Figure 3.7. You can also use a piece of translucent plastic (acrylic or polycarbonate).

Figure 3.7: A diffused photo light, turned on, produces high-contrast images for creating tool silhouettes.

3.5.2 Mounting Home Tags

Nitto brand double-stick tape works well for attaching whiteboard tags to clean, flat surfaces. 3M VHB tape, which is much thicker, accommodates more surface variation.

Screws can be used, but consume space on the front of the tag and could be visually distracting, however there is also a long history of riveted or screwed labels that offer examples of handling the mounting holes gracefully.

---

[16]We copied this from our internal SOP—your SOP will provide whatever information is needed for your staff and tools.

3.5. HOME TAG SOP

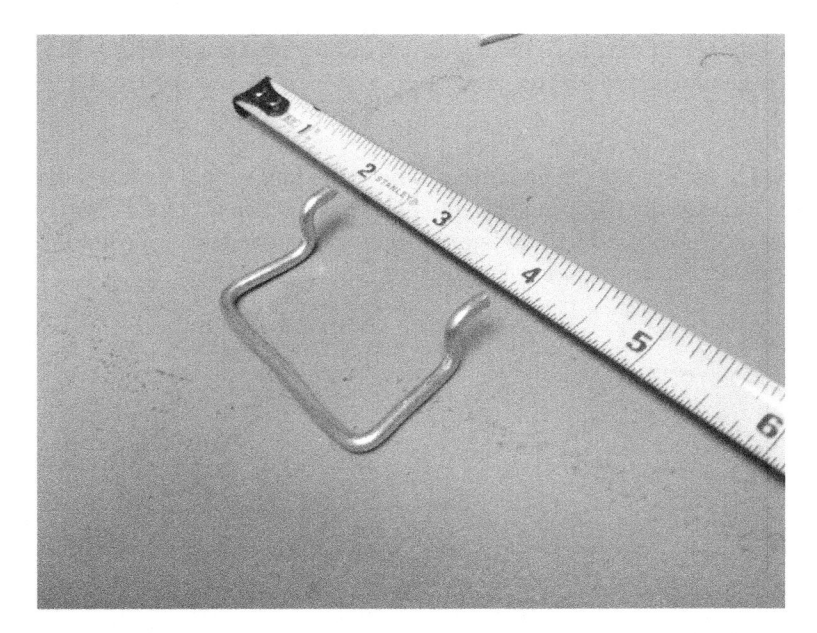

Figure 3.8: Shop-made pegboard hook for the back of a home tag.

Pegboard: To attach the Home Tag flat to a pegboard (there are a couple of examples of this in the photo of the Electronics pegboard), take some 1/8" or 3/16" aluminum wire and bend into the form shown in Figure 3.8. The spacing between the ends should be 2" center to center, to fit a standard pegboard.

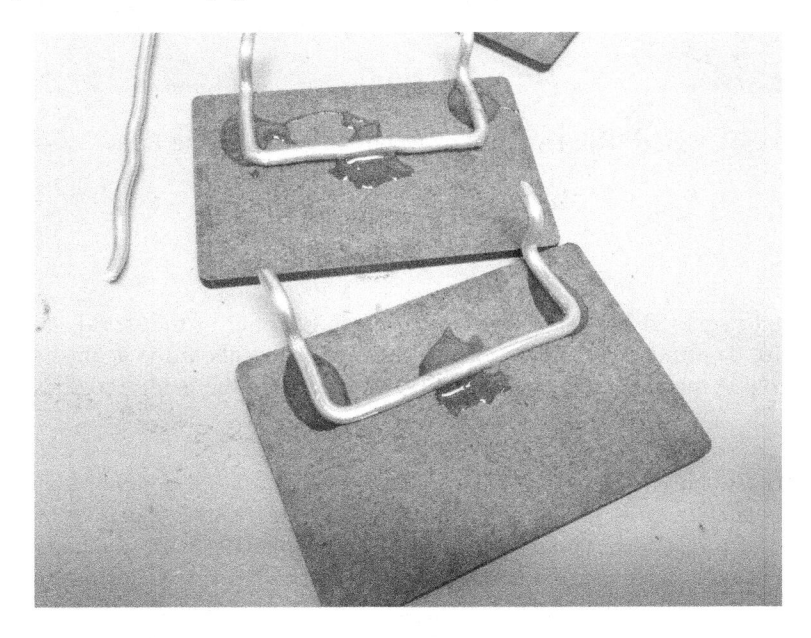

Figure 3.9: Epoxy attaching pegboard hooks.

5-Minute epoxy[17], as in Figure 3.9, will secure it to the tag. Be sure to position the ends of

---
[17]Hot glue may also work.

the wire past the top of the tag so the tag can be installed in the pegboard—the wire has to go into the pegboard at a 90 degree angle.

To stand the tag off from the pegboard or to have the home tag also act as the holder for the tool (see the majority of examples in the Electronics pegboard photo), you can laser cut a hanger out of 1/8" Baltic Birch and glue together. Use two strips of Nitto tape to attach to the back of a 2x3 home tag—see Figure 3.10.

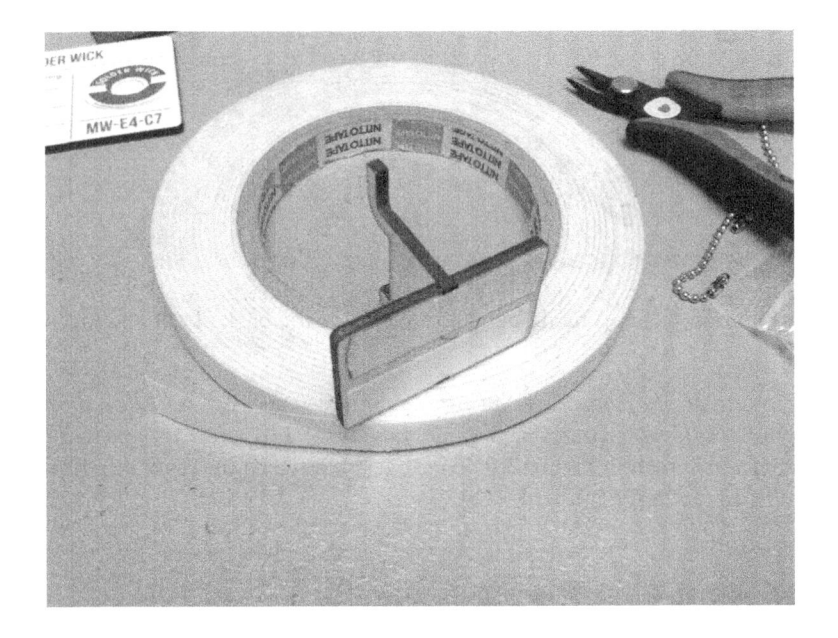

Figure 3.10: Laser-cut plywood hanger for Home Tags.

The plywood pegboard hanger is not the most robust thing in the world, but very fast compared to 3D printing a hanger/holder. Note—if the pegboard is against a wall, you may need to pull the pegboard away from the wall to install the holder.

The tag may also have embedded magnets[18], as with the wax carving tools in Figure 3.11: Cut 0.248" diameter holes on the laser out of whiteboard, which is a snug fit on 1/4" x 1/16" rare earth magnets. Rough up one side of each magnet with sandpaper (pick the same pole for each), make sure it is clean, place with smooth side facing out, put tag flat, face-down on a piece of paper, push magnets flat, fill hole in back with 5-minute epoxy. Use plywood pegboard hangers (two, one at each end).

---

[18]Magnets won't work with some stainless steels.

3.5. HOME TAG SOP

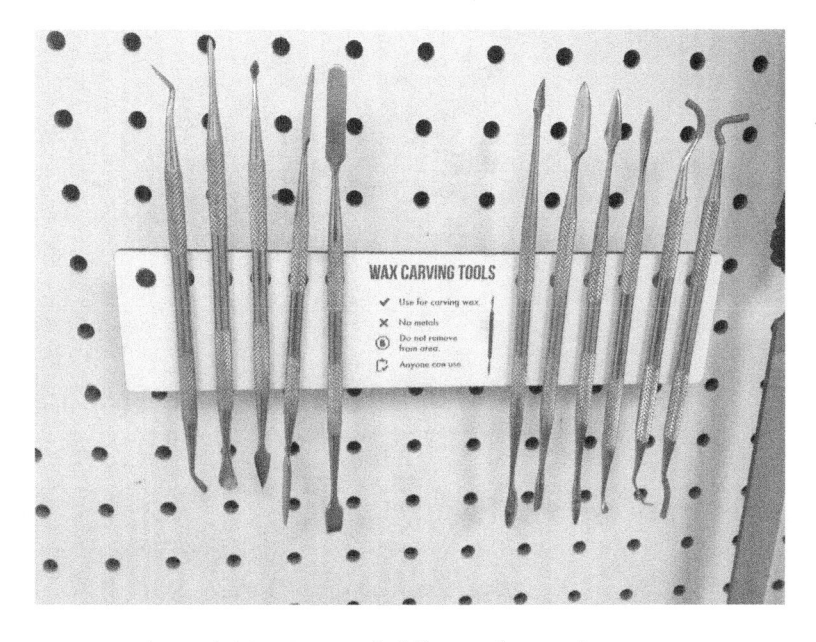

Figure 3.11: Magnets holding tools on a home tag.

Add a block of solid wood to the plywood pegboard hanger and drill a hole to hold a single pointed tool like an auto-punch in Figure 3.12.

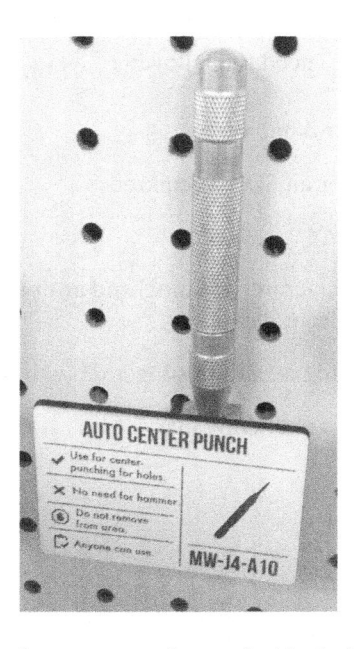

Figure 3.12: Example of a home tag on front of a block that holds a tool in a hole.

Attach two of just the pegboard hanger pieces to the ends of a block of wood with holes for things like files or tubes, then tape the home tag on the front as in Figure 3.13.

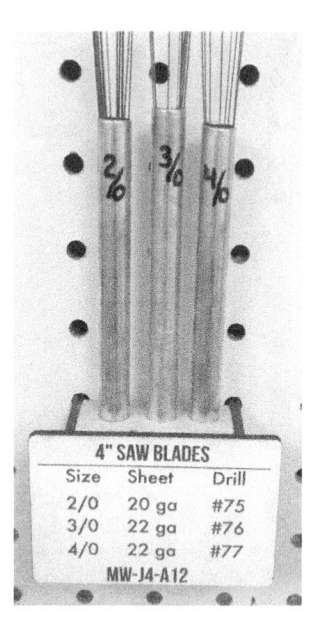

Figure 3.13: Using tubes for storing thin objects like saw blades.

3.6 Process Tool SOP

Use this SOP to process a tool at Maker Works—that is, make it ready to be put out for use. At a minimum, for each tool we need the following:

- Entered in any tool list or database
- Determination of whether an SOP is required
- SOP created if needed
- Manilla folder with manufacturer's manual and any other (non-purchase) material in the filing cabinet by the front desk
- Provision made for keeping accessories together with tool
- Tool (asset) ID number permanently marked
- Tool address marked
- Color coded mark
- A home prepared for it

3.6.1 Marking Tools SOP

Tool marking should not interfere with tool operation, should be reasonably resistant to wearing off, be easy to find and read, and not interfere too much with appearance. A member should be able to quickly figure out who owns it and where it lives.

3.6. PROCESS TOOL SOP

Note that even though we want it to be clear that the tool belongs to Maker Works, our top priority is not marking the tool to prevent theft. It is slightly more important to be able to change the tool address, for example. If someone really wants to steal a tool, it's very easy to. We assume good will on the part of our members, and just want to make it easy for them to do the right thing, harder to do the wrong thing (which in this case is about returning tools as well as not mixing up our tools with theirs).

Important Point: We may want to make it easy for members to mark their own tools!

What to mark on our tools:

- tool address (which includes "MW" as the owner)
- color mark (see Tool Address SOP)
- tool or asset ID #

3.6.1.1 Marking Tool Addresses

The following are examples of marking the tool address. The best approach will vary with the tool.

Direct ink mark: Use permanent marker (Sharpie) to mark if sufficient contrast is possible. Check after ink dries—ink smears on some plastics (especially metallic Sharpie). Mark in areas easily visible but not subject to regular wear, like the inside of handles. See Figure 3.14.

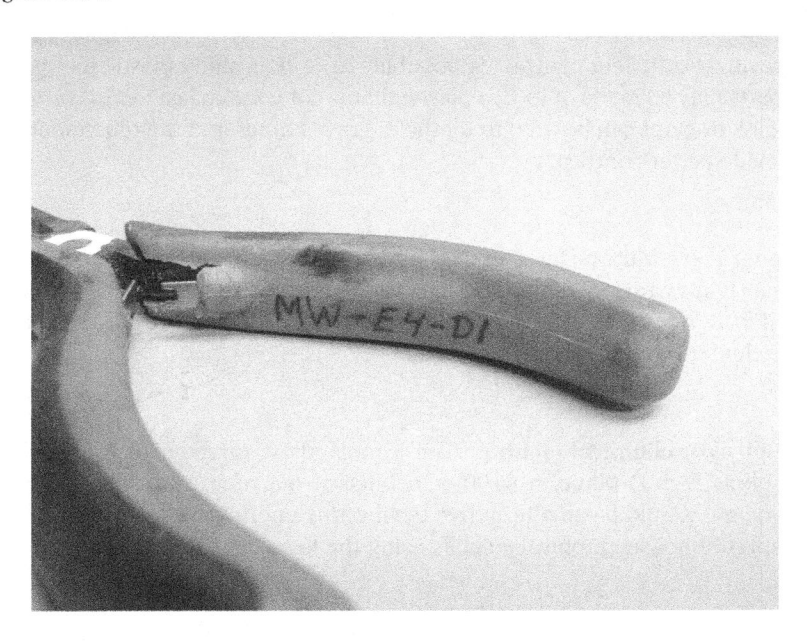

Figure 3.14: Direct ink marking of an address.

Ink mark on heat-shrink tubing: Tools with round or roundish handles can be marked by first putting white heat-shrink tubing on the handle, marking the address with sharpie, then covering with clear heat-shrink. See Figure 3.15. The first priority is clarity; a white background does allow for the address to be color coded to the area (in this case, red is associated with the Electronics area).

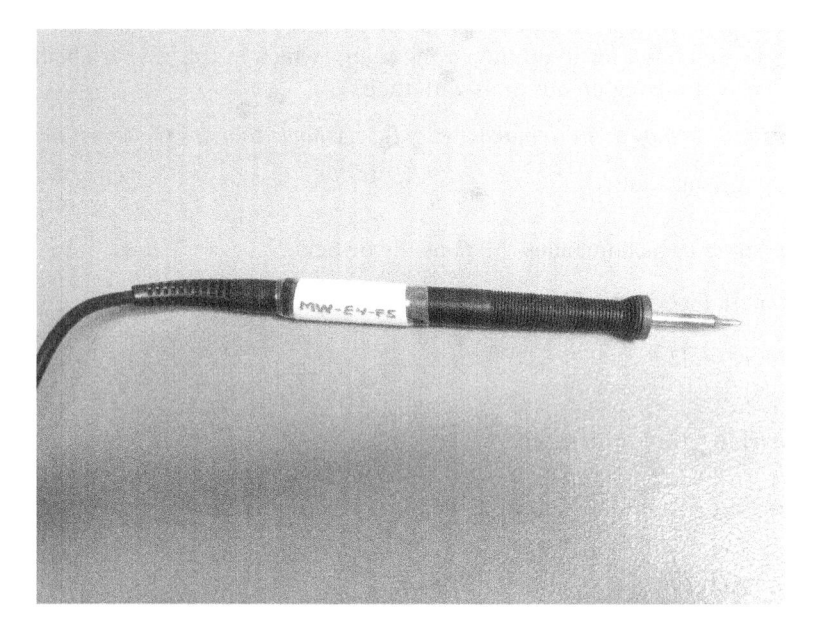

Figure 3.15: Example of ink on white heat-shrink tubing.

Laser engrave: If sufficient contrast is possible. Note that many plastic handles or other tool parts may be made of PVC, a plastic that is not good to laser engrave. If engraved deep, ink or paint can be used to fill the engraved areas and the remainder wiped off, to provide better contrast.

Vibrating engraver: Must be large enough to see easily. Probably more easily visible than using a (non-vibrating) carbide scribe. Might work on some hard plastics, but metals with dark surface treatment might be easier to see. May be better for asset numbers, which do not have to be as easily read.

Electrochemical or chemical etching: These tools allow directly marking metals. One example is Etch-O-Matic, a $100 stencil-based machine, or acid etching pens like Gimark, etc. Could be an alternative to vibrating engraver. May be possible to create (cheaply) in-house graphical stencils using the laser, for example.

Tag: (screwed, double-stick tape, ball-chain on cord, through spindle, around narrow part, etc.) Whiteboard material (Lowes in 4' x 8') engraves very nicely and is incredibly cheap. Nitto double-stick (no foam) tape works great on many clean surfaces, or 3M VHB double stick foam tape. 1" x 2" seems large enough for 1–2 lines of tool name, and address. Can also use anodized dog or luggage tags (laser engraved). See Figures 3.16 and 3.17.

3.6. PROCESS TOOL SOP

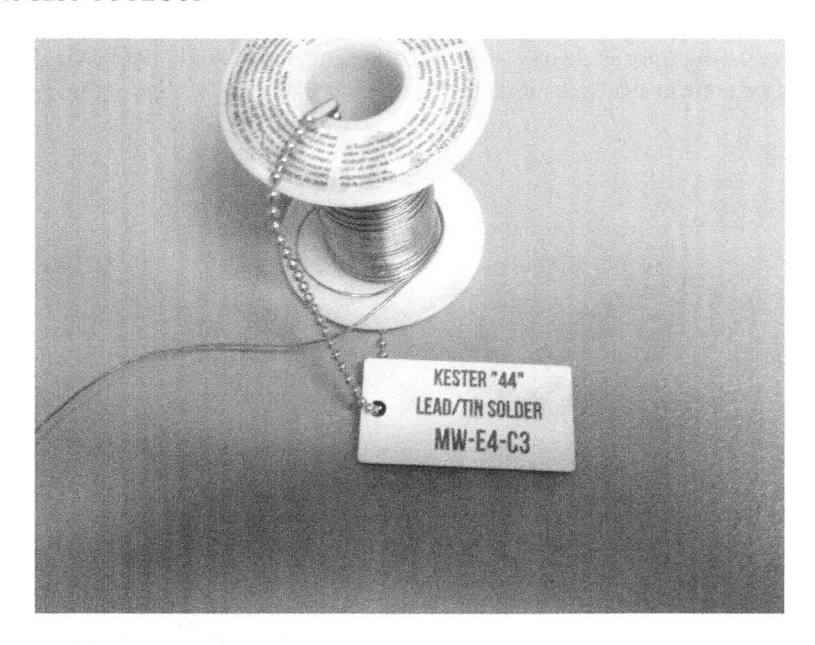

Figure 3.16: Two ball-chains are linked together to form a longer chain for a tag.

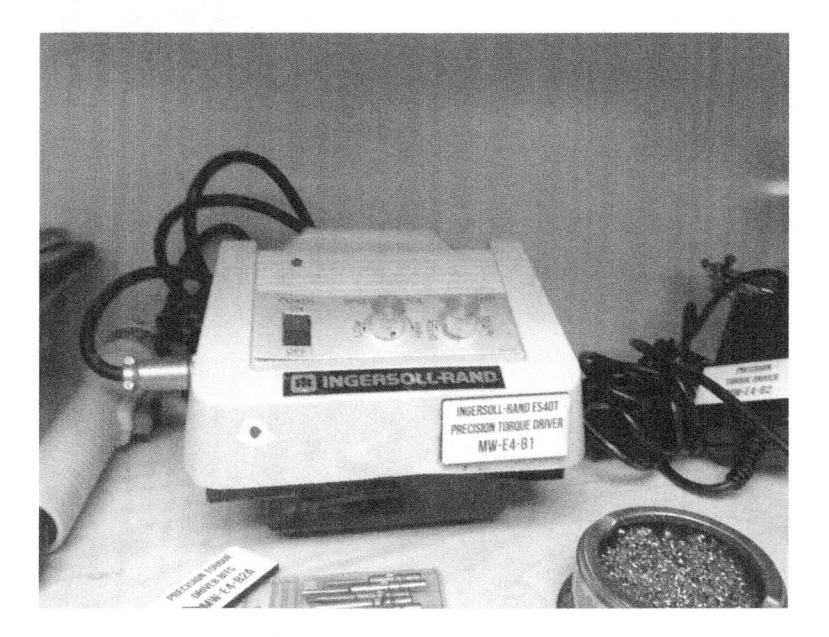

Figure 3.17: Double-stick tape holding an address tag to a tool.

3.6.1.2 Color marks

Maker Works has been using a white dot to mark tools for a while. We augment that with a center dot corresponding to a specific area like Wood (green), Electronics (red), Metal (blue), etc. See the Addresses SOP for details.

Use Testors Enamel paint to make the mark. The white circle should be ½" to ¾" in diameter and in a place where it is visible but not exposed to lots of wear. The inner dot should be big enough that the color is clear—say 1/8" or so. The mark should not be visually jarring, and should be done as neatly as possible. See Figure 3.18.

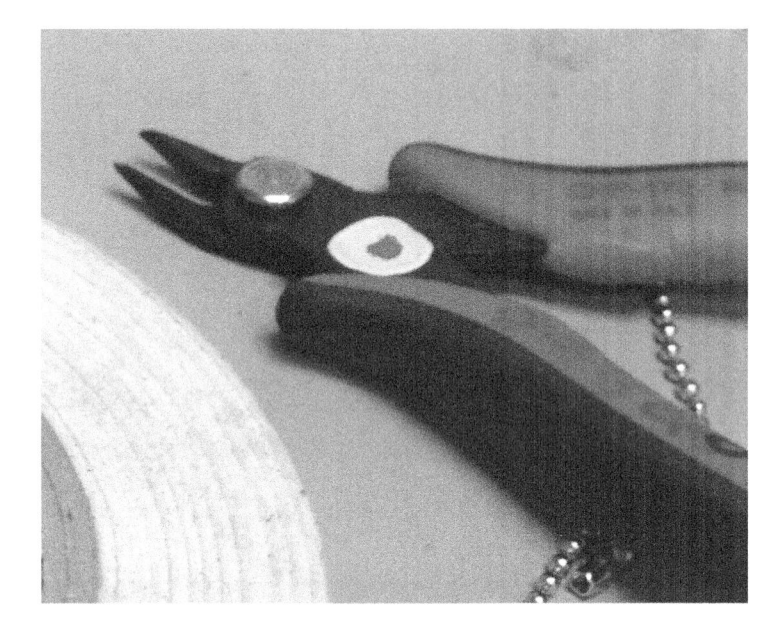

Figure 3.18: Example of a color mark for a tool from Electronics (red center dot).

Again, the major point is to make it easy to identify the tool as ours, and not necessarily for theft prevention.

Stationary tools do not need a mark.

3.7 Area Labeling SOP

So we all can quickly locate tool addresses, each shop or area needs to be well labeled.

In at least one place in a shop, spell out the shop name and if there is a symbol, show it. Vinyl is good for this. Use Bebas Neue font. The size will have to scale to make sense visually—fairly large in a space like Wood. See Figure 3.19.

3.7. AREA LABELING SOP

Figure 3.19: Example of a shop name and some area labels.

For each tool crib or similar (e.g., ShopBot), list the shop letter in addition to the tool crib number. So a tool crib in Metal would be labeled "M3" for example, rather than just "3". Make it easy to see from anywhere in the room.

Use somewhat smaller letters for the actual locations.

Each shop should have an overall map for tool addresses, and a map of the specific tool cribs in that area (unless the area is so small that all the tool cribs are easily seen by looking around). Maps should include colors—perhaps example white/color-dot in each area as well.

Chapter 4

An SOP for Business: The Business Perspective Chart

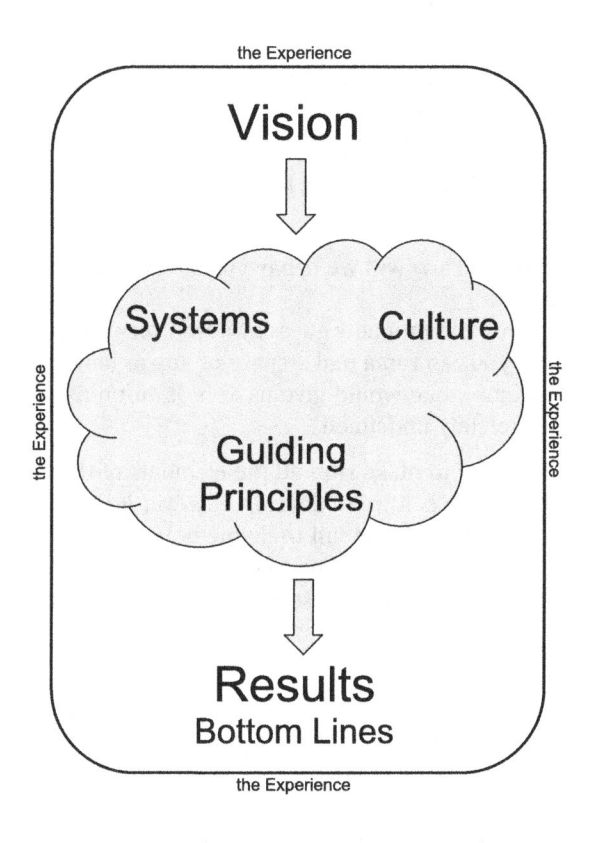

Figure 4.1: The Business Perspective Chart.

The previous two chapters have gone into a lot of detail on two useful systems for operating a makerspace—SOPs and 5S. Now we'd like to step back and give you a framework showing you how the other business elements we'll discuss fit together.

The business perspective chart (Figure 4.1) is a framework for the various elements that nearly any organization requires in order to deliver value sustainably. Much of the usefulness of the chart comes from showing not just that some element is required, but how it relates to the other elements. We can omit or at least not be intentional about some of these elements, but doing so would lower the odds that we could deliver the most value we could on a sustainable basis. In fact, we're going to claim that you'd have to be pretty lucky to have a sustainable organization without being intentional about each of these elements.

The chart was developed in the Zingerman's Community of Businesses, and has been used within Zingerman's and taught to other businesses for quite a few years. It's felt to be so useful, most internal Zingerman's business classes begin with a review of the chart.

The elements are as follows:

Mission[1]: The "north star" of the organization, a goal that may never be reached. The answer to "why are you doing this?"

Vision: A specific point on the path, a preferred concrete future image. In contrast to the mission, this is a specific set of goals that we intend to reach.

Experience: What different groups of people will experience in the space (members, staff, vendors, instructors, etc.)

Bottom lines: How will the progress towards the mission of the organization be measured?

Systems: What systems will be used to contribute to the bottom lines?

Culture: What will it be like, on a day to day basis, to be in the shop? What will the ground reality be?

Guiding Principles/Values: How will we behave in carrying out the mission?

Now, Tom and Dale are (you can probably guess by now), very much systems-oriented. And we'd love to tell you that you can run a makerspace or any organization just using systems, but we can't. Using systems alone would give us at best an uninspiring makerspace, with critical elements left completely undefined.

It is a responsibility of leaders to make sure all the elements of the organization are intentional. If we do not, if we leave culture to develop however it will, if we fail to put systems in place that reinforce our values, if we fail to define bottom lines that reflect our mission accurately, then we risk at a minimum failing to realize the full potential of our efforts, and in many cases may see the enormous investment of time and money in our makerspace evaporate.

4.1 Flying to San Francisco Using the Business Perspective Chart

We're going to use Tom's favorite example to show how the various elements of the business perspective chart tie together.

---

[1] Comment from Dale's Dad: "I don't see Mission on the chart." True. In Zingerman's case, they might say that their mission (page 82) is to deliver the Zingerman's experience. For most of us, there may be a reasonable argument for replacing "experience" in the chart with "mission", and perhaps placing "experience" under "results" with the "bottom lines".

Let us say you're a Michigander, fortunate enough to live in our little city of Ann Arbor, and have decided to take more trips to warmer, sunnier locales in the winter. Seems reasonable to us. We'd say this is your mission. Will winter always be cold and snowy in Michigan? Probably. So your mission won't be completed with one trip. There will always be winters.

However, you can pick a point in the future, say a few days hence, and say that your preferred future on that date is one in which you're looking at the Golden Gate Bridge. Add a few details to evoke some emotional connection, and you have your vision. (Note that our vision didn't say how we're getting there, at least not specifically.)

What about your bottom lines for this project? In this case the qualitative state of being by the Golden Gate Bridge is probably fine, but often it's useful to have quantitative bottom lines ($X net profit, Y people served free meals, etc.). So let's use miles from Golden Gate Bridge as a bottom line—if you got as far as Palo Alto or Menlo Park, you'd probably feel you had made substantial progress even if you couldn't see the bridge.

We see from the chart that the three elements of Systems, Culture, and Guiding Principles are the tools that will get you from Vision to Bottom Line. We'll begin with Systems.

Let's say your system will be to get in a plane and fly to San Francisco. Your initial flight plan is simplicity itself—you'll plot a course directly from Ann Arbor[2] to SFO at, say, 10 feet above sea level. What could go wrong?

To start off with, Ann Arbor is 840 feet above sea level. Even San Francisco is mostly roughly 50 feet above sea level. Even if we change our system to flying 10 feet above the average ground level, in between here and there are a few things that stick up more than 10 feet—trees, buildings, people on stilts, telephone poles. Perhaps the stray mountain or two in Colorado.

By just setting your course at 10 feet above sea level, you've ignored the way things are on the ground, the way things are in reality. We define the term "culture" as "the way things really are". And believe us, imposing a system on a makerspace when it's at odds with its culture is about as useful as flying the route above. Try to enforce a "clean work tables at the end of the day" policy when everyone—staff and members alike—normally leaves their stuff on tables just as a regular thing, for example. You can post all the signs you like, but if staff and the "old timers" are all leaving their stuff out, what do you think new members are going to do?

So this plane trip needs to take into account the ground reality (culture). Excellent—we'll fly 10 feet above the highest feature.

Problem solved? Well, what would this trip feel like? You'd be okay for a few hundred feet beyond our little airport, but then there's a line of trees—zipping up, over, and then down is going to be an interesting experience. You'll get a respite over Lake Michigan, assuming calm water, but our Illinois neighbors have some fairly tall buildings in Chicago that are going to be real roller coasters going up and down. The Rocky Mountains should be entertaining as well.

Long before your arrival in SFO you'll be wanting to modify your flight plan one more time. This time taking into account an outside constraint—a guiding principle that informs how you'll go about operating. That guiding principle in this case may be that you want the flight to feel comfortable for the passenger (you!).

---

[2]The Ann Arbor airport happens to be across the street from us. We keep our corporate jets there, which is handy.

Now the flight plan has a gentle arc going up to an altitude well above any obstacles, and assuming no turbulence, you'll arrive in as reasonable a shape as can be expected from a lengthy flight.

In the same way, even after we modify our system-only approach to include a consideration of culture in our makerspaces, we still need to apply our values/guiding principles.

To wrap up this overview,

- The mission tells us our direction
- The vision gives us a specific preferred future to work towards
- The bottom line describes how we're going to measure our success in meeting the vision
- The set of systems, culture, and guiding principles are the tools that help us realize the vision and produce the desired bottom lines.

We'll take each of these elements in turn, describing in more detail each element, how it is created, how it's used, and an example, in the following sections.

Chapter 5

Mission: The North Star

The organization's mission answers the questions "Why are you doing this? Who are you serving and how are you serving them?" For example, a mission could be to create a world where every child can read. Or to create a space where teens in your neighborhood can hang out. Or to create a shop where blacksmiths can ply their noisy trade.[1]

The mission—at least in our usage[2]—is the "north star". It guides us towards a destination, but we may never fully get there. There are exceptions—a disease may be eradicated. The Burning Man vehicle makes it to Burning Man. But for many organizations, there will always be more to be done to realize their mission. There will always be new children to teach, teens to support, blacksmiths who need a forge.

(Recall that we can, and should, have shorter-term, realistic goals. In our framework, this is the role of a Vision. See Chapter 7.)

A mission can be to "maximize monetary value to investors". If that's where you (or your investors) are, that's where you are. But note that having this as the primary mission of the makerspace organization may be challenging, since this maximization is almost certain to occur at the expense of the member, the community, and the larger society. You may now be engaged in a continuous conflict with members who may, quite understandably, adopt a similar attitude of wanting to extract maximum value for themselves. (There's no need for us to pause while you bring some business to mind with this mindset—it would be strange if you hadn't had several such interactions so far just today.) That this may often seem the norm doesn't mean this is your only option, especially if you'd rather spend the energy that would be lost to conflict with the member in other more productive ways.[3]

---

[1] Ask Tom and Dale about the wisdom of having the jewelry studio, with its nice anvil, adjacent to their office.
[2] Please note that "mission", "vision", "goals", and other terms like this are defined by different people in different ways.
[3] The Business Roundtable (think CEOs of Amazon, IBM, Johnson & Johnson, etc.) just (mid-2019) released a new statement on the purpose of a corporation, which moves away from "Shareholder Primacy" (i.e., maximizing investor returns) that they've been preaching for the past 20 years, and instead states the corporation is for the benefit of all stakeholders including communities and the environment. This is a pretty radical, but welcome, departure! https://www.businessroundtable.org/business-roundtable-redefines-the-purpose-of-a-corporation-to-promote-an-economy-that-serves-all-americans Accessed 8/21/2019.

5.1 Characteristics of a Useful Mission

In order to be useful, the mission statement should be memorable, meaningful, clear, and concise. It will describe what value the organization or project provides and to whom. Avoid buzzwords—and do note that under international law, anyone can come over there and slap your face if your mission statement uses the words "actualize", "monetize", or "recontextualize". Instead, your mission should be something you could say to your aunt to explain what you're doing with your life.

Be concise. It's a mission statement, not a mission novel.

Will your staff more or less be able to repeat the mission statement? How is it different from other missions? What is surprising about the mission statement? Is there a hook?

As an example, here's Zingerman's mission statement:

> We share the Zingerman's Experience
>
> Selling food that makes you happy
>
> Giving service that makes you smile
>
> In passionate pursuit of our mission
>
> Showing love and caring in all our actions
>
> To enrich as many lives as we possibly can.

The mission of this book series is:

> Our mission is to increase the quantity and quality of makerspaces by collecting, vetting, and sharing best practices for safe and sustainable operations.

At Maker Works, we did something a bit different. Our mission statement is a mission blueprint—a diagram that we draw as we tell a story. See Figure 5.1.

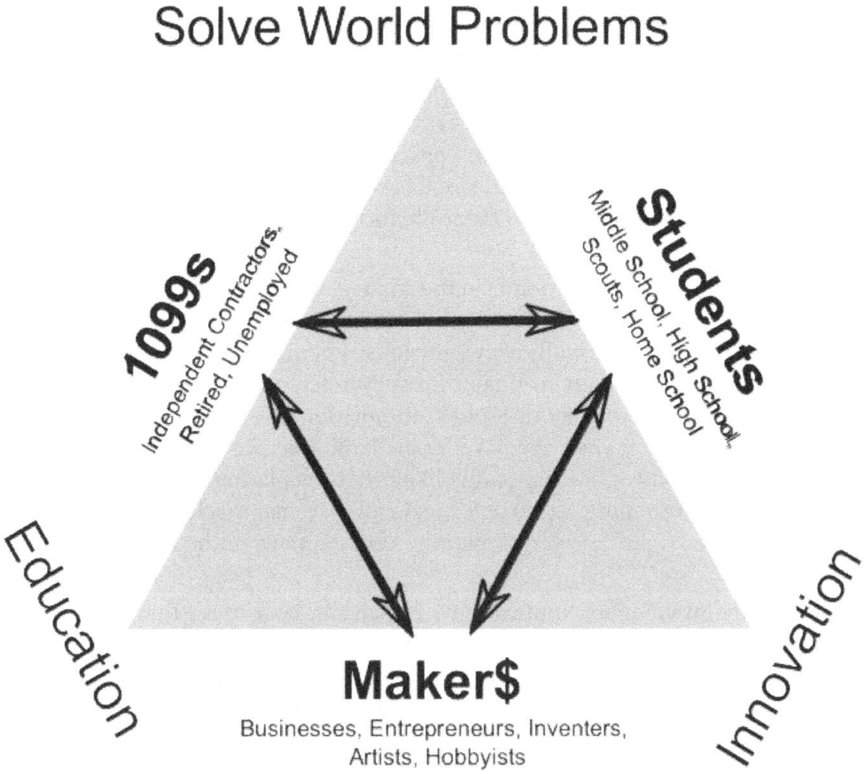

Solve World Problems

(Triangle diagram)
- Top-left side: **1099s** — Independent Contractors, Retired, Unemployed
- Top-right side: **Students** — Middle School, High School, Scouts, Home School
- Bottom: **Maker$** — Businesses, Entrepreneurs, Inventors, Artists, Hobbyists
- Outside labels: Education, Innovation

Figure 5.1: Maker Works' Mission Blueprint.

Here's how we usually narrate the mission. We'll start by drawing a triangle—or a pyramid, if you like. The sides we use to list some of the core groups we serve. The base we label "Maker$". These are the people that are interested in having access to the tools, space, instruction, and community, and have the ability and willingness to pay for that access. (That's the $ at the end.) These are often entrepreneurs, local businesses, inventors, and other folks for whom making is part of their livelihood, but can also include hobbyists.

The left side of the triangle we label "1099", from the number of the US tax form that self-employed people fill out. This includes a lot of different people in our community, including many highly-skilled workers from the automotive industry who found themselves underemployed or unemployed during the financial crisis of some years ago. As Tom says, it's one thing to invest in some equipment and then, when the business climate changes, let it go. It's another thing when it's our neighbor. Shouldn't we find ways to upscale their skills, from manual machining to CNC, from drafting boards to CAD? And what if they could pass along some of their hard-won knowledge to the young people in our community?

The final side is our students. At least locally, our schools had moved away from shop classes where the emphasis was on hands-on engineering and making. Physically making things was no longer in the course plan. On the other hand, students today are comfortable around computers, and many have skills in CAD or at least a solid familiarity with manipulating a 3D model on a 2D screen. (Minecraft, anyone?) So we hoped to serve students by providing an opportunity to make, hopefully reinforcing science, engineering, art, and mathematics. (In the past few years we're seeing a realization that STEAM topics are important in schools, so our message about students resonates a lot more now than when we started. We even have a local elementary with a STEAM focus now.)

Next we draw arrows on the inside of the triangle, because we don't serve these groups separately, but as members of a community of makers. The entrepreneurs (Maker$) draw on the skills of the 1099's for fabricating prototypes, for example. Students see (and hopefully learn) the skills of the manual machinist, even as they're able to share their knowledge of computers and CAD. It's not uncommon for students to find gigs with the Maker$ or 1099's.

Not leaving well enough alone, the points of the triangle get used too. What is going to happen in this space? Starting at the lower left, that point is labeled "Education." Sometimes it's formal, in classes, but we usually view our most important contribution to education as providing the resources and environment for self-directed education. Dale can attest to the difference between learning about 3-phase motors for an exam in a course, and learning because you want to run your new (well, old) lathe that has a 3-phase motor but you only have single-phase power. We especially like robots as platforms for students learning about mechanics, programming, electronics, control systems, machining and fabrication, etc. When you get the "right" answer, something cool happens in the real world.

The right bottom point we label "innovation". Which can be a tricky thing in makerspace, since we do draw in, from time to time, folks who have jumped right over the education part and into the innovation area. In our minds, however, innovation is what happens at the edge of what is known, so must have a solid basis in existing knowledge. And we do have innovation of the type you might expect—new inventions, etc.—but we also want to encourage innovation in other ways—for example, in how we run a business. We know several small businesses that started in our space that are now using SOPs, 5S, open book management, and other practices in their shop, having seen it in action here. (One even hired away our shop manager—*you know who you are, Quentin, and we know where you live. Watch your back.*)

At the top we label the point "Solve world problems." Which seems pretty grandiose for a little makerspace in a smallish city in the midwest. But makerspaces in general, including ours, we hope, do increase the probability of some pretty big solutions—whether it's a technology solution, or the way we treat our members. And yes, several members are working on solving world problems in energy usage, empowering women in third-world countries, and assistive technologies.

By around the 14th paragraph you probably started thinking to yourself that this is not a brief, zippy mission statement. It's a picture and story, it's a good 5 minutes long (or longer if you tell some anecdotes on the way), and unless you are going up a very tall building, not elevator ride material. We can't disagree. It's a choice, and it feels like it works for us.[4] The diagram guides us through the discussion—makes it harder to leave out an element. If a diorama or saxophone solo is what captures your mission, good on you. Just be intentional. And remember that Aunt Margaret hasn't a clue what "recontextualize" means.

---

[4]Actually, there are some things that are obviously important to us that have not been captured in the mission diagram. We're thinking of a revised mission statement something along these lines: "Maker Works empowers people and businesses in technical, creative, and educational fields in our local community by providing a wide range of tools, a place to use them, and a community of makers that supports the acquisition and sharing of knowledge; and globally by promoting the establishment and sustainability of makerspaces everywhere through the sharing of best practices."

5.2 Creating a Mission Statement

This might be an easy one, if this is a one-person show. Who are you serving, how are you serving them? Be specific when appropriate—if you serve only students in the fine arts department, that should be in your mission.

Shortly we're going to discuss the Vision in more detail. If you started with a vision, it may give you insight about how to express your mission. If you're hung up writing a mission that feels right, you might try coming at it from the other direction and start with a vision, then extrapolate to the mission.

If you have a large decision-making group and there is not already a mission, this may be more challenging. For example, you could have a diverse group of people from the local geek meet-up who are interested in starting a makerspace. Among other things, there may not be one mission that will satisfy everyone. But even though crafting a mission may be more difficult in that case, it's incredibly necessary that there is a mission. The folks that support it support it, and maybe there's another group that wants to follow a different path. (For example, see the earlier note on "freedom from vs. freedom to".)

This divergent path happened here in Ann Arbor around co-working. In May 2008 there were some meetings of people interested in the co-working in Ann Arbor, and it became clear that there were some divergent needs—the "laptop" co-workers wanted a place with more of an office/coffeehouse vibe, while some engineer-types wanted a shared makerspace-like setting with lathes and welding, as two examples. We ended up with both shortly thereafter. The Workantile is downtown Ann Arbor, and is about 3,000 sq. ft. of clean office-like space for the "laptop" co-workers. The A2 MechShop eventually moved into a space at Maker Works where it still is today, and has about 3,200 sq. ft. of CNC and manual machinery, an auto-lift, electronics, etc. Both groups are much happier with the results, we're sure, than if there was one compromise co-working facility.[5]

Getting good work done with a large group will be easiest with an experienced facilitator. The facilitator will help you craft a clear message around the goals for the meeting (e.g., "Tonight we're going to brainstorm some elements we feel are part of the mission of our proposed makerspace, and gauge support for these elements."), the process to be used, and what will happen later on. The large group is an excellent place to generate ideas and get a sense of what elements have a lot of support, but it may be useful to take that information and have a small group or individual process that information and even propose a draft mission statement at a later time to the larger group (if, in fact, the larger group is the decision-making body).

By the way, now seems a good point to raise the following: a sustainable group must bring everyone along who needs to be a part of the group. If, under the banner of "efficiency", discussion is limited about an issue, anyone who does not feel heard by the group will have less energy or interest to contribute. If a decision is made that doesn't seem to take into account people's input (the input wasn't sought in the first place, or isn't acknowledged), that's another place for energy to leak out of the organization. Decision-making processes like consensus, processes for making changes like the BOTTOM-LINE CHANGE process, and even skilled facilitation during meetings can all preserve and enhance the feeling of members about the organization itself.

---

[5] Which does lead to the interesting question of who would win in a fight—geeks with milling machines or geeks with PCs?

5.3 How to Use the Mission

Everyone who comes in contact with your makerspace should have at least a rough idea of your mission. It's the elevator pitch for your organization. It's in your member handbooks, brochures, on the website (maybe in a few places)—if it's short enough, it's probably on your sign and on the door.

It is not written, approved, and filed away, to be brought back for a 5-year review every 10 years. That serves no purpose, and is a waste of your time. If the mission isn't something you'll print as a big poster and have in your front room, why not?

Chapter 6

Measuring Success: The Bottom Line(s)

How do you measure the success of the organization? That is, what is the measure of your progress towards your mission and the more concrete vision?

A purely for-profit entity, by definition, will measure its success in terms of profit. Nothing tricky there. "In our last fiscal quarter we succeeded in the amount of $780,437." End of story.

Having a single bottom line of profit is a common thing for most businesses, so common that to have any other measure of success may strike you as strange, at least in the for-profit sector. But depending on your vision and your values (guiding principles), if you have just one bottom line, you'll likely have challenges acting consistently.

For example, say the local FIRST robotics team wants to use your makerspace for a few weeks during their build season for free. You might think this is great, and the staff are all excited (hey, half are probably FIRST alumni), but it's clear that not only is this not going to contribute to your bottom line of profit, it's going to cost you money (in wear and tear, staff costs, impact on paying members, etc.). If your support of STEAM programs is part of your vision, but the only way you have of measuring success is in a profit figure, this is a problem. What do your investors expect you to do? What about your staff, your members, your community? Isn't realizing each part of your vision something that should show up as a positive element of the bottom lines?

We're going to suggest that if your vision and values point your makerspace towards goals including other than profit, then from the start you should define what those goals are and make them explicit. If you serve the community in a particular way, then one of your bottom lines needs to capture and measure that. For example, at Maker Works, we have adopted the popular TRIPLE BOTTOM LINES of:

People: We want to support the development of our members, staff, and others in our community.

Planet: We want to minimize our negative impact on the environment through our activities, and create education and opportunities for people to change their behavior around consumption.

Profit: We want to provide a good living for our staff, reinvest in improving the business, and repay our investors.

(These three triple bottom lines date back to 1981 when they were introduced by Freer Spreckley as a way of more accurately measuring the social and environmental performance of an organization in addition to the traditional financial bottom line.)

Your bottom lines may be different, either in broad categories or the specifics. But you should be intentional, and create bottom lines such that all the elements of the business are in alignment.

By the way, Zingerman's three bottom lines are:

- Great Food
- Great Service
- Great Finance

6.1 For-Profit or Nonprofit, You're Still a Business

If you are contemplating setting up your makerspace as a nonprofit, that's great. But if you have not been part of a nonprofit before, know that 1) there can be even more administrative overhead than a for-profit, and 2) it is still a business. In particular, you will still have income and expenses, and income had better exceed expenses over the long haul or it is not sustainable.

At the end of the day, a nonprofit isn't going to distribute its net profits to owners, but will instead use them to better deliver value in accordance with its mission. All the other stuff a business worries about—cash flow, income/expenses, balance sheets—are all present in the nonprofit world.

Being a nonprofit does have some advantages:

- It is clear to staff, members, the general public, the state, the IRS, and everyone else that you have a public good as your main bottom line. (Not just that you say you have it, but it's actually a legal requirement with penalties for non-compliance.)
- People and organizations may be able to receive a tax deduction for donations.
- The organization may pay less or no taxes.
- The organization may be eligible for grants or in-kind donations[1] from a variety of sources.

You may be fortunate enough to have your income side taken care of—that's excellent. Perhaps some major organization (or your parent organization) is happy to foot the bill indefinitely. But for many non-profits, if the operations (e.g., classes, membership, space

---

[1] Here's some free advice. The most costly machine you can have in your whole shop is a donated, used, industrial CNC machine. They can be deadly expensive to repair, the tooling may not be industry standard (or might be an expensive style), it may be hard to find the right software, it may be much bigger than you need, may have incredible electricity requirements, and so on. The odds are pretty high you just lost 80+ square feet to an 8,000 lb. paper weight. Be careful what you ask for!

6.1. FOR-PROFIT OR NONPROFIT, YOU'RE STILL A BUSINESS

rental) do not bring in enough income, there can be a never-ending cycle of grant seeking that is non-trivial in terms of time and energy. You can build it, but there's no guarantee that they will come (with checkbooks open).

Many states or areas will have nonprofit resource centers. Consult them early as possible to make an informed decision on the business structure that best fits your mission. If you do go the nonprofit route, they can also be incredible resources for board development and other key ingredients for a successful nonprofit organization such as referrals for legal, accounting, and other services.

In this book, that's all we're going to say about legal business structures. And certainly the for-profit vs. nonprofit division is a big one. But you still have a number of decisions to make if you go the for-profit route. These decisions will include considerations of liability, tax treatment of profits, decision making, and the costs and overhead associated with various business forms. Figure out your mission, vision, guiding principles, and bottom lines, then talk it over with a professional who can match your organization with the best legal and governance structures.

Chapter 7

Vision: A Key Document for Leadership

Your makerspace—and virtually any other organization or project—projects into the future. This potential is one of the most exciting elements of a makerspace, especially when it is just starting out and there are vast areas of the canvas with rough pencil sketches. Members of your community may have a ton of energy to put forward to make a makerspace happen, to realize this dream, and it is a gratifying thing indeed.

But, we have to ask, what dream is it that they're working towards?

"Why, a makerspace, of course!", again showing the tolerance you, dear reader, have for our apparent inability to see the obvious.

If we were talking about a McDonald's, we'd have to agree that just mentioning the golden arches gives us all a pretty good idea of what we're talking about. It will serve a specific type of food, at a certain range of prices, and so on. There's probably even an approved color scheme. And it's unlikely to include a sauna, does not rent bicycles, and probably does not have a liquor license.[1] A "makerspace", however, covers a pretty big range. There's no corporation defining what each makerspace will be[2]. It is much more like a local library, with a wide range of variation in media available, lending policies, space, etc. For example, we note with pride that our local library loans out telescopes, infrared cameras, sewing machines, musical synthesizers, and giant chess sets[3]. In addition to there being no entity overseeing what makerspaces are, at this point, most folks haven't even heard of a makerspace, much less even been in one.

So when Valerie is working towards her image of a makerspace, it's likely going to be different than the one Amy has. Valerie, as everyone knows, is very focused on serving youth through STEAM education, while Amy's dream of a laid-back space for late night parties is pretty specific down to the size of the dance floor. At a minimum, someone is going to be disappointed if these images are incompatible. Probably a lot of energy is going to

---

[1] And we're pretty sure that if you're reading this book and thinking about operating a makerspace, you're the kind of person that just went off for a brief moment thinking about what a Mickey-D's would look like with a sauna or bicycle rental. Maybe even serving micro-brews. Or all three. Happy Meal, indeed.

[2] "FabLabs" on the other hand have a specific tool list, which does mean they can share processes without worrying about different equipment.

[3] Though, at this point, we've never met anyone with a burning need for a giant chess set, even on a temporary basis. What kind of conversation ends with "I've got it! We just need a giant chess set!"?

spent down the road resolving issues, and time and money spent ineffectively. We've certainly heard of many organizations that imploded or suffered major setbacks when internal groups with different goals could not figure out a path forward.

Not only may we lose people in our group who don't see their future in the future of the makerspace, but we may also fail to attract people in the first place, who may not understand where they would fit in, or have an incorrect image that actively repels them.

It is the responsibility of leaders to make sure there is a clear, shared vision for the makerspace.

Note that it is not necessarily the responsibility of leaders to create the vision themselves—that can be done in many ways, with various subsets of the membership, community, etc. But leaders are responsible for seeing that it happens.

This vision tells the reader "this is what is in it for you." It tells everyone, this is the path we are taking. When we make decisions, keep this destination in mind. Ari Weinzweig, one of Zingerman's founders, puts it this way: Visioning is "the idea of beginning our work by first figuring out what we want success to look like at a particular point in the future, then working backwards to the present." We often use phrases like "Begin with the end in mind", and that the vision is our "preferred future".

Zingerman's teaches[4] that a vision should be:

1. Inspiring
2. Strategically Sound
3. Documented
4. Communicated
5. Time Bound
6. Measurable

Let us take each in turn.

Inspiring: "Necessary" is not necessarily (sorry) inspiring. Having a vision of getting up in the morning so you can get to work on time is probably not going to lift your heart the way starting a new art project will. Does it thrill you inside? The language of a vision should evoke emotion. We often recommend writing it in the first person—for example, beginning with "when I stepped through the door this morning..."

Strategically Sound: Winning the lottery is certainly inspiring, but would not be something you could count on. Writing a book on group facilitation based on your years of facilitating experience seems much more reasonable, even if you might feel it will be a stretch.

Documented: Writing the vision down allows you to capture your thoughts and continuously improve them. It's unlikely that every element of your vision for your makerspace, project, day, business, relationship, etc., is something you could remember each time you want to share your vision with someone, and once it is written it is easy to add to and improve. (Just like with an SOP—writing it down lets us be consistent and improve it.)

---

[4] See for example Ari Weinzweig, A Lapsed Anarchist's Approach to Building a Great Business, 2010, Zingerman's Press. And note that ZingTrain has entire classes on visioning and other business topics. www.zingtrain.com

Communicated: If you can accomplish the vision without interacting with anyone else, we suppose you could skip this, but even then you're missing getting useful feedback. And if anyone else is involved—as other investors, founders, members, staff, your family, etc.—then sharing the vision will be necessary for reasons we discuss in a moment.

Time Bound: This is an important element. The vision is not a vague, hazy arm-waving in the general direction of the future with bits of glitter[5] tossed in for good measure. It is a description that is specific, describing a concrete state of affairs, and this is aided by describing the time. "Later this afternoon" may be a good time for a vision of baking a cake or hosting a party; we'd suggest 3-5 years is a good range for a makerspace getting started.

Measurable: Again, making the vision as specific as we can. How many members have joined? How many classes were taught? For aspects that may seem unmeasurable, you may be able to come up with proxy measures, like a survey. All this because we want to be able to ask ourselves when those 8 hours or 5 years are up, did we reach our vision?

7.1 Why is Vision Important?

We'd even say that having a vision is *critical*. Here are some reasons:

1. Positive impact on others. Most people, when they can see themselves in the vision, will want to help you. They'll make connections. They'll keep their eyes open for real estate. Tell you about the upcoming equipment auction. And so on. None of this network effect happens if they don't know what your vision is.

2. It attracts good people and keeps them. There will be long slogs through mosquito-infested swamps. (Metaphorically speaking. Unless that's where you're building your makerspace, in which case we're really sorry but we have something we already said we'd do that weekend. Yes, that weekend too.) But if they know where you're heading, it's much easier for them to keep slogging along with you. We don't want to exploit people by giving them a vision that is unlikely, but if we're really creating something special, share that and bring them with you. Because creating this makerspace is something that they value, too. We need to make sure they know what's possible.

3. It allows us to create reality instead of reacting to problems. It's very easy to slip into the mode of reacting to each day to day problem. Well, the reality is that nearly every day is going to be filled with problems (makerspace-related or not). Having a vision and keeping it in front of everyone (including yourself!) gives you a useful perspective, and can keep everyone from losing focus on where you want to be. Sometimes, we even see that some of the problems we think we have are actually ones we can side-step—they're really not on our path to our vision. Keeping your brain where you want it to be (your eyes on the prize) is a valuable brain hack.

4. It is a statement of optimism in the future. Hard to argue with that. We're saying that our makerspace is going to still be here, and be doing this and that in the not too distant future.

---

[5] We recently heard glitter described as "the herpes of crafting."

5. Forces us to act on and model that there is no safe path. Passively sitting on our behinds is not going to move us forward. There is no guarantee that our path will be successful. But as a leader we choose our preferred future, our vision, and we do what we can. We have to be active, and more than that, intentional.

6. It forces us to hold ourselves accountable. Putting out our vision means we may fall short. It says "this is how I want the future to be". Sometimes this push is going to be the thing that keeps us going—we said very publicly that we're going to do this thing, and we don't want to let people down.

7. It tells us what we aren't going to do. This is a very useful aspect of a vision, particularly with a makerspace. We get emails all the time—would Maker Works be interested in doing X or Y? If it is not in our vision, our discussion is going to be "why should we say yes?" If it is in our vision, we are more likely to start from yes and check if there's anything that points to no.

8. It tells everyone what's in it for them. Being specific is good, even if it takes more effort than some hand-waving and saying "you'll see, it'll be great". If you're worried that in being specific you'll lose some potential supporters, we'd suggest that if someone is wanting to help you based on an inaccurate image of how things are going to be, everyone is better off without that situation. Paint the most accurate, compelling picture you can, and then find the people that it resonates with.

9. It creates positive movement within the organization. There's energy in contemplating a shared, preferred future—energy that will otherwise be dissipated in contemplating the past (sometimes useful, but not our ideal focus) or in multiple directions. We have limited hours and limited dollars. A vision provides a focus to our efforts, a pulling towards, a positive outlook that cannot help but add to a positive experience (for staff as well as members). *In the absence of a unified vision, everyone will have their own.* Let's not count on the random chance that everyone will be pulling in the same direction.

7.2 What Should You Create a Vision For?

We've given you some reasons why having a vision for your makerspace is important. But there are benefits from creating a vision for even very short term things, or visions that are not directly about your makerspace.

For example, at the start of each day at Maker Works, the staff fills in the blanks of a form listing their team and personal goals for the day, how they're feeling[6], and what is motivating them. Literally just a couple of minutes for all three staff, but now there's a clear vision for the end of the day (and some idea how people are doing at the start). Well worth the effort.

When we started this book, we crafted a vision. Did that help create forward momentum? Did it help us decide what would go in the book and what would be left out? Do we ask lots of questions? (Yes, you know we do.)

---

[6]By the way, we're not asking how people are doing so we can penalize them. We're asking so that everyone on staff knows that Bob's mom is in the hospital, so we can as a team give great service to everyone, members and staff alike.

At the start of each class we teach, we let the students know what the future holds—by the end of this class, you'll know how to use the laser engraver to do X, Y, and Z. (See How to Instruct.)

What about asking your staff to create and share their own personal visions for where they'll be in 3 years? We've had some great experiences with this. Several years ago, we learned that one of our staff wanted to complete a comic book he had been working on for some years. Maybe that doesn't sound like something we'd like to know (you haven't read the servant leadership part yet), but in fact it let us know how we could support him in his development as a person. We knew some people who could help him with this, it turned out.

Another staff member had in her vision—shared with us—that in several years she would no longer be on staff, but be renting space here and producing a line of hats as a member. As we write this, her kiosk with her line of products (in a slightly different but related area) is up and running, and she's reduced her hours with us. Yes, it's a bummer that she's no longer working as much for us in the makerspace, but it's far outweighed by her development as a person, so of course we've helped her on that path. (Again, in case this sounds too strange or touchy-feely, we'll talk more about this in Servant Leadership a bit later on.)

In both cases, we had no idea about these personal goals. You have to ask—and be willing to find out what is real for that person. You'll also need a culture and guiding principles at your makerspace that place value on the development of staff, so that your staff is willing and maybe even eager to share this with you.

What about your own personal vision? And sharing that with your family, friends, and co-workers? No one can help you towards your vision if they don't know what it is. Here's a good one—have your family create a family vision.

The point is, many activities will benefit from having a vision. They don't have to be long or take a lot of time—scale it with the nature of the activity.

7.3 What is in a Vision?

The vision tells every constituent what's in it for them. For a makerspace, these people could include:

- Members
- Staff
- Management
- Investors
- Members of the community at large

The vision tells the reader here's what it will feel like. This is the experience you will have as a member, or staff, and so on. This is the value you'll get from being here. It will be written to evoke feelings. For example, this place feels supportive. This place feels exciting. This place feels (fill in the blank). But while the vision does need to be strategically sound (reasonable and possible), the vision need not and in fact should not go into how we're going to do it. That's not its purpose. By sundown we'll be at the top of that ridge—that's a vision. We're not going to specify—and nor should we—the exact path we'll take, how we solved getting across the river, etc. (By the way, it will often be natural to discuss the broad path leading to your outcome. That's fine—that's assuring ourselves and our readers that this is strategically sound. We just don't need the details.) Not discussing the "how" is why we can write a vision early on in the project. We're really not sure where our building will be. We don't know the exact contents of the book yet. We're not sure how we'll market our new line of hats. That's fine—you're not supposed to know yet. We are picking our destination as a first step. We need only believe that there are realistic ways to get there.

7.4 SOP for Writing a Vision (Solo)

We'll begin with an SOP for an individual writing a first draft of a vision. (At the end we'll have some comments about the process and some alternatives.)

Requirements (Ingredients)

Belief in the process. We'll ask that you put aside any doubts you have and, at least for the moment, believe you will get something of value from this process. Over the years, many people have successfully created visions using this process, so we're fairly confident you're going to end up with something in the range of "hmm, that's interesting" to "oh my goodness I never realized I need to open a makerspace in my child's school."

Your gut. You can come back later and put in all the nice facts and figures. (And you'll want to.) Right now we need your gut. That's where the power, the greatness of the vision is going to come from. It's going to be the framework that this vision hangs on. *Don't sit down to create something mediocre*—there's not enough time to waste for that. We'll say again, do be prepared—when we allow ourselves to start imagining an extraordinary future, it can bring up some strong emotions.

Some time. This is a process that is not very amenable to interruption. At the very start of this process there's a step to get your mind into a particular frame of thinking. Answering the phone or a text is going to at least partially reset that. Try for 30–45 minutes or so of uninterrupted time.

Willingness to make yourself vulnerable. Yes, you're creating a wonderful, positive future, but it may still feel scary to put down on cold white paper some pretty serious things. Will people laugh at me? Is this just a pipe dream? If it helps, you can make this first draft for your eyes only.

Readiness to do something great. Many of us haven't been told that we're capable of great things. That's not a common message—we're much more likely to hear from the nay-sayers (who themselves usually are not doing great things—funny, that). But great things are done by "ordinary" people all the time. Most truly great things are done by someone because they decide they can.

You gotta wanna. Here's some help: In 30 minutes, you will have at least a page in front of you with the exciting core ideas for a vision of your makerspace 5 years hence. There will be spelling and grammar errors, sentence fragments, and *it is going to be great*. You're going to feel pleased and excited. You can build on it and use it to make your makerspace really happen. That was a vision, by the way. (Did it help?)

A willingness to stick to the process. Writing a great vision may be challenging. It may take several drafts to click. But the time will almost certainly be worth it. And we have to ask, what is the alternative? How will you convey to interested (and non-interested) people what you are trying to build? Interpretive dance? An oil painting—"Still life with router table"? (Actually, if you do that interpretive dance thing, at least send us the video.)

Sidebar: What's the Alternative?

It's not uncommon for people to question us if one or other of the time-consuming practices we recommend are really worth it. Is it really worth creating SOPs? Is it really worth creating a Vision? And so on. We often respond with something along the lines of "well, what's the alternative?"

There are two ways you can take that. One is perhaps a tiny bit snarky—that while this way might involve a lot more work than we'd like, we don't know of any better alternative. Dale's favorite quote along these lines comes from Tom's response about staff training. At Zingerman's Mail Order (and actually all of the Zingerman's businesses), new staff spend dozens of paid hours in classes, getting up to speed. People often ask him, isn't that terrible when someone goes through all the training and then decides to leave? "What's the alternative? Wouldn't it be worse if we don't train them and they *stay*?"

The other way of taking it is as a statement of genuinely being open to the possibility—and, to be honest, probability—that we may not always have the right answer. And if even we have the right answer now, situations change. So, is there a better alternative? If we let our egos get too much in the way, we'll miss opportunities to deliver more value to our stakeholders.

Procedure

1. Pick your topic. "My makerspace" is great. ("The world" is probably a bit ambitious.)

2. Pick your time frame. We'd suggest 3–5 years is a nice time frame for a vision for an organization like a makerspace. If you are starting out, that's enough time for things to realistically have grown and logged some accomplishments. It needs to be short enough that the vision feels "in reach" and possible. Too short and the vision may not be able to offer realistic goals that are compelling.

3. Put together a list of "prouds". Write down, on paper, a list of achievements that you are proud of. Emphasize achievements that are inspiring and perhaps related to the topic. The point is not so much to create the list (though it is going to be a fun list) as it is to get our brain primed and in an optimistic, forward-looking, positive state of mind. Take 5–10 minutes. (Set a timer.)

4. Now we're ready for the first pass. Silence your phone, close your door.

5. Set a timer for 15 minutes.

6. Pick up your pen (or keyboard) and start writing.

7. Begin with the phrase "It is (a specific date 5 years in the future) and I just locked up the makerspace after a great day!". We find it is useful to write in the first person, and as though we are writing a journal entry at the time of the vision (e.g., 5 years hence). Looking back over the past 5 years, tell your present-day self what it is like in your makerspace.

8. Go for Great! You will not hit what you don't aim at. We are not predicting the future, we're describing our preferred future. You probably don't prefer in your heart of hearts to be mediocre. When you are stripping carpet off of concrete (or one of a hundred other exciting jobs to make your makerspace happen), your motivation cannot be a mediocre makerspace, but a great one.

9. Write from the heart. Later on you'll want to add in specifics about membership numbers, revenue, etc. Right now see if you can capture the elements of the vision that make it compelling on an emotional level.

10. Make it personal. One of the most important people the vision has to work for is you. It is fine, and important, for the vision to include you—after all, everyone should see themselves in the vision. It will also tell other people just what role you intend to play, and why you're motivated.

11. Use the hot-pen technique to avoid writer's block: Write what comes to your mind. Don't stop writing to edit, or organize, or at all—just keep writing. There will be time later to edit. If you don't know what to write, write "I don't know what to write". Very quickly you'll likely find your mind shifting and getting into content. As we said earlier, don't be surprised if you find the vision leading to interesting places.

12. Once you have your rough draft, you can start editing and revising. Your first draft may be heavy on the experience aspect of your future makerspace; review your list of who is being served and how they're served. Have you described what's in it for the various groups involved in your space? Take statements that are vague ("we have lots of active members") and turn them into measurables ("we have over 200 active paid members"). Use proxies like survey results to make statements like "everyone feels welcome" into a quantifiable goal like "when we survey members, over 95% percent agree or strongly agree that High Ridge Makerspace is welcoming." Review the characteristics of a vision to see what other improvements are possible.

13. Get input from "content experts." Who is a content expert? Anyone who can read the draft vision from the viewpoint of one of the groups you are serving. Small business owners. Students. Artists. Your spouse or significant other. Are they excited? Do they "get it"?

14. The most important step: Share it. With whom? Everyone. Your parents. Your next door neighbor. And of course the organizers of the local geek meet-up, the science teacher at the local school, etc. Post it on your website. Include it in your member handbook. Make it part of the application process when you hire staff.

15. Use it. This is not a one-time read. The vision describes your preferred future, and should influence every decision that you and your staff (and members!) make. Does this decision move us towards or away from our vision for where we will be in 5 years? Make reading the vision an expectation on a regular basis.

16. Make a new vision. Each vision is time-limited. You'll need to periodically create a new vision—certainly by the time the vision is set in, but perhaps earlier if it's clear

that, for whatever reason, the current vision isn't useful. We recommend not just revising your vision to create an updated one, but to start from scratch each time. You'll have different staff, and be in a different place (particularly after your first vision). You'll know what types of things are easy and what are more difficult. You may want to explore other techniques to produce the vision.

Comments

This was a "cooking" recipe—variations are welcome. There are some specific goals this SOP tries to address:

- It can be hard to focus on the positive
- We can get writer's block by getting caught up with how we're expressing some idea
- Self-censoring can prevent us from expressing our scary, big dreams

There's a place for logic, but in order for our vision to inspire people (including ourselves), it has to make an emotional connection with the reader. The hot-pen method, writing from the heart, priming our brains with exciting examples, and so on—these introduce from the very first draft the excitement, the energy that our vision must have if it is to serve us. But if you'd prefer to be more analytical to start with—"let's see, our members should find a selection of top-notch tools ..." and then add the more emotionally-connecting layer on top, great. In the end, when the person you handed your vision to has finished reading it, did they laugh at parts? Are they smiling? Did they look up at you and ask when can they come in and help make this happen?

7.5 SOP for Writing a Vision (Group)

Here's an SOP for creating a vision when you have a group of people involved. When we've used it, it has worked well to bring up a load of exciting ideas and build excitement and support in the group. Your group may have some other ways of working together that will give you better results. Feel free to use this as a starting point.

We'll preface this by saying that your responsibility as a leader is to make sure there is a vision. You don't have to do it all yourself (and in anything but a small organization, probably shouldn't), but at the same time you can't abdicate responsibility for the content. The process below generates ideas, which can later be vetted for strategic soundness, support (among various groups), and other criteria.

Requirements (Ingredients)

Your group: Who should be involved? The argument for inclusiveness includes 1) getting more ideas, and 2) letting people know that they are being heard. Owners. Managers. Staff. Members. Others from the community with a significant interest in the long term success of the space. (A caution: strong facilitation and an explicit process and goals will be crucial if you find it unavoidable to include people with disruptive tendencies or views/values that are contrary to or misaligned with the mission or guiding principles of the makerspace.)

Time: Set aside enough time for the process, and use good meeting skills to honor the time people are spending by starting and ending on time.

Space: Appropriate for your group.

Strong facilitation: A skilled facilitator can be someone from outside the organization, and can be quite successful at creating great value from a meeting without necessarily being an expert in the matter at issue. Key point: *a facilitator exercises power in the service of the meeting, not for themselves.* If you are using an internal facilitator, or facilitating the meeting yourself, know that facilitation is a skill worth developing. (See resources on running a meeting later.)

Explicit process and goals: Every meeting should have clear goals, and everyone should be clear at how the group is going to get there. At a minimum, you'll help everyone be prepared to give the process their best effort, while in the case of a group with disparate viewpoints and motivations, having the process and goals clearly stated will aid in facilitation. It is also important to note what you won't be creating—a finished vision, for example.

Supplies: For this exercise, bright round stickers (any size from 1/4" to 1" is fine—smaller are cheaper), big flip chart paper, easel or tape to tape paper to walls[7], dark markers.

Existing Vision: If you have a previous vision or some examples you admire, that can be useful.

Roles: Scribe (with readable writing). Facilitator. Possibly a time-keeper, or the facilitator can also time-keep.

1. Thank everyone for making time.

2. Describe the goal of this exercise—for example, to identify a potential set of elements to include in the new vision, and to gauge the level of excitement and support. If you want to be clever, make this in the form of a vision. "It's 3 o'clock, and we just got done with our initial visioning session. We have 60 different ideas, organized into broad areas, with dots showing how much support they have."

3. Go around and ask for *brief* introductions. Do they represent an unique point of view? Have they ever participated in creating a vision before? Do they have one or two words to describe an element of their vision they're excited about? (We're trying to build excitement here—we'll record the actual ideas in just a moment.)

4. Describe in whatever detail is appropriate the characteristics of a vision:

    (a) Inspiring
    (b) Strategically Sound
    (c) Documented
    (d) Communicated
    (e) Time Bound
    (f) Measurable

---

[7] If you tape paper to walls, make sure you don't have markers bleed through to the wall. Just saying.

7.5. SOP FOR WRITING A VISION (GROUP)

Describe any other characteristics you want your vision to have. Hand out your current vision, or a short example vision. You could even use the vision for this meeting as an example.

5. Describe the process (below).

6. Stage One: Brainstorm. Here we want to gather as many ideas as we can, unfiltered. In particular, we want to avoid having ideas shot down by someone since 1) the "shooter" may not know what they're talking about, and 2) once someone has been shot down, they're less likely to want to contribute more ideas. So, the rules are:

   (a) State your idea as briefly as possible (they will have to be written down)
   (b) You may add on to a previous idea (We will ask for support later on, so it isn't necessary to worry about noting your support during the brainstorming section.)
   (c) No critiques of other ideas—we will handle that outside this meeting

   Have the scribe record each idea on either a large whiteboard or large notepads attached to the walls. Depending on the dynamics of the group, you may want to call on people in addition to having them shout it out. (In particular, you want to make sure you are not just hearing from the outgoing, verbal members, but everyone at the meeting who is willing to share.) Be sure to ask for and write down useful adjectives. Not "gas forge" but "awesome gas forge", "2-burner gas forge", etc. Not just "member lounge", but "cozy member lounge." Recall that our final document has to be compelling for the reader, even while it presents a strategically sound future. You can explicitly ask for descriptive words for ideas—"can you tell me more about that?" or "how would you describe that?"

7. Stage Two: Organize. Have the larger group take a break and do the following in a small group, though if your facilitator likes a challenge you could try this in the larger group. Your goal is to condense and organize the ideas for the next stage, when people will indicate their support. Sometimes several specific ideas will lead to a more general theme (e.g., "paper towel dispenser" and "soap dispenser" for the bathrooms might lead to "upgrade the bathroom"). Some ideas may be duplicates, so combine. Post these on the whiteboard or new note pads. Try to carry through adjectives and anything that could help craft a compelling vision ("awesome", "humongous", "heavy-duty", etc.), since these will be important later on when crafting the vision itself.

8. Stage Three: Dot Storm (aka "Dot voting"). Each person in the large group is given the same number of dot stickers—say 1/3 the number of items plus 1^8. Briefly describe the organizing that was done by the small group. Explain that the goal is to gauge the level of support for each idea. Give the group 5 or 10 minutes for each person to place their (say) 8 stickers, 1 per idea maximum, on their favorite 8 ideas.

9. That's it. Thank the group, and explain that a smaller group will take the results and use it in crafting the vision. If the larger group is a decision-making body, give a date for the vision to return.

10. A small group is then responsible for vetting the ideas and organizing them, along with other elements the small group may want, into a coherent vision. These ideas are input, and useful, but even a well-supported idea may not be strategically sound at the moment.

---

[8]For example, if you had 21 items, 21/3=7, plus 1 is 8 dots. Some folks use a number more like 1/5 the number of items.

Comments

This is just one way of beginning the vision process with a group. The advantages of this, as stated above, are that we hear many different ideas, and people feel heard. We also get a quick read on the support and excitement for elements.

It will be trickier to go further in a large group. Above a handful of people, evaluation of how strategically sound an idea is is not necessarily very efficiently (or accurately) done. A smaller group, or even an individual, can be charged with the subsequent stages. If the larger group is a decision-making body, then the elements can come back for a decision once they've been evaluated by the smaller group, and then likely again after a smaller group has word-smithed them into a vision document. (In general, it's rarely a good use of large-group meeting time to "word-smith" a document. Charge a smaller group or individual with the job, and then have the larger group approve.)

7.6 What to Do With Your Vision

The vision has absolutely no value if it is not shared and used. Does your staff have the latest copy? If a proposal is made that seems problematic or perhaps not in the mission of the organization, is anyone likely to think of looking at the vision document? Do your members have the latest copy? Visitors to your website? Investors? Is it posted in the common room?

7.7 Creating an Updated Vision

If you are starting a makerspace, the initial vision may be yours, and you might have a rough draft in the matter of an hour or two. With an established organization, the process may involve many more people and numerous stages. So when year five comes around (it seemed so far off at the time!), start planning ahead of time for the next 5 year (or 3 year, or whatever) vision.

We would recommend not just editing the old vision and adding in some new numbers and dates. It's very unlikely that you didn't learn some very important things in the past 5 years. The makerspace is a different place, you're a different person, likely a fairly different staff. Writing a completely new vision (informed by the old, if appropriate), is almost certainly worth the effort.

Your vision should surprise everyone in at least some aspect.

Your vision should ask as well as provide.

7.8 Example

Here's the vision for this book:

It is a snowy December day in 2021. It's hard to believe it has been three years since we started this book project!

7.8. EXAMPLE

In one book, we've outlined the basic content of our Makerspace Operations Bootcamp, including key tools like the use of SOPs, 5S-ing, but also more background like what we can learn from Lean, TWI, open book, servant leadership, the Improvement Kata, and so on. The goal is that it can provide 80% of the impact of attending the bootcamp, at least if the reader is willing to work with and absorb the information.

Everyone at the shop has contributed stories and other content.

We've distributed 1,000 copies of the book as of last month. About 20% were print volumes, and the remainder a name-your-own price e-book. It has contributed to our makerspace's financial bottom line, but the biggest impact is on our "people" bottom line.

The book is still printed on-demand, and so benefits from the latest information we have, plus we carry no inventory. We often have a new update every few months.

Over 100 makerspaces openly subscribe to major elements (SOPs, 5S, etc.) and are on the list of Intentional Makerspaces. When a person looks for information on starting a makerspace, this network and approach is one of the first things they come across.

We've built into our website and the book a means for soliciting and receiving feedback. We've had hundreds of emails and made dozens of important improvements to the book. Plus we've included many new stories from a variety of makerspaces—successes and failures.

The book was a core part of our project to launch the Intentional Makerspace project, sharing best practices (SOPs in particular), open book finances, etc. (This has its own vision!)

We've also used the book to launch an annual conference of Intentional Makerspaces which is held at Maker Works. Last year Jeffrey Liker spoke at the conference.[9]

The Maker Works Makerspace Operations Bootcamp has been fully-booked three times a year for the last year, and we're looking at other ways we can get this available to more people (including in other countries). The bootcamp experience of course involves seeing an actual makerspace and other tours, and is interactive. The book delivers much of the content, but is a very different experience.

---

[9]We can dream, can't we?

Chapter 8

Values/Guiding Principles

Your organization's stated values (or guiding principles) describe how you're going to behave. In the plane flight earlier, values were what turned a roller coaster ride into a (somewhat) civilized mode of transportation—specifically, the value that the comfort of the passenger was important.

As with every statement an organization makes publicly, there's the chance for its guiding principles to be read in a cynical way. "Do they really mean that?"

There are plenty of famous, large companies that claim they value and respect their customers, but our own experience (particularly around companies with limited competition) is too often that these are not reflected in the actual experience we have as a customer. In these cases, these are not guiding principles—these are marketing points.

Paul Saginaw (one of the Zingerman's founders) has an excellent definition of a guiding principle: "A guiding principle is a best practice that costs you." Maybe we can rephrase that a bit as "A guiding principle is a best practice that you'll do even if it costs you." This is useful because guiding principles are not just what we should do, but what we will do, and in the short term sometimes (though not always) that could be to the detriment of the financial bottom line.

In the absence of clearly-stated guiding principles, decision-making is much more difficult (except for the dictator) because the organization's guiding principles must be inferred—or more likely, projected by each individual in a way that best suits them. It is a duty of the leaders to make clear the guiding principles, and to ensure the decisions and behavior of the organization are consistent with them.

8.1 Values of the Maker Movement

Since 2014 we've been asking current and potential makerspace operators if they think there are values that are essential to makerspaces. It's an interesting question, given the wide range of makerspaces our audience represents—elementary schools to corporations. But we think it's a useful question to consider, since at least some people will join our makerspaces with a set of preconceived ideas about the guiding principles a makerspace will have. When we walk into a restaurant, our expectations are that our comfort (heat, lighting, seating) will be valued; the time it takes for the food to be served will fall into a reasonable range since we're likely hungry and have a not-unlimited amount of time to spend waiting; the food will be uncontaminated, warm or cold as appropriate, tasty, and so on. Are there likewise values that members expect in makerspaces?

As we said in the first chapter, there are some values that seem to come up all the time:

- Sharing Information. Generally speaking, the expectation is that members freely share information—"Where did you find that part?" "How did you make that casting?" "What type of wood is that?" If anything, the most sharing members tend to be most admired—as long as the information is accurate and delivered in a respectful way, which may sometimes be a challenge for some members.

- Self-directed learning. There can be formal classes, of course, but makerspaces generally also support individuals pursuing their own development.

- Failure is seen as an opportunity for and part of learning. Put another way, the member (and makerspace as a whole) values even a failure in a makerspace since it increases the member's knowledge. Risk and exploration is welcomed and supported for the same reasons.

- Another value can be phrased in the negative—makerspaces typically do not support "rent seeking" and often (but not always) actively support routing around it. "Rent seeking" in this case is defined as when an entity collects value by imposing artificial limits on some activity. For example, companies that restrict sales of repair parts, prohibit repairs by consumers, or otherwise limit the use of items sold to consumers would in general, run counter to the usual makerspace value system. At the other extreme, makerspaces often actively promote open-source software, open-source hardware, and the sharing of alternatives to products and policies that extract wealth without providing corresponding value.

- Many makerspaces (again, not all) expressly value diversity of various types in their membership. (We will discuss diversity a bit later.) This can include racial, socio-economic, educational, gender conformity, and so on.

- Entrepreneurship. A very common value is the support, often very active, of entrepreneurial efforts by members. Many makerspaces, in offering high-capital or physically large equipment, make possible small business opportunities without the large investment in equipment and infrastructure that might be necessary for prototyping and first run production. However, size, capacity, and mission of the makerspace may limit this type of support. In a few cases, the mission or nature of the organization (or a parent organization or a funder) may even preclude entrepreneurial enterprises making use of the space. This might be the case when makerspaces are a part of an educational or other nonprofit entity. In other cases, the equipment just may not be up to the task of commercial production.

(By the by, Maker Works has a starting place of "prototyping yes, production no", and then we see if we can make small-scale production work on a case-by-case basis. Not all our tools are industrial, for example, and up to the rigors of large-scale production runs.)

A few other values to consider:

- What about supporting formal education in the community?
- Should the makerspace prioritize helping local non-profits?
- What about contributing to the support and development of other makerspaces?

8.2 Discovering Your Guiding Principles

If you are part of a larger organization, some of these values may be either explicitly listed or can be extracted from existing documents. In that case, though, there are probably values specific to the makerspace environment that may not come up, for example, in the typical church, library, etc., so you may need to augment them. But in the more common case, as a leader you'll need to guide the creation of the values/guiding principles.

The sole proprietor or partnership can draw upon the vision. But it's likely your vision doesn't explicitly mention some core values that you want—actually, need—to be reflected in the makerspace. There may be implicit, or in the background, but even if it's obvious to you, it will be useful making it very clear to everyone. *You should not underestimate the ability of people to project their own viewpoint and values onto any situation.* And of course it is your responsibility as a leader to make sure the guiding principles are written down, just as it is with the other elements.

You might try an exercise similar to visioning, but this time focused on values that you would find necessary to feel happy in the makerspace.

To create guiding principles with a group, you can use a process similar to that described for creating a vision. That is, carefully describe the process, brainstorm to generate possibilities, organize, use a dot-storm to gauge support, then refine in a small group before bringing back to the larger group for approval.

8.3 Writing the Guiding Principles

Guiding principles probably lean towards statements of fact vs. the emotional appeal we hope to see in the Vision. Again, the actual writing is best left to a small group or individual, working from raw material in the form of existing documents (vision, mission, etc.) and the list of guiding principles compiled using brainstorming or other techniques. These can be brought before the larger group (if there is one) for approval.

8.4 Integrating Values

Writing down your guiding principles is a waste of time unless you take active steps to integrate them into your organization. This means sharing them during hiring, sharing them with your members, listing them in your handbooks, but most importantly reflecting them in your day to day actions.

Chapter 9

Instruction and Learning

We're convinced that a core system in your makerspace should be the use of SOPs. See Chapter 2 for details. As a reminder, SOPs standardize our work so we are more efficient, reduce waste, produce consistent results, and allow us to continuously improve since we can make controlled changes to what we do. SOPs can be applied to member use of machines, but also nearly all the aspects of a makerspace, from front desk operations (renewing memberships, signing up for classes, etc.) to teaching classes (we call ours "Train the Trainer" SOPs). Just as a point of reference, we have 28 SOPs at the moment for our monthly bookkeeping tasks (paying bills, recording payroll, projecting cash flow, etc.).

It also turns out that the process we use for instruction, "How to Instruct" (or "Job Instruction"), has as a core requirement that the work to be done is broken down into closely defined steps, as do most of the techniques for system improvement (which we'll also discuss). That is, *SOPs are necessary for instruction and improvement*. Let's now talk about How to Instruct in the context of the intentional makerspace.

9.1 How to Instruct

9.1.1 TWI and How to Instruct

As a reminder, Training Within Industry (TWI) was a voluntary World-War II program of the US government that sought to improve efficiency of wartime production in the face of reduced labor and increased demand. There were several training sessions available, each delivering a different set of skills aimed at the supervisors. Later on we'll discuss some of these other sessions, but one that is particularly useful in a makerspace is called "Job Instruction", or as we'll call it, How to Instruct (HTI).

9.1.2 Should You Be Instructing in the First Place?

Before we jump into How to Instruct, we remind you that while How To Instruct is a system, the fact that we're asking someone to learn something may not be the best solution to a situation. Are members forgetting to turn on the dust collector when they use the table saw?

Well, should we solve that problem with more instruction (and perhaps shock collars[1]), or is there a change to the system that we can make, so the dust collector automatically comes on? (Make it easy to do the right thing, hard to do the wrong thing.)

We're using How to Instruct in the wider context of all the possible solutions to delivering value to our members; when we instruct, this is how we'd like to do it, but maybe a better solution involves changing a system or element of the culture.

9.1.3 Back to How to Instruct

It may be hard for some of us to fully appreciate the work environment of the 1940's and earlier. Instruction in how to perform a job often fell into two categories—apprenticeship, a fairly lengthy and often inefficient[2] way of teaching a set of skills or knowledge; and instruction by academic instructors, that is, people whose primary area of knowledge was in education (vs. the subject being taught). But in a wartime scenario, apprenticeship was not going to have bombers rolling off a production line quickly enough. And maybe, just maybe, there were better people to do the instructing than academics. Perhaps—and this might be a long-shot—but perhaps people who actually knew what the job was?

Put another way, is the core talent the ability to teach, with the content considered either simple enough to pick up or largely irrelevant to instruction; or is knowledge of the work more important, and instruction something that can be accomplished following a recipe?

There were some other aspects of working in the 1940's and before, including discrimination (race, gender, marital status, sexual orientation, etc.), cronyism, and so on. A bit later we'll talk about other lessons TWI had for these times, and some that are still applicable today. But Job Instruction—How to Instruct—had a big impact at the time.

How To Instruct begins with the idea that the people best suited to instructing were the supervisors. (Before you get too concerned, we should say that TWI actually spells out the skills the supervisor should have, and central was knowledge of the work. So there's an understanding that these were not pointy-haired bosses[3], but people experienced in doing the work.) What the supervisors needed was a recipe for instructing the front-line staff, a 5-step[4] plan:

1. Prepare to teach

2. Prepare the learner

3. Present the operations and knowledge

4. Try out performance

5. Follow-up.

---

[1] You weren't expecting that, were you?

[2] Of course, the apprenticeship may have several different goals, only one of which was the actual conveyance of knowledge.

[3] We were surprised that Dilbert's "pointy-haired boss", or PHB, even has a Wikipedia entry: https://en.wikipedia.org/wiki/Pointy-haired_Boss

[4] Or, preparation plus 4-steps.

9.1.4 The 5-Step Plan

1. Preparing to Teach

Before the learner shows up, the instructor has some preparation to do.

First, we should have answers to at least the first 3 of the following 4 questions, the Zingerman's Training Plan Questions:[5]

1. What is expected of the trainee — and by when?
2. How will the information that the trainees need to know be provided? (What are the training resources?)
3. How will we know (measure) that the expectations are/are not being met?
4. What are the rewards/consequences for meeting/not meeting the expectations?

(And actually, if there are rewards/consequences, we should probably share that in the context of the class.)

For example, "At the end of this class, you'll be able to make a spot weld in mild steel using the spot welder." The instructor will actually need a more detailed list of what the learner needs to know in order to do the job "efficiently, safely, economically, and intelligently."[6]

Second, HTI requires that we have a job breakdown—that is, an SOP. If we don't have one, HTI isn't going to be helpful.

Third, the instructor needs to have all the tools, supplies, equipment, and materials at hand. (Not just for efficiency, so the class isn't continually delayed as bits and pieces are retrieved, but so we can model that in instructing, we're following an SOP and our SOP for teaching the class says we'll be prepared in a certain way.) Note that HTI requires that the learner try out their knowledge—classes must be hands-on. (This can place constraints on class size—we find at Maker Works that for more than 3 learners, there's too much dead time for students as they wait for others to try out an operation, since we usually have just one tool.)

Finally, fourth, have the workplace arranged in the way you want it kept. This is a pretty important point—during instruction, the learner will be open to information about this job in a way that will never happen again. We have one chance during this critical moment, and if we begin with a cluttered, dirty, disorganized workplace, we've sent the message that this is okay. (One idea to help maintain this state and remind people is to use a photo of the ideal state.)

A few years ago Ben, one of our staff who teaches some of the metal working classes, had a brilliant idea about the third item. Each of our classes has a binder with an SOP describing how to present the class. (We call them the Train the Trainer SOPs.) He put a pencil holder bag in the milling class binder to hold all the end mills, rulers, and other small tooling that is needed when we teach the milling machine class. Saves tons of time over running around trying to locate all the pieces each time you teach the class.

By the way, everyone received a training booklet at the Job Instruction (How to Instruct) session, and printed at the bottom of every page was the phrase

---

[5] http://www.zingtrain.com/content/essential-guide-staff-training
[6] The Training Within Industry Report, 1940-1945

"If the worker hasn't learned, the instructor hasn't taught."

We'll have a bit more to say on that later, but keep in mind this attitude—as instructors, we are expected to use the best practices we know, and to take responsibility for the results.

2. Preparation of the Learner

Step 2 is about getting the learner mentally here, ready to learn, and even excited about learning.

First, put the learner at ease. Introductions (brief, please), name tags, and icebreakers can all help.

Second, find out what they already know about the job. This is helpful to the instructor in that they can customize their presentation, reviewing information everyone already knows, and spending more time on topics they don't. In the makerspace, this is also an opportunity to acknowledge the learner's knowledge and to frame the presentation in a way that may be more palatable. For example, we've had members who have quite literally owned and operated multiple machine shops join our makerspace, and we ask them to take our milling machine checkout class, just like the 16-year old FIRST robotics student who may never have drilled a hole. You can see where this could get a little dicey! But if we ask about experience, it gives us the opportunity to say something like:

"Clearly, Mike, you have a lot of experience on this machine, and we hope our other members will learn a lot just by being around you. We appreciate you taking the class to learn about our shop-specific ways of doing things, and the quirks of our specific machines. After the class I hope you'll share with me thoughts about how we can improve the class." Something like that.[7]

When we ask the learners about what they already know, we also get them thinking about the job, getting more into a receptive mental space.

Third, HTI asks us to get the learner interested and desirous of learning the job. In a traditional work environment, that may be a challenge, but in a makerspace we're usually in the wonderful position that our members have come already motivated. Heck, in many cases they've shelled out good money for the class. However, it never hurts to provide examples of the things you can do with the addition of this tool to their skill set and get them even more excited.

3. Presentation of the Operations and Knowledge

Our learner is hopefully ready to learn, and we have everything in place. How are we going to convey our information? HTI lists 4 main points as follows:

a. Tell, Show, Illustrate, and Question to Convey the New Information

First, what are we conveying? The contents of the SOP. Actually, this is pretty important. If our checkout classes are teaching something other than what is in the SOP, we have a big problem. *If we expect the member to act on something, it must be in the SOP.*

---

[7] Ideally, we'd have this talk with the person long before the class, probably as soon as we identify this potential issue. It often comes up when we do a tour, for example, and we can take that opportunity to tell them why we need them to take the checkout class.

9.1. HOW TO INSTRUCT

And we're going to model the use of the SOP (even for something we've done a dozen times before), rather than going by memory. We will have two SOPs open during class—the SOP for operation of the tool, and the SOP for teaching the class. Recently in some classes we've been printing out additional copies of the SOP for students to follow along with. It seems worthwhile.

How do we convey the information? The four modes are:

Tell: We're all familiar with this one, and we probably default to it too quickly. For some types of information, an element of telling is just fine, but we can often delude ourselves that only telling someone is really getting across what we want. Not everyone may know the specialized language or concepts, and even vigorous handwaving[8] has its limits with abstract or complicated concepts.

Take the example of tying a taut-line hitch. Wikipedia offers the following instructions: "It is made by tying a rolling hitch around the standing part after passing around an anchor object." While accurate and concise, this is not very helpful for most people.

Show: An actual demonstration of the operation is a big step up, but even here if we only show, we run the risk that important elements are difficult to see or are not immediately obvious.

Continuing our taut-line hitch example, imagine that someone is tying the knot in front of you. It's possible that this will be sufficient, but we can equally imagine the demonstrator has a hard time tying the knot such that it's clear what is being done. What about the situation where you are facing the instructor but left and right are important to an operation? You'll have to mentally flip all the lefts and rights.

Illustrate: Here we may use diagrams, pictures, or other methods to draw attention to the important aspects of the job and simplify the details. Many simple knots can be clearly shown with just a single (sometimes broken) line.

Question: Until this point we've been feeding the learner information. Asking the right questions requires the learner to take what they've learned and apply it. In our knot example, we could ask things like could you tie the knot with ropes of two different diameters. Do you have to keep going the same direction around the "standing" part? Could you have just one wrap on the inside of the loop instead of two? (These all happen to lead to other types of knots.)

We shouldn't be surprised that the elements of the SOP parallel the above steps (with the exception of Question). Our SOP text (operation and key points) are the telling, and the illustrations are the show and illustrate.

b. Instruct Slowly, Clearly, Completely, and Patiently, One Point at a Time

What's a point? A step of the SOP.

---

[8] "I am waving my hands as hard as I can! Why can't you understand what I'm saying!"

c. Check, Question, and Repeat

Here's where we get feedback on how we're doing so far. Are they getting it? We can't just ask them, because if they say "yes", we don't know if the "what" they got is correct. So find out what they understand by *asking questions*.

When is the best time to correct errors of understanding? Now.

"Now" is always the best time to provide feedback.

As you go, use whatever means you can to make sure that the learner has a correct understanding. Ask questions that go beyond repeating back what you just said, but that require the learner to demonstrate they get the underlying information and can apply it. Repeat whatever content is necessary and then verify again.

For example, if you discussed how to hold down thin, flimsy material in the laser cutter with magnets, later on you might want to ask "So Bob, how would you go about cutting a piece of fabric in the laser?" It can also be valuable asking questions to explore the negative—operations that are not possible, or things they don't know yet. On the laser, we might ask "How would you hold down a piece of PVC plastic in the laser?" If you've taken the laser class, you'd hopefully know that PVC is a no-go in the laser due to the caustic and toxic fumes it produces, so the answer is that in fact we shouldn't cut it in the first place.

Remember—"If the worker hasn't learned, the instructor hasn't taught."[9]

Every moment that goes by will make correcting errors harder. If we fail to catch errors during the initial instruction, things get even worse—now the learner has had time to feel their understanding is their own, whereas during the initial instruction they're much more willing to accept what we say, since they haven't had any experience. We provide the most value to our members when we do our best to make sure they have correct understanding at every stage.

Now is always the best time to provide feedback.

And if you didn't catch it earlier, when should we then act?

Now is always the best time to provide feedback.

d. Make Sure the Learner Really Learns

Just asking if everyone "got it" may not give you accurate results. The learner's body language can often warn you that you're losing their attention or something isn't clicking for them.

Move on when you feel confident.

4. Performance Try-Out

HTI now asks that the learner try out the job.

Let's be clear about the situation. The learner may be in a group of several other learners and may be anxious not to screw up. This may be the first time they've ever done this sort of thing, and it might be on a big, expensive, fancy machine. Are they feeling relaxed?

---
[9] If you promise not to tell anyone, we're going to give you an "out" a little later on.

9.1. HOW TO INSTRUCT

Let's hope they don't realize what the real situation is—you're the one being tested! Did you follow the SOP? Did you make sure each learner "got it"? What about when Marty wasn't clear about how to install the collet—are you sure he figured it out?

a. Test the Learner by Having Them Perform the Job

Model using the SOP. *This is not a memory test.* Make sure this is clear—*in the class and on their own, using the SOP is part of the SOP for using the tool.*

b. Ask Questions Beginning With "Why", "How", "Who", "When", or "Where"

Again, we're not asking for parroting back facts, but exploring have we taught the underlying concepts well enough that the learner can synthesize responses to new situations.

"How would you hold down a piece of cardboard on the ShopBot?"

"When would you use soft copper jaws in the vise?"

c. Observe Performance, Correct Errors, and Repeat Instructions If Necessary

Again, "Now is always the best time to provide feedback."

d. Continue Until You Know They Know

Here's the temptation. These are your members. You want them to feel good about the class. You want them to be happy. You don't want to say "Hey Bob, I'm not sure you understand how the automatic feed works yet." You'll be tempted to just let them slide. However, it is a disservice to "let them slide". We and our staff need to care enough about our members to make sure we know they know.

5. Follow-Up

HTI isn't done with us yet. We've done our best to convey the information, but we have 3 more steps:

a. Put Them "On Their Own"

In the makerspace, we're probably going to check them off in the database—they're good to go on that machine. However,...

b. Check Frequently To Be Sure They Are Following The Instruction

This is probably best framed as seeing if we've given them everything they need to know. "I just wanted to check that we've given you all the information you need, or if there are any points that aren't clear. We're always looking to improve our SOP if it seems like something is missing."

c. Taper Off Extra Supervision and Close Follow-Up Until They Are Qualified to Work With Normal Supervision

This last point implies there's a normal level of supervision. In a makerspace, we'll want to be walking around more in the mode of providing customer service rather than wanting to make our members feel like we're monitoring them. "How is it going? Need anything or have any problems?"

9.1.5 Summary of HTI

1. Prepare to teach

    (a) What is expected of the trainee — and by when?
    (b) How will the information trainees need to know be provided? (What are the training resources?)
    (c) How will we know (measure) that the expectations are/are not being met?
    (d) What are the rewards/consequences for meeting/not meeting the expectations?

2. Prepare the learner

    (a) Put the learner at ease.
    (b) find out what they already know about the job.
    (c) get the learner interested and desirous of learning the job.

3. Present the operations and knowledge

    (a) Tell, show, illustrate, and question to convey the new information.
    (b) Instruct slowly, clearly, completely, and patiently, one point at a time.
    (c) Check, question, and repeat.
    (d) Make sure the learner really learns.

4. Try out performance

    (a) Test the learner by having them perform the job.
    (b) Ask questions beginning with "why", "how", "who", "when", or "where".
    (c) Observe performance, correct errors, and repeat instructions if necessary.
    (d) Continue until you know they know.

5. Follow-up.

    (a) Put them "on their own."
    (b) Check frequently to be sure they are following the instructions.
    (c) Taper off extra supervision and close follow-up until they are qualified to work with normal supervision.

9.2 The 4 Levels of Competency

This can be an interesting way of looking at the progression as we acquire and make knowledge our own. Having this model in mind can let us talk about the different stages that makerspace members (and staff) are in, and help us understand where they're coming from.[10]

1. The student begins by not knowing that they don't know. They are *Unconsciously Incompetent* (at least about that topic). "I had no idea you could cut metal out like this on a plasma cutter." Makerspaces are wonderful places to expose members to new tools, ideas, materials, and designs, and move them into the next stage. However, until the student knows about this new area, there's no way for them to be excited or motivated to learn.

2. The *Consciously Incompetent* student now knows that there is this particular knowledge or ability they don't have yet. Combined with an active excitement or interest, this may lead them to take steps to acquire this knowledge. Perhaps they take a class. Or it could be a skill that is developed with practice (e.g., welding).

3. Eventually the student may become competent, but like a beginning driver, spends a lot of effort on the task. They are very conscious of each movement—there is not yet a smooth "flow", but the result is acceptable. At this stage, the *Consciously Competent* student may be able to express each step of the task quite clearly, since each step requires careful thought. Depending on the student and the task, progress may end with this conscious competence, and we're generally pleased when our members gain this level of ability, since they can consistently produce a good result. There's also something to be said for an instructor who is at the higher end of this stage—their consciousness of each step may make it easier to convey to members details that are automatic for instructors at the next stage.

4. With additional experience and practice, less and less conscious thought is required to competently execute the task, until we are driving across town and hardly remember getting from point A to B. We may have a real "flow" to our behavior, and can use our thoughts to concentrate on higher aspects of the task ("I wonder if it would be more efficient to sand in this direction?") or perhaps on other things altogether. However, this *Unconsciously Competent* person may not be a great person to write an SOP, for example, since the steps are automatic in their mind. They reach unconsciously to adjust a lever without it registering, observe some aspect of the way a cut is going and make subtle corrections, all below their conscious thoughts. Wonderful for them, but not the "beginner's mind" we need to put ourselves into when we create SOPs and other aspects of instruction.

9.3 4 Levels of Learning

Another lens to examine learning through is the 4 Levels of Learning from ZingTrain (a part of Zingerman's that does corporate training). They're listed by Maggie Bayless as follows:

Level 1: Listening/Reading

---

[10]Gordon Training International, as referenced in http://www.zingtrain.com/content/essential-guide-staff-training

This is described as a fairly passive mode. We're listening or reading, but this doesn't necessarily mean we're integrating what's being said.

In our makerspaces, we'd like for people to listen, and we want them to read material we feel is important, but this level reminds us that just listening or reading isn't a guarantee that the information stuck.

Level 2: Reflecting

Here we're actively thinking about this new information. Does this make sense given the other things I believe are true? What are the implications?

This is getting better than the passive mode above, and the new information bumping up against the other stuff in our noggins, but we haven't done anything with this information—it's rather theoretical right now. We don't have any experience ourselves.

Level 3: Assimilating and Implementing

Here we actually act upon this new information. But Maggie points out that merely adopting a practice is not as significant as adapting that practice or information to fit your own situation. Again, drawing a parallel with the How to Instruct, we're asking for a synthesis of the information, not just a repeating of what someone else has said or done. And of course, we want our members to actually practice using the new information (i.e., how to operate a tool).

Level 4: Teaching

The ultimate level of learning. If you've ever taught a non-trivial subject, you've no doubt had a new-found level of understanding. There is a world of difference between understanding something well enough to do it yourself (especially if no one is watching!), and understanding it well enough to teach and answer questions about it.

Again, this is just another perspective on the learning process that may be helpful as you think about the instruction and the development of people that happens in your makerspace, especially the staff. The implications are interesting—it sounds like we need to provide a path to teaching if we want to offer the deepest possible mastery of a subject.

9.4 The Training Compact

Back at the start of this book we introduced the training compact:

The trainees agree to:

- Take responsibility for the effectiveness of their training.

The trainer agrees to:

- Document clear performance expectations.
- Providing training resources.
- Recognize performance.
- Reward performance.

9.4. THE TRAINING COMPACT

We can now discuss the trainer's responsibilities in a bit more detail.

Document clear performance expectations. In the context of our classes in a makerspace, this is the Training Plan:

1. What is expected of the trainee—and by when?

2. How will the information trainees need to know be provided? (What are the training resources?)

3. How will we know (measure) that the expectations are/are not being met?

4. What are the rewards/consequences for meeting/not meeting the expectations?

As you may recall, How to Instruct requires we answer at least the first three, and for classes that allow a member to use tools, the reward for completing the class is being able to use the tool.

Providing training resources. This applies not only during the actual class, but any resources necessary for the overall training. As an example, at Maker Works this could include what we call "bridge projects"—simple, documented projects (documented in SOPs) that serve as an intermediate experience between the heavily guided class and the member's own open-ended explorations. The bridge project is completed on the member's own time (the class includes a membership for the time it takes to complete the bridge project, usually just an hour or two), and often with materials supplied by the shop.

Recognize performance. Reward performance. For most of our member-oriented classes, successful completion leads to an entry in our membership database and the ability to use that tool. Depending on the culture or situation of your makerspace, you might choose more public recognition or some incentives. Educational institutions in particular would have more obvious connections between grading and completion of classes. A makerspace will have other instruction going on. For example, all of our staff are required to take several classes, such as How to Instruct and How to Give Great Service, and other classes may be optional but rewarded with compensation. (Our actual mechanism we call a "passport"—it's really just a list of things that a staff person is expected to complete in order to remain on staff or, for an existing staff person, to move up to a higher level of compensation. A list for a new hire would include the classes above, a few checkout classes—picked with the staff person—and becoming certified to teach one or two classes.) Looking ahead, we'll see later on that the training compact is related to the stewardship contract.

Here's a challenge for a makerspace that adopts the use of SOPs and the idea of mandatory checkout classes: the member who "already knows how to run that machine." This can range from the handy-person who has had a table saw in their garage for years and "still has all their fingers" (they will wave them at you just to make sure you see them), to the retired machinist who has owned four machine shops and, in truth, has forgotten more than most of us will ever know about metalworking. Here's why you can't just give them a pass: They don't know your shop's procedures and practices. They don't know your SOPs, and so may be operating machinery in a way that will be confusing to other members. They won't know the quirks, limits, improvements, or changes to your machinery, local materials, tooling, etc. And even if the checkout class was only about the basic operation of the machine, it is difficult and time-consuming to "test" someone—probably an appreciable amount of the time it takes to just take the darn class. Some people have an inaccurate view of how much expertise they have and how safely they can operate a tool. If anything happens, you're going to have a harder time explaining things to the insurance company if you just took someone's word for the amount (and relevance) of experience they have.

What you can do is acknowledge their experience, and even ask for their help in improving. Just make sure that they're clear that you're asking for their feedback after class, not during it, and not contradicting your SOPs for no good reason.

Different, but related to this, is the member who basically says that they don't want to follow the SOP and that they're willing to accept the liability for doing so. We had one of those a few years ago. The problem is, this doesn't really work. If they got hurt, they could change their mind—we have nothing on paper. It makes for a confusing space ("but Bob over there didn't take the class" or "but Peggy isn't using the push-board"). And even if they are sincere in their statement about accepting responsibility for their own actions, in the worst case, you may be dealing with their next of kin who may have no such feelings.

This is a particular sore spot, and it is one of the places that the rubber hits the road. It is no fun to tell someone with years of experience that they have to take (and maybe even pay for!) a class on the basics of a tool they've used professionally for years. The good news is that if someone is really pushing back, they may not be a good fit for other aspects of a shared making space. And the other good news is that most folks understand. That retired machinist turned out to be a loyal member and understood where we were coming from. To those that just don't get it, we may say something to the effect that if they'd like to open their own makerspace (and have their skin in the game), we're always happy to see more.

9.5 "If the Worker Hasn't Learned, the Instructor Hasn't Taught"—The Out

Okay, "if the worker hasn't learned, the instructor hasn't taught" is a rather definite statement without any wiggle room. But in practice there are circumstances where a learner just isn't prepared for the current learning, isn't actually excited about learning this piece of knowledge, or perhaps isn't willing to take responsibility for the effectiveness of their learning (which could include paying attention, not falling asleep, etc.). How can we tell what's a valid exception?

Actually, there's a comforting answer. *Did the teacher follow the SOP ("How to Instruct") for teaching?*[11] If so, then we can be satisfied that we did all we currently know how to convey this knowledge, and it is just not a fit right now. (We're usually going to use this language—it's not "never", but "not right now".) "Right now we just don't feel comfortable about your safety operating this machine. Could we spend some time later today going over a few of the steps? Our board/owners/lawyers/insurance company really are sticklers that everyone who operates these machines can do so safely." And if we can't get to a place where we feel comfortable? We may have to say that we're sorry, we just don't seem to be a good fit with them right now. (Yes, we'll of course refund their money.)

---

[11] The sentence "Did person X follow the Y SOP" is going to be extremely useful in any number of situations in a makerspace. Did the member follow the laser SOP? If so, we can't blame them for the auto-focus getting messed up. Did the staff person follow the closing SOP? No? Then we need to have a discussion. Follow an SOP and we're never going to be upset at you—you did everything we asked.

9.5. "IF THE WORKER HASN'T LEARNED, THE INSTRUCTOR HASN'T TAUGHT"—THE OUT

Who should make this final determination? Normally Tom and Dale want our staff to feel empowered to make things right (see the Giving Great Service, coming up). In this case, though, it really needs to be at least one step, if not two, up from the front line staff. It can take some heat off the front line staff, and allows us to bring an outside perspective to the situation.

Chapter 10

Other Systems

In this chapter we discuss some systems we've found useful for organization and improving in the makerspace. We also talk about techniques for improving meetings.

10.1 43 Folders—Expensive, But Worth It

We use SOPs for most everything, but "43 Folders" is the glue that holds much of it together. We don't normally recommend multi-thousand dollar pieces of software, but when you see the power and flexibility of "43 Folders", well, it's just a no-brainer. The 43 Folders software lets you schedule processes effortlessly days, months, or even years in the future. It handles an incredible range of item types—invoices, bills, reminders, SOPs, nearly anything you can think of. Adding items is nearly instantaneous, and querying the system is intuitive. It uses "folders" to hold "paper". These are contained in a "plastic file folder holder".

Okay, actually 43 Folders (also known as a tickler file) is in fact just a collection of file folders. (Figure 10.1) Regular manila file folders. 43 of them. In a plain brown plastic file folder holder. (Yours can be any color you like.) It's a completely manual system, devoid of any operating system to upgrade, maintenance fees, bugs (unless a fly happens to expire above it), or crashes. It's going to cost you $10, and it will be the best $10 you ever spent.

Here's how it works. There are 43 folders, each the same type: 31 are labeled for each day of the month, 1 through 31. 12 are labeled for each month of the year: January through December.

To set up the files initially, arrange the month files in order, beginning with the next month at the front, and going back through the remaining months in order. The very last month folder will be that of the current month, but it actually is being used for that month a year from now. Now take the day files and order them starting with today's date on up through the last day of the month. These go at the very front of the file. The remainder go behind the next month's file. Here's what the files on October 6 would look like:

6, 7, 8, 9, 10, . . . 30, 31, November, 1, 2, 3, 4, 5, December, January, February, . . . , September, October

Let's say you have some maintenance you want to do on the Bridgeport mill on the 7th of the month and every 3 days thereafter. Turn that goal into a piece of paper—it could be an index card, or better yet it could be the entire SOP. You can directly file it in a day folder—the one labeled 7—since we currently have day folders for October 6 through November 5 (always one month). Anything past November 5 would be filed in the corresponding month folder (regardless of the year). So November 6 goes into the November file. December 15th goes into December. March 5th of 2030 goes into March.

Now each day our SOP for starting the day says to take out that day's 43 folder and process what's in it. Anything that doesn't get done can be put into the next day's folder. Put today's empty folder at the end of the next month's folders of days (in the example above, just before December). On the first day of a new month, you may have items that are in that month's folder. Take them out and distribute them among the days. Or, if it is for a future year, leave it in the month folder. Now move the month folder to the end of the stack. You should have 28 to 31 folders representing the days of the new month. (For months shorter than 31, make sure the folders are empty and move them to the next month.)

If you like, you can label binder clips with the days of the week and use them to label the next 7 day folders to make it easier to file based on the day of the week.

What can go into 43 folders? Anything that will fit into a folder, such as

- Bills

- Membership transaction reminders (e.g., email a member to tell them their membership will be ending in a few days)

- Maintenance SOPs

- One-off reminders (e.g., call to check on the roof repair schedule)

- Reporting reminders (state taxes, federal reporting, etc.)

We have found 43 folders especially useful for regular maintenance. Most every machine in the shop has one or more maintenance SOPs that should be done regularly, either by calendar time ("every 5 days") or by usage ("every 100,000 stitches"). The SOP is written up as usual, and then a log is attached. This just has columns for when was the maintenance done, who did it, and space for any comments. At the top of the SOP we note how often the SOP should be done. Then it is filed in 43 folders. At the start of the day the crew will open the folder, do any SOPs they find, and then file the completed SOPs for the next day the SOP should be done.

This may seem like a decidedly low-tech solution. Tom and Dale are quick to point out that they both come from a long background of relational databases, web portals, and custom programming of all sorts. We love nothing more than nice software. But as we alluded to above, we haven't had a single bug. The system has never crashed. It shrugs at power outages, and from time to time accepts unusual items into its system with nary a complaint. Training is quick. Custom reminders are as quick as grabbing a stray piece of paper and scratching out "Put this on Dale's desk to remind him to check on the new laser tube." A few weeks ago, a paper showed up on Dale's desk. It was the reminder, filed 5 years ago, to renew a registration. It works!

(One downside to the use of 43 Folders for recurring items like maintenance is that if an SOP is removed and then not replaced in 43 folders, we might not realize it. So consider having a log in the back of the file holder where you can record the recurring items. Then put an SOP in to be done once a month to take an inventory of the SOPs that should be in there. Just don't lose that SOP!)

Figure 10.1: Our 43 folders (plus a few).

10.2 Effective Meetings

Meetings serve a number of purposes—not just information sharing and decision making, but group building and other social purposes. The frequency of and attendees of the meetings will depend on the governance and decision-making structures, among other things, but it's very likely that, formal or informal, meetings will play an important role in your makerspace.

It's worth developing some skills in facilitating meetings. A well-run meeting is respectful of everyone's time, gets done what we want to get done (which often involves information-sharing and decision-making), and leaves people with more energy and motivation than when it started. It maximizes the value produced, and minimizes waste (e.g., time). It is the role of the facilitator to help the group accomplish their vision for the meeting, consistent with the group's values and culture, and using whatever systems are appropriate. The outcome of the meeting should, in many cases, be measurable (i.e., the meeting should have a vision associated with it—see below). For example, we reached a decision on the milling machine purchase., or we brainstormed 10 ideas for a new class.

It is important to point out that the person facilitating the meeting need not be the group's leader. The facilitator is a servant of the group[1], helping the group reach its collective vision for the meeting—*not necessarily the personal vision of the facilitator*[2]. They need not necessarily be a content expert. The skills of facilitation are general, and apply to all kinds of situations. So it's not unreasonable at all to bring in an outside facilitator to run a meeting, especially if the topic is contentious, or the regular facilitator needs to participate in the discussion. (It really is best to avoid having the facilitator participate in the discussion. If it

---

[1]Though as we'll see, so is the leadership.
[2]Dale would be—the word is not "happy" but perhaps "willing"—to share with you over a cold root beer what happens when a facilitator comes in with their own agenda and sets the group back quite literally a year or two in its progress on a topic.

really is necessary, they should symbolically take off their facilitation hat, perhaps by sitting down in a chair, to make it clear they're now talking as a participant.)

The vision for the meeting is the responsibility of leadership. However, if the group is authentically the decision-making body, then the vision can be that a decision has been made, but not that a particular choice was made. If the goal is to share information, spell out the information to be shared. At the end of the meeting, has the vision been accomplished?

As part of our respect for the attendees, the total time allocated to the meeting and to each topic within should be defined ahead of time. For example, the meeting will be 1-1/2 hours long, the introduction and icebreaker will be 10 minutes, the report from the committee on logos will be 20 minutes, etc.

If you don't already have a template for your meeting agendas, consider the following elements:

- Welcome
- Introductions (i.e., new attendees)
- Agenda review and approval
- Icebreaker
- Committee reports / standing agenda items
- Proposals in progress (old business)
- New proposals (new business)
- Announcements
- Review of new tasks[3]
- Evaluation (of the meeting)
- Appreciations[4]

A daily meeting will obviously have different elements from a more formal weekly or monthly meeting.

Share the agenda ahead of time, as well as any material and proposals. The group will be better prepared to contribute, and if a decision is to be made, everyone will be aware that their attendance (or perhaps proxy) is important.

With larger groups, having even a simple template for crafting proposals will be very useful, such as:

- Title of proposal
- Background: context and information
- Proposal: the proposal itself, clear and concise
- Pros: benefits of the proposal

---

[3] For reasons we'll reveal later, we call these tasks "monkeys".
[4] More on this in section 17.4.

- Cons: (potential) negative effects

With regard to decision-making, you may be (legally) required to give prior notice of a certain amount before meetings or decisions at meetings. Even if you're not required, though, your decision-making process (an SOP?) should be intentional. Making important decisions over two or three meetings (e.g., introduction of the decision and fact gathering; discussion; decision) can lead to well-informed decisions with good support. (We'll have more to say about decision-making in section 17.5).

Honor the agenda. In larger groups, assign a person to help the facilitator keep track of time.

Evaluate the meeting. What things went well and should be kept? What things should be done differently next time?

An excellent method of facilitating meetings, especially for large groups using consensus decision making, is Berit Lakey's "Meeting Facilitation: The No-Magic Method"[5]. Whatever method you choose, apply the business perspective chart to see how you will accommodate a vision (goals), systems, culture, guiding principles, outcome, and the experience of those who attend the meeting.

Decisions are not the only outcome of a meeting. Some issues will require we do something about it. Someone needs to make the poster about Fix-It Friday. Someone should replace the spindle with the backup spindle. *A task without a person and a deadline is just a wish.* If you want a task completed, assign a person, a deadline, and sufficient resources and authority to make it happen. If appropriate, check in with them at the next meeting to see how it is going. But unless there's a name and a date, nothing is going to just happen.[6]

10.3 Improving a Process with How To Improve

Briefly put, How To Improve [7] is an SOP for improving an SOP.

In a makerspace, that means we could use How To Improve if we felt some process, documented in an SOP, needed overall improvement. Because it examines the entire process, it's probably not the optimum approach if it's clear there's a problem with a specific step—you can concentrate on that single step. And likewise, it is limited to examining one process, and some problems span multiple processes (whether those processes are documented in SOPs or not). For the latter cases, see the Improvement Kata that follows next.

There are 4 steps to the How To Improve process, each of which is simple. What you'll (hopefully!) find is that the usefulness of How To Improve comes from trying to examine each step as though you've never seen it before by asking at least 6 questions of each step.

---

[5] https://reclaiming.org/consensus-process-facilitation/ Retrieved 9/4/2019

[6] Earlier in his time with Zingerman's, Tom became aware that it was sometimes hard for people to remember what tasks they had agreed to do at meetings. So he went looking for a small physical object that could serve as a reminder. Somehow he ended up picking the monkeys from the Barrel of Monkeys game. For a while, if you were assigned a task at a meeting, you'd get a little plastic monkey labeled with that task. It was in a sense a "monkey on your back". The term has now permeated meetings there, including phrases as "Let's monkey that committee", which sounds pretty weird out of context.

In a weird coincidence, long before Dale met Tom, his neighborhood (a cohousing community) had been using the term "monkey" for tasks since its beginning. It was a few years into knowing Tom that Dale discovered Tom had started the term, and one of Dale's neighbors had brought it with them from Zingerman's. And now we're gifting it to you. You're welcome.

[7] ("Job Methods" from TWI)

The goal is to find unexamined assumptions or changed circumstances that can lead to improvement in the process, but the reality is that this is also repetitive and not necessarily very fun. (If it was easy, we'd probably already have found the improvement.)

Step 1: Break down the job.

1. List all the details of the job exactly as done by the current SOP.
2. Be sure details include all
   (a) Material Handling
   (b) Machine Work
   (c) Hand Work

   Do this at the job, as it is happening, not later at a desk.

Just like How to Instruct, How to Improve requires that in order to improve the process, we need to have defined the process (i.e., have an SOP).

Note that How to Improve says that we need to go and see the actual work. "Genchi genbutsu"—literally "real location, real thing"—is a very important principle in the Toyota Production System. Sitting at a desk and imagining what the situation is will never be as useful as seeing what is actually happening.[8]

Step 2: Question every detail.

---

[8] A fun story from Tom about Mail Order: The line at Mail Order snakes back and forth, a conveyor line moving totes down the line as workers add items, wrap them, insulate them, etc. Towards the end the contents of the totes must be placed into cardboard shipping boxes. Unlike some companies (not mentioning any South American rivers, you understand) that seem to have a thing about shipping mostly empty boxes, Zingerman's Mail Order tries to pack as responsibly as they can.

Some years ago, Tom became aware that there was a weird problem happening. He could tell that the final station, where boxes get their shipping labels, was feast or famine. They'd work like crazy for 20 minutes, then have nothing to do for 20 minutes. The problem seemed to be right upstream, at packing. What was going on? (By the way, some other aspects of the Toyota Production System tells us that we should strive for level production, so this feast or famine thing is indicative of a form of waste that needs to be addressed.)

There was nothing in the SOP for the packing station that seemed like it would lead to this uneven output, so Tom went to actually see. And actually, nothing seemed up at first. The packers were packing constantly, it was just that their output had these bursts of lots of boxes, then few. So he stepped in and worked a station to see for himself.

Now he's doing the actual work, consistent with what Genchi Genbutsu asks, but there was another thing going on that turned out, somewhat coincidently, to be very helpful. Here's one of the owners, one of the people writing the SOPs, and now he's trying to do the actual job. And in that circumstance, like everyone, he of course wants to do a good or even great job since the employees on the line are watching him.

The thing that might not be obvious is that figuring out the best box is a really tricky thing to do sometimes. It takes some skill when there's a real mix of items, though it can be really easy when there are just a few items.

So when a tote comes down the line with a fairly simple match to a box, what would anyone of us do, especially if the alternative was a box with all kinds of complications? Tom took that easy tote and boxed it. Success. Now another tote or two comes down the line—what tote did he work on next? The easy one.

See where this is heading? It was natural for everyone to do exactly that—pick the easy totes over the harder ones. And the easy ones go quick, so there's a long line of boxes coming out of the packing station. But eventually all you have left are those tricky boxes that take longer. Now the flow slows to a trickle as everyone works through those. Aha!

The solution was to add a system—a couple of markers that say to take the tote between the markers. Now there's no choice about what tote to process, and the production is smoothed out. There's an evenness to the flow. But seeing the problem required looking at the work as it was happening. Sitting at a desk, even knowing at what station the problem was occurring, was not sufficient to understand the issue.

1. Use the following types of questions:
    (a) *Why* is it necessary?
    (b) *What* is its purpose?
    (c) *Where* should it be done?
    (d) *When* should it be done?
    (e) *Who* is best qualified to do it?
    (f) *How* is the "best way" to do it?
2. Also question the materials, machines, equipment, tools, product design, layout, workplace, safety, and housekeeping.

This is the core of the improvement process, but is not necessarily fun. Start with a notebook, devoting one page for each step. Then on each page, list the six questions above—Why, what, where, when who, how. For each step, see if in answering the questions, you can find an opportunity. Is the step necessary? Should it be done now, or at a different time? Is the way we're doing it the best way—and what are the criteria we're using?

The repetitive questions may feel silly or inefficient, but the systematic questioning of what might seem obvious can lead to some big wins. For example, Tom was asked to improve a lengthy invoicing process at a local business that hosts events. These events are relatively large affairs whose planning can span months—think weddings and such. One step in the invoicing that took a quite long time involved figuring out the laundry order for the event. It involved going back through laundry invoices and calculating what amount was attributable to that particular event versus another. But when Tom started asking questions like who should do the calculation and when it should be done, it turned out that there was a point much earlier in the whole event cycle where this information was readily available and just needed to be written down for later use: when the event details were first approved. The accounting person was actually not the best person to figure this out ("who is best qualified to do it?"), and it should have been done months earlier ("When should it be done?"). The best way was for a completely different person to write down the figure at a much earlier point in the process, not work backwards from other documents.

By the way, when we ask "why is it necessary", we're asking specifically "is this a value-add step?" (See chapter 12.) If it is not value-add, then we need to establish whether it is necessary or not. Not value-add and not necessary? It's a candidate for removal in the next step.

We shouldn't give short shrift to things like materials, tools, layout, the workplace, and so on. 5S-ing could dramatically improve a workplace. For example, the use of a browser-based online form that automatically calculates figures could reduce mistakes and make a task more efficient. Even housekeeping could play a role—cleaning the lighting in an area that generates dust may be a much-appreciated improvement.

Step 3: Develop a new way.

1. Eliminate unnecessary steps of the SOP.
2. Combine steps when practical.
3. Rearrange for better sequence.

4. Simplify all necessary steps:
    (a) Make the work easier and safer.
    (b) Pre-position materials, tools, and equipment at the best places in the proper work area.
    (c) Let both hands do useful work.
    (d) Use jigs and fixtures instead of hands for holding work.
5. Work out your idea with others.
6. Write up your proposed method.

Your answers in the notebook to the why, what, where, when who, and how questions now inform the steps above. Why is some SOP step necessary? If it is not value-add or necessary, then eliminate the work. When and where can help identify places to improve by combining or rearranging steps.

Item 4 above resonates a lot with the idea of making it easy to do the right thing. And the idea of "Poka-Yoke" or mistake-proofing from Lean, which is just another way of looking at "make it hard to do the wrong thing", would certainly not be out of place in this list.

Step 3 asks us to work out our ideas with others. Who? Almost always the answer starts with the people doing the actual work. No one else knows what it is really like to do that process, not even the person who may have written the SOP. And finally we must document the new proposed method.

Step 4: Apply the new way.

1. Sell your proposal to leadership.
2. Sell the new method to the operators.
3. Get final approval of all concerned on Safety, Quality, Quantity, and Cost.
4. Put the new method to work. Use it until a better way is developed.
5. Give credit where credit is due.

A sole proprietor of a makerspace may not need to "sell" the improvement to someone higher up, but note that even in the 1940's we're told we have to sell the new method to the operators—in our context, this is often the member (who is actually using the SOP, actually doing the work). And note that it is "sell"—not tell.

10.4 A Scientific Approach to Improvement: The Improvement Kata

How to Improve gives us a straightforward, if at times tedious, method for improving a single process (e.g., an SOP). But we often have issues that span multiple processes/SOPs

10.4. A SCIENTIFIC APPROACH TO IMPROVEMENT: THE IMPROVEMENT KATA

or are not reflected in an SOP. The Improvement Kata is a general purpose tool you can use in these cases, and has as its core the systematic application of the scientific method.[9]

The recipe is best conveyed in the Figure 10.2.

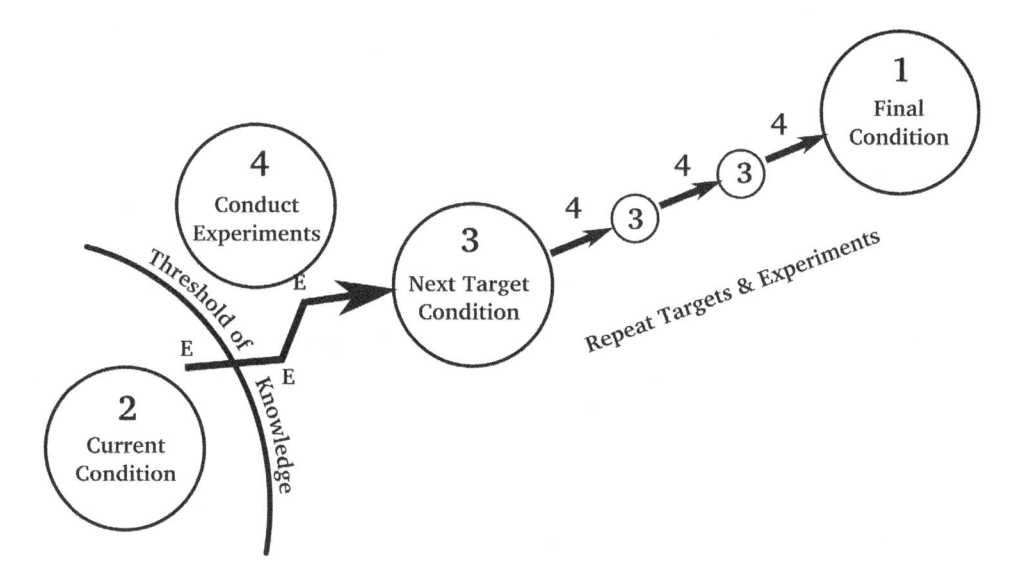

Figure 10.2: The Improvement Kata.

There are several important points here:

- It is critical to agree upon the final condition/direction/goal. This is step 1.

- You must be able to quantify the current condition (step 2) so you know if you've improved.

- You may not be able to reach the final condition right away. For all but trivial situations, you may need to set intermediate target conditions.

- Our knowledge about the situation has limits—otherwise we'd immediately know what the solution is. We expand this "threshold of knowledge" by conducting experiments. Often multiple experiments will be necessary to reach the next target condition.

---

[9]The Improvement Kata is a different kind of platypus from the other tools we've discussed. First, it's been reverse-engineered from the culture at Toyota, rather than being some element of the Toyota Production System that is documented and explicitly taught within Toyota like SOPs and 5S. Ask about the "Improvement Kata" and you'll get blank stares. But describe the elements and the response will be more along the lines of well, of course fish live in water.

Second, Mike Rother, the researcher who created the Improvement Kata, believes strongly that it is the combination of the recipe (scientific thinking) with the repetitive practice (with the assistance of an Improvement Kata coach) that is important. Patterns, repeated over and over like the beginning Karate student's forms ("kata"), become habits after a while. This way of thinking becomes a part of the organization's culture.

Can you apply the recipe without a coach? In the same sense of having a second person to help write an SOP, the coach can provide a dispassionate perspective, asking the "stupid" or repetitive questions that are too easy to ignore when it's just ourselves working a problem. But if you're the only one you've got, you can write an SOP and you can apply the scientific method.

See Mike Rother's book "Toyota Kata" (2009) for the whole story.

- Once we've reached a target condition, we can repeat the process, picking a new intermediate target condition and conducting experiments to reach the condition.

The path to the goal isn't necessarily straight or predictable. As you progress, you may learn a lot more about the problem, including that some things don't actually have to be solved in order to reach your goal. This reality is built into the Improvement Kata—we assume the path will wind a bit.

Conducting experiments is the way we expand our knowledge. If we already knew how to process new memberships in 2 minutes or less of member time, we could just do that. But in the more likely case that we don't know how to do that, experiments will give us more information with each iteration.

Rother's free "Kata in the Classroom"[10] curriculum illustrates an application of the Improvement Kata using a catapult, and can be a nice way of introducing the Kata to staff or other groups. (It was designed for kids, but grownups enjoy it as much if not more.) In the exercise, a challenge is set to launch a ball from a catapult so it ends up in a cup located a certain distance away, and the students are guided through the steps as they iterate towards the goal. Applying the diagram above, the steps might look like:

1. The challenge is to launch a ball so it ends up in a cup exactly 10 feet away. (Step 1—identify the final condition or goal.)

2. The students pick a certain starting state (i.e., a particular ball—say, the ping pong ball, and a pull-back angle of 60 degrees and a release angle of 45 degrees for the catapult). To establish the starting condition—the output of the process given the starting state—they make multiple launches[11] using the same settings, and record the result. It's not uncommon for the initial condition for the exercise to be pretty short—say an average of 4 feet. (Step 2—understand the current condition.)

3. Given the result above, the next target condition is picked (somewhere between where you are currently and the goal). The students might pick 8 feet. (Step 3—set next target condition.)

4. Now experiments are run, changing one parameter at a time, to try to improve and reach the next target condition. Their first experiment may be to vary the pull-back angle to 80 degrees. This might give them 6 feet. The second round of experiments may increase the pull-back to 90 degrees, giving them 7 feet. And so on. (Step 4—experiment to reach the intermediate target.)

5. Once the next target condition is achieved (i.e., 8 feet), a new target condition is picked, and the process of experimentation repeated until the goal is finally reached. (Repeat steps 3 & 4.)

In our makerspaces, this iterative process can be used to improve any operation where we can define what success looks like (the challenge), we can define a measure or set of measures, and where we can vary some element of the process. It is therefore quite general.

A key requirement for the successful application of the Improvement Kata is the willingness to believe in reality. By which we mean that we must be able to set aside our beliefs and intuition and see what the facts say. Our intuition is crucial—it provides us valuable

---

[10] Free material available at www.katatogrow.com.
[11] In the real world, you may need to take a lot of samples to get a good estimate of the average and variation.

10.5 K-Base (Knowledge-Base)

shortcuts virtually every waking moment, and living without a high degree of trust in our intuition would be impossible. But intuition is based on knowledge, and often has nothing useful to offer about situations that are beyond our threshold of knowledge. Intentional experimentation has proven a powerful tool to expand our threshold of knowledge.

10.5 K-Base (Knowledge-Base)

Makerspaces are information hydrants. Every moment people are producing new knowledge, often on purpose, and sometimes serendipitously. A fair amount of this information will be useful to you as the makerspace operator, and even quite often necessary—to the extent that if you don't somehow record the information, you'll have to re-discover it later on. For example, what size blade a bandsaw takes, what switch port an Ethernet jack is on, where to buy laser lenses, or what size filter the rooftop air-conditioning units take.

Some information can be preserved nicely and locally—for example, it is general practice in most shops to write down the bandsaw blade length on the inside of the cover to the blade, right where you are when you discover you need a new one. But there's going to be a ton of information that won't have such an obvious home.

File folders are necessary for preserving and organizing physical documentation, so set up a file cabinet or two. But for information you can capture electronically, an online Knowledge Base (or K-Base for short) is extremely handy.

We use Google Sites to set up what amounts to a simple wiki. Whatever software you use, think about the following attributes:

- web accessible
- easily created/updated[12]
- changes are tracked
- allows different access permissions on different pages
- can store other files (PDF, zip, photos, etc.)
- searchable
- can accommodate both organized (hierarchical) and non-ordered content

Examples of what we store on our k-base:

- Tool information, including current status, when and where we bought it, where to buy supplies, part numbers for replacements, service history, problems and cures, usage information, etc.
- Daily and weekly meeting notes (and templates for them)
- Vendors and account information
- Building infrastructure info (HVAC, phone, internet, alarm, lock key-codes, power)

---

[12]Note that only one person can edit a page at a time in a Google site.

- "New for Crew"—updates for the front desk staff

We expect that when one of our staff comes across updates to the above information, they'll make the changes in the k-base. There's an argument to be made that members should have direct access, and even perhaps write privileges to make changes. We currently do not do that.

10.6 Creating and Organizing SOP and Other Documents

We find Google Drive/Docs to be very helpful with SOPs and other documents when the visual form of the printed document is important. Google Docs is not terribly sophisticated as a word processor, but allows easy collaboration among multiple staff. It is even possible to embed a Google Doc in a Google Site (the wiki-like software described above).

Similar to the K-Base, we're looking for the following characteristics for the creation and organization of SOPs:

- can create decent[13] printed documents
- web accessible
- easily created/updated[14]
- changes are tracked
- allows different access permissions on different pages
- can store other files (PDF, zip, photos, etc.)
- searchable
- can accommodate both organized (hierarchical) and non-ordered content

We also use Google Sheets for spreadsheets such as event pricing, to-buy lists, bookkeeping spreadsheets, and the like, and Google Forms (which then populate a Google Sheets spreadsheet) for registration for events, surveys, and other form-driven input.

10.7 Membership

You will need a system to track your members. Often this will be a database or member management software of some sort, though you can do it on paper. The things you'll want to track are pretty obvious:

- Member name, birthdate, contact information (especially cell # and email), emergency contact, and any special status (e.g., student, veteran, etc.)
- Membership activity (at a minimum if they are currently in active membership—your front desk staff will need to be able to query this quickly and easily)

---

[13] This is a good example of an 80% solution—it's not perfect, but it's good enough.
[14] Multiple people can edit a Google Doc at the same time.

10.7. MEMBERSHIP

- Classes taken or other permission to use tools or engage in other activities (we separate taking a class from having permission to use the tool)[15]

We also keep track of agreements they've signed (liability waiver, all-hours membership, renting a space, etc.), if they're staff or some other special status, any interactions we've had (e.g., perhaps safety issues), shop credits, and connections to other members (e.g., children). Obviously your activities will drive the type of data you want to keep track of.

Keeping historical information will allow you to analyze activity in your makerspace. But whatever information you have, you should have clear policies around access and disclosure. (E.g., we don't give out contact information about other members or staff, but will forward email for example.)

Tom and Dale both have a long background in using relational databases, but strangely enough we used a paper to prototype our membership system until we understood what information we really wanted and how we wanted to use it. Then Tom created the database and user interface. We can't say it's an extraordinary system—it is the 80% solution, nothing more. But you definitely need some kind of solution unless you are embedded within a larger organization that can provide these functions. Before rolling your own (unfortunately, often our first response as makers[16]), you might check out existing makerspace (or more general purpose) membership management software.[17]

10.7.1 Machine and Access Control

Before we opened our doors, we crafted a very nice RFID access and tool control system[18], the worry being that people would be using machines they weren't checked out to use, or folks would be wandering in and creating a problem. We've found that in our community and with the culture we've created (see Chapter 11), it just isn't a problem. We don't find people using machines they shouldn't, and it's much nicer to have our front desk staff wave at folks when they come in the front door, rather than have them scan in. (Yes, sometimes a member might have their membership expire without us noticing, but it's pretty rare and not worth us worrying about.) Blame our fixation on an RFID system on our failure to realize that our membership is relational, not transactional.

However, every makerspace will be different, and you may choose to enforce safety and usage limits through systems like access control. As a side effect, you may be able to collect useful usage information. But please don't jump immediately to a system to solve a problem, especially if the system is not in complete alignment with your guiding principles or desired culture.

---

[15]Why? They may have paid for and taken the class, but we don't feel that they're safe to use the tool yet. Having them seperate is also a pain, though, because once in a while we miss updating permissions. Just one more system we can improve upon.

[16]All makers seem to suffer from this. Dale recalls the half-serious warning in a blacksmithing book that once you learn how to make tools like pliers, tongs, etc., you have to watch out that your first response when you can't find a tool in your shop is to just make another.

[17]See for example https://wiki.hackerspaces.org/Hackerspace_Software

[18]Elements are actually in use, collecting temperature and machine usage, but not tied to a particular member. Handy information to have when assessing whether tools are being utilized well.

10.8 Classes, Tools, and Other Resources

Most every tool in the shop has the unfortunate characteristic that only one person can use it at a time. Likewise, classes will often have a finite capacity (especially since we require hands-on work by all the students if we're following How to Instruct). There are also other resources such as conference rooms, courtyards, or perhaps even Zoom accounts where multiple people may want to use the same thing at the same time.

In some cases cultural norms can address potential conflict, and in fact for tools that typically are used briefly such as the table saw or drill press, we don't bother with reservations. We instead may need to, very occasionally, assist members in sharing, but for the most part members can practice generosity and understanding. In other cases, though, members may be spending a long time getting to the makerspace and want to know that they can use the tool they want, or have a space in a particular class, so we find that some kind of system for reservations is necessary just from the desire to give great customer service.[19]

But there's another strong reason to provide reservations for tools especially, and that is safety. Accidents are much more likely to occur when people are anxious or rushing, and that's exactly what would happen if our kind and generous members were working on a tool and someone came by to check "how long are you going to be using that?" With a reservation, everyone knows when they can use the machine, and can take their time to properly secure workpieces, take gentle cuts, and just in general be more thoughtful and careful. So we'd argue even if your makerspace's dominant system is one of negotiation, safety is a strong argument for having tool reservations.

We've used a couple of "software as a service" (SAAS) products for scheduling. There's always a tradeoff between ease of use and ability to do more complicated things. For what it's worth, we currently use Acuity for scheduling classes and reserving tools and rooms, but some things are harder to do than we'd like. As we'll mention later, a useful feature of scheduling software is the ability to charge for a class. Makes it much more likely the member will show up.

---

[19] A few details on our policies: Members can make reservations for up to 2 hours a day per machine. (The two lasers count as one machine—yes, we had to plug that loophole!) But if no one is waiting to use the machine after you, you can keep using it. We just need to make access fair to everyone. You can find our complete member handbook at our website, www.maker-works.com

Chapter 11

Culture

Recall our somewhat eventful airline ride a few sections back. We said that culture was "the way things really are." Culture isn't like vision, systems, guiding principles, or any of the other elements we've mentioned in that, regardless of what you do, you will have a culture[1]. It just may not be the one you want. Let's be more specific. Here's what culture really is:

- How do people (i.e., staff and members) act when the "boss" isn't around?
- How do leaders treat others in the organization in casual situations?
- Are people laughing at work?
- How do people respond in truly unique situations?
- How do people respond to failures? (Their own and others.)
- What do people say about the organization with friends and family?
- What pronouns are used when discussing the organization—"us" or "them"?
- Do staff follow the same rules as members? (E.g., safety equipment, how they use tools, etc.)
- How do members talk about the makerspace? "My" makerspace?

The good news about culture is that we strongly believe you can create and influence it. This is going to surprise you, but we even have an SOP for doing that. Here it is:

1. Define it.
2. Teach/share it.
3. Measure it.
4. Live it.

---

[1] Actually, the problem isn't that you won't have any vision, any systems, or any guiding principles—it's that if you aren't intentional, you'll have twenty different ones. Your job as a leader is to make sure there's exactly one of each, and they're shared.

5. Reward it.

In a little more detail:

Define it. Is it okay to make fun of a newbie? How important is following the Principles of Safety? How should we act towards each other?

In the early months of Maker Works, we had a few times when our members weren't behaving like we expected. Didn't they automatically know what the culture we expected was?[2] Well, you can argue that the staff was modeling the culture we wanted, but we had not defined to our members what we expected. So perhaps we shouldn't have been surprised when not everyone knew what we wanted. We fixed that by writing up a poster we called "The Code".

> Everyone is Welcome Here: We don't discriminate. We celebrate a diverse community of makers from all kinds of backgrounds, experience levels, and ages
>
> We are Positive and Supportive: We make this a great place to work, learn and create
>
> We Care for Tools and Space: We do our best to do no harm to tools. We return the workspace to a clean and usable state for the next member
>
> We Care for Each Other: By being safe and by being kind

Which leads us to:

Teach/Share it. We have this posted in the main hallway where folks will see it. We don't tend to teach this as aggressively as the Principles of Safety, but you could make a good case that we could and should. It is listed in our member and staff handbooks. However you have your definitions, you do need to make sure everyone who needs to know it sees it.

Measure it. Measuring an aspect of culture lets us evaluate our progress and identify where we need to put more effort. For example, tally up how often members are seen wearing safety glasses (or not!) in the woodshop. Use a survey. Etc.[3]

Live it. Nothing is as corrosive as saying one thing and doing another. If safety glasses should be worn in the woodshop, then everyone better wear them. If someone acts racist towards another person, address it. Model the behavior you want.

Reward it. Can you create a reward of some kind, a recognition that the aspect of culture you've been measuring has met some goal?

11.1 Who Do You Serve? Who is Helping You Do That?

Who does your makerspace serve? If you want to serve a wider, diverse audience, your makerspace may have some challenges to face.

---

[2] Slowly reaches for the box of shock collars...
[3] The dark side to measuring is that sometimes the measured effect is *all* we get—other unmeasured aspects get short changed.

11.1. WHO DO YOU SERVE? WHO IS HELPING YOU DO THAT?

Not all the members of our communities may see themselves as welcome in a makerspace. The activities may feel like they don't belong to their gender, their race, their age, their economic or social position, and so on. They may not be able to imagine themselves in a makerspace having a positive experience. Just passively opening our doors is not enough to overcome the messages people have received about what they should and shouldn't do, can and can't do, or where they're welcome or not.

Social psychologists have a concept called Stereotype Threat. At its core is the idea that the performance of members of a social group (gender, race, etc.) can be influenced by stereotypes about that group. For example (and this was an actual experiment) when researchers told a group of women that a math test they're about to take was usually more difficult for women than men, the results were lower scores for the women. But if a second group, identical to the first, took the same exact test but with the message that this math test has been specially prepared so there's no gender differences, the difference actually goes away.

Now, people and cultures are complicated, but it does seem reasonable to take the implications of ideas like stereotype threat seriously. Using the recipe for changing culture, we can decide what message people get in our makerspace. And that message can be that everyone in our community can weld, can machine steel, can embroider, can laser engrave, can create jewelry. When they walk in the door or take a class, the staff and instructors they meet can, as much as we're able, reflect the diversity of the community we're in. We can give each of our members (and potential members) great and supportive customer service, since we never know if they might have had to overcome a concern that they might not be welcome in a makerspace. We can continuously improve our systems if they're failing to help a group to succeed.

We have to insert a brief "aha" moment here. Dale had a good friend of many years and his family come to the shop. The whole family are real geeks, and almost without thinking Dale was about to tell the staff something along the lines of that these were very important guests, please treat them very well, and so on. You get the idea. But Dale's office is right across from the front desk, and day in and day out he hears exactly how the front desk staff treats people, from our longest-time members to people who are just dropping in without knowing the first thing about a makerspace. Dale ended up saying nothing. The way the staff treats each person through the door is the way we'd want even our dearest friends to be treated. (Stay tuned for How to Give Great Service, coming up.) Likewise, we're not saying that we need to give extra great service just because someone seems to fit some category—our level of service is going to make everyone feel welcome.

Is it hard to find staff that reflects the diversity of the community we serve? Here's some good news—we (and you!) can hire people for their ability to deliver great customer service, and we can use our systems (like our SOPs) and our classes to allow them to deliver on the technical side. We don't expect our members to join with all the knowledge they need to work in the shop—why expect that of our staff? Just because people might not have previously had access to experiences and tools doesn't mean they can't be valuable staff members—and in fact, because they have recently learned material, they may be even better at serving our members because they remember what it was like to not know. There's no one on staff that came here knowing everything, so it's not even that the choice is between hiring people who require not training vs. those that require some. It's our feeling that the ability and desire to give great customer service is harder to pick up, and that our SOPs and other systems will help develop the other sides.

We can see the need to serve everyone as part of our mission, and any lack of diversity as a problem to solve. But we can also approach this from the view that "diversity is the solution, not a problem to solve."[4] Diversity in our staff and membership is not just the right thing to do for our mission, but it is good business. Studies of businesses show diversity will lead to better outcomes for our members, increases innovation, and allows us to attract and retain better staff. Your organization benefits from diversity, regardless of whether that is an explicit part of your mission. As such, it is well worth explicitly incorporating into your guiding principles, ensuring it is supported by your systems, and baked into your culture using the recipe for changing (and maintaining) culture just presented. It is another example of a win-win situation, where our interests can not only be in alignment with a wider good, but we derive benefit for our organization and in turn can deliver more value.

11.2 Mind the Gap!

So let's say you have crafted wonderful systems, cultivated a powerful set of guiding principles, and defined and created a culture worthy of your makerspace.

These three items do not stand alone. They don't represent 3 parallels paths from mission to bottom line—they are the three legs of a stool that all must be in place. They must be compatible and overlapping.

Here's a tiny Venn diagram of the ideal overlap: O

(That's 3 circles on top of each other, if it wasn't obvious.)

In practice, there may be gaps between systems, culture, and guiding principles. But like gaps between roof tiles, the end result is decay. The roof tiles may look very nice from the outside ("oh look, what a nice set of guiding principles"), but the rain flows freely below to rot the walls and floors over time.

A common example of the gap between a system and culture is embodied in a rectangular sign with numbers on it. You've seen them along the highway—"Speed limit 70 MPH" or something similar. Around here, the culture is to drive at least 2-3 MPH over, on average. And you can indeed drive 73 MPH past a police officer, because while the system says the maximum is 70 MPH, ticketing actually (usually—we can't guarantee) starts higher.

Does this minor transgression really pose a threat to any other areas of our civil life? You may have had the interesting experience of explaining this system-culture gap to a child—especially if it is your own. Let's just say no one needs to give a 5-year old another arguing point about the need to follow rules.

Perhaps we can ask at what point we should be concerned, where tolerating a cultural norm of not following a system is a real problem.

Is it okay for staff not to wear safety glasses when "just passing through" the woodshop?

Is it fine for a member to work up until closing time, then begin cleaning up?

What about a member who brings their young child into the woodshop, not for a very brief visit (which we generally allow, under continuous close supervision), but to "hang out" while the parents work on a project?

If your guiding principle is to deliver great customer service, and a knowledgeable and otherwise valued staff person is continually grumpy, is that okay?

---

[4]"Diversity is the solution, not a problem to solve" The Diversity Project, https://diversityproject.com/resource/diversity-solution-not-problem-solve

11.2. MIND THE GAP!

Gaps between systems, culture, and guiding principles are fundamentally unsustainable in the long term. A tiny leak isn't going to spell immediate doom, but if you have members sawing rough lumber in flip-flops and dollar-store sunglasses, that's a gap too wide.

Gaps can corrode the trust our members have for us. For example, if our guiding principles say we want to maximize value for our members, but our systems nickel and dime the member at every turn, that's hardly a sustainable position.

Here's a story from Tom about the gap he found between a system he wanted and the culture that was already in place.

> I started my career at Zingerman's as the chief information officer, and being a good systems guy, I thought about problems from a systems point of view. That worked out okay from the point of view of the business perspective chart in that systems are clearly there. So I figured I was in good stead.
>
> So as a good systems thinker, it became apparent to me that the organization needed email, and that the first thing we needed to do was to set up the server and other equipment, and create accounts for everybody. In my mind, the vision was very clear: everybody should have an email address. The results are going to be very measurable. We are going to be able to say we had succeeded when everybody in the organization had an email address and was using it.
>
> Clearly all I needed to do was set up the systems in order to do that. And in my mind, there was going to be like some ticker-tape parade or something. They were gonna hoist me up on their shoulders and there was going to be much jubilation.
>
> I learned a valuable lesson about the business perspective chart when I rolled out that there was now an email address for everybody and that there was an expectation that people would use them. And there was a parade, but it involved something more like pitchforks and torches.
>
> What I had failed to account for was that as an organization we placed a very high value on interpersonal communication, that the culture of the organization was that they didn't want anything to interfere with that sort of one-on-one, face-to-face sort of personal interaction.
>
> I'll give an example of the sort of the value placed on that at Zingerman's Deli. It was very important that the order takers not stand behind the counter, but rather come out from behind the counter, stand shoulder to shoulder with the guest, and look at the menu together.
>
> So what I had inadvertently done was I had signaled the intent to take away interpersonal communication by emphasizing email communication and by failing to account for that cultural norm. I interrupted my ability to achieve the desired result of everybody using email as a communication form. So once we went back and retooled and did a new rollout where we tried to address the cultural norms, we were far more successful getting people to adopt the email.
>
> The way we did that, by the way, had to do with that it was very common in those days to write an email usage policy that said don't use email for anything that isn't business related. We came out and made the exact opposite statement. We wanted people to use it, to talk to their grandparents and their friends and to email however they saw fit, whether personal or professional. The thinking was simply that this policy was far more culturally normal for us. It was

an expression of trust in the staff member. That was the cultural norm. And there was the backhanded idea that if they were already checking email because they were looking for emails from friends, that maybe when we emailed them periodically, they might actually read it.

So there was my personal example of how I ran afoul of, and then finally figured out how to utilize the business perspective chart to make my way from from vision to results.

Mind the Gap!

Chapter 12

Value-Add

We'd like to define a useful concept from Lean called "value-add". In Lean, value-add is defined as an activity that

- transforms the product or service
- the member (customer) is willing to pay for
- is done right the first time

It's very helpful to us in a makerspace or any other organization because it helps us see which of the following three categories an activity falls into:

- Value-add: let's offer and do more of that! (as long as there's demand)
- Necessary but not value-add: let's minimize the resources (time, etc.) that these consume
- Not necessary, not value-add: let's eliminate this!

For example, at Maker Works we offer members the option of booking one-on-one consulting time with a staff member. This "project partner" time is theirs alone, and members often use it to tackle more complicated projects or come up to speed more quickly on more advanced software. This is value-add activity—members are (obviously) willing to pay for it, and so long as we've priced it in a sustainable way[1], we'd like to encourage this activity.

We'd say teaching classes is value-add. Likewise answering member questions—except when it's not. If we're answering questions because our SOPs did a bad job, we didn't instruct well, or something is broken on the machine, we don't get to pat ourselves on the back for answering questions—*we didn't get it right the first time*. Our recipe says if it's necessary but not value-add, then minimize it. Fix the SOP, instruct well, fix problems with machines.

What about machine maintenance? We already convey to members that we have tools for their use—they probably, and reasonably, assume that the machines will be usable. Do

---

[1] Let us assure you that even in a makerspace, if you price something below your cost, what you lose on each individual sale you won't make up in volume.

members come up to us all excited because we did the weekly greasing of the bearings? (Short answer—no. Longer answer—still no.) Would we get a good reaction by charging a regular membership for $100, but for $150 we'll make sure the machines work? And yet, is the work of maintenance necessary? Definitely. So it's clear that we do need to do the work, but we should minimize the time we spend. Let's get a better grease gun, so greasing takes 1/10th the time. Let's set up a maintenance cart with all the supplies right at hand (5S-ing) so we waste as little time as possible tracking them down.

And if we identify an activity that isn't necessary—eliminate it. For example, early on we built a half-wall with a gate and RFID reader so members could swipe in to get access to the shop. It was never really necessary, and we've never used it—our front desk staff wave at the member as they come in, and folks have been great about keeping their memberships up to date. The access control wasn't value-added (no-one would want to pay extra to have to swipe in), wasn't necessary, so we got rid of it.

So far we've discussed value from the viewpoint of our member (our customer). We can also talk about "value-add" for our staff—the idea being that we can then classify activities from the staff's point of view into "value-add", "necessary but not value-add", and "neither".

What we cannot do is think that because we're paying our staff for their work, that that is enough. It may not be. If any of our staff uses the phrase "soul-crushing"[2] to describe their work day, that is not sustainable.

For the customer, we said a major criterion for value-add was that they would willingly pay money for it. We didn't go into more detail about what it was that made them willing, and that's fine—it could be a long list, and in the end, the proof is the exchange of money. For our staff, it's a bit trickier because the corresponding measure—is our staff member willing to remain employed by us—may be clouded by the fact that we may be talking about dozens of different activities (some are valued, others may not be), over a long period of time (vs. a single retail transaction, for example), and the disincentive we all have around quitting one job and having to find another. So a criterion like "wants to keep working here" is not going to help much, at least at the individual level.

Instead we can look at what, besides money, motivates people. There are long lists (and not all the possibilities are noble) but some do stand out so much that our confidence level can be pretty high that if the activities we're asking our staff to perform have these elements, our staff will find them value-add:

- Learning ("Did I learn something?") / Mastery of a skill
- Completing a task
- Reaching a goal as a team
- Helping others
- Making a lasting impact

Armed with some characteristics, we can evaluate activities as likely value-add for our staff. Things like teaching are definitely value-add (recall the 4 levels of learning), ideally even when the class is being taught for the Nth time. 5S-ing or making a jig—probably Yes's. We could even argue that some things that are not value-add from the customer's point of view may be value-add from for our staff—there was a mastery of a skill, completing a task,

---

[2] Just this morning we read this in someone's description of their work in retail sales.

reaching a goal as a team, learning something, etc. But unless our staff is willing to pay us for allowing them to do that activity, if the customer doesn't see it as value-add, we need to examine it and perhaps reduce it (maybe via a system) or eliminate it.

We can't guarantee to our staff that they will spend all their time in value-add activity. We can, however, make it clear in our guiding principles, that our goal is to maximize the value-add time of our staff—specifically including things that aid their development as staff and as people. We then need to back that up with systems and an active culture that supports that goal, allowing staff to identify and work on issues that they feel are important to maximizing their value-add time.

What happens when we have an activity that is clearly value-add for the member but not for the staff? We might question whether that service is one we want to provide. We can ask if there's a system or change to our culture that would minimize the non-value add time of our staff. We can ask our staff to look for solutions. We may also see if we can frame the activity so that while it may not entirely fit the value-add definition for our staff, they can still feel that their time produced something of value. We'll have an example in the next section when we talk about constructing cathedrals.

Chapter 13

Giving Great Service

So what does Great Service[1] look like? In our bootcamp, we'll ask for examples of when people remember receiving great service. Some common themes:

- Their problem got solved quickly.
- They felt heard and understood.
- The service provider went beyond what was expected.
- There was a genuine apology.
- There was a genuine smile, eye contact.

If you like, and it's a bit more fun but also sad, you can also ask for examples of poor service. Funny how long we can hold onto those stories—which should be a warning for us. Bad service sticks around in people's minds for a long time. In either case, we can ask "how did that interaction make you feel?" Or, "how likely would you be to recommend that place to a friend?", or "How likely are you to return to that place?"

13.1 Why Give Great Service?

Let's start with perhaps the best reason to give great service:

It's the right thing to do. The other reasons below are good ones, but even if we took them all away, isn't giving great service what we'd like to do? What kind of service do you want your children to see you giving? What kind of service do we want to model for the community?

Here are some others:

Great service makes you something special. It's a differentiator, since (as we'll shortly discuss), it can be hard to find.

---

[1] For more on Zingerman's recipe for giving great service, see the book "Zingerman's Guide to Giving Great Service" by Ari Weinzweig, and the 2-day class "The Art of Giving Great Service" by ZingTrain.

Great service is sound marketing. If you receive great service, whose name is at the top of your mind when someone asks you for a recommendation?

Great service keeps customers coming back. Who is the most valuable member? The one who keeps coming back, renewing their membership month after month. You've already spent the effort to on-board them, and now they're making very valuable contributions to your community and financial bottom lines.

It yields better bottom-line results. Economic, social, educational—giving great service to members makes sense even when viewed from just our bottom lines.

It makes a better place to work. Just today we saw an article on how a single negative customer interaction with call center operators can affect those operators the rest of the day. We're not going to avoid or eliminate all possible negative customer interactions, but the 3-step recipe we'll get to in just a moment is going to make everyone's lives that much easier.

It attracts better people to work with you. Come by and meet our staff some time—or the staff at any of the Zingerman's businesses around town, where the Giving Great Service recipe was developed. These are some wonderful people. They're who you want working for you—but before you ask, no, you may not hire any of our staff away. (We tag them, just in case. They won't get far.)

It's easier. Yes, in a moment we're also going to say it's harder. But it is easier in the following way: we do not need to split ourselves into two: the caring person we are to friends, and the hard-nosed business person at work. We are nice, caring people. We want to help others. Of course we'll look up our competitor's phone number and address because you might live closer to them. We don't have to spend energy maintaining two different sets of values.

In the section on Value-Add, we asked what we can do about activities that are value-add, or perhaps necessary, from the customer point of view, but may not be value-add from the staff point of view. There is a story (one source attributes it to Iphigene Sulzberger)[2] about a medieval traveler who visits a construction site where three stonecutters are working. When the first stonecutter is asked what they're doing, they respond "I am cutting stone." The second is asked, and responds "I am making a cornerstone." The third says "I am building a cathedral." Which stonecutter is enjoying their work the most?

At Tom's "day job" at Zingerman's Mail Order, they're asking staff to pack and ship boxes of baked goods and other tasty foods, usually as gifts. Is picking product and packing a box "value-add" to the staff? Not very much on the surface. Maybe mastery (of box packing?), and completing a task, but it's not very compelling. And if people need a job hard enough, just monetary compensation may be enough to keep them for a short time, but it is not sustainable. So it turns out to be important to share with everyone in the company what the people on the phones hear each day. In many cases these are gifts for significant people in the customers' lives, celebrating events or conveying condolences, but always expressing affection. Yes, you're packing cheese and bread and olives in a cardboard box, but it's a real person opening the box and smiling, receiving a message from another person just as any of us would feel in receiving a gift. Not every job is working on a majestic cathedral, but we're lucky at makerspaces in that much of what we do is allowing our members to realize some

---

[2] https://theprepared.org/features/2019/4/28/building-a-cathedral retrieved 5/5/2019

amazing projects. Yes, often we're going to be just whacking at stone[3], but we can share as well as we can the impact that the space and the staff has on the many lives we'll touch. When we're sweeping sawdust, we can also see that we're also contributing to a beautiful wooden dinner table for someone's family.

13.2 Why is Great Service Hard to Find?

So if this giving great service is so great, then why can it be hard to find?

It's unfamiliar. For many reasons, organizations often don't value giving great service. Perhaps they hold a monopoly (e.g., governmental units, utilities, or dominant companies in a field). Or the primary interface with customers is technology-mediated (online, phone, mail), so face to face service is a small part of their interactions. Or their staff have used so much energy serving their managers that there's little left over for serving the customer. (See the section on Servant Leadership.) But the bottom line is that many people do not experience great service as the norm.

It's not respected. This is a good one. For a lot of people in our American culture, the ultimate goal is to reach a level where *you* are served. Butlers, servants, maids, chauffeurs—the more people serving you, the better, according to this.

It requires more work in the moment. True—saying "no" is going to make for a shorter conversion. But in the long term, delivering great service is less work. Great service solves problems, and you can not solve other people's problems without some benefit coming back to you, however indirectly.

It's hard not to be "macho". We do have a thing in this culture for equating serving someone with weakness. The characters John Wayne typically played don't serve people—they were tough guys who people served.

It's not fair. As Tom likes to say, "Fair is a different planet, and we don't live there." True enough. The customer is often not going to meet us halfway (or what feels like a fair, halfway to us). That's okay. It doesn't have to be fair each and every time.

There's a lot of talk and not enough walk. Lots of places claim they give great service, as though if they say it enough times, we'll believe that we're getting great service.

Systems often don't reinforce great service. We can ask our staff to give all the service in the world, but if it takes a manager to approve any adjustments, for example, we've made it hard to do the right thing. Systems must support culture and guiding principles. (See the discussion about Minding the Gap.)

It's not defined. This can be true on a number of levels, but especially if the organization has not defined what constitutes great service, then how can we expect anyone to deliver and even to improve over time? We can't apply the culture recipe unless we have a definition. There's nothing definite to support with our systems. Zingerman's defines Giving Great Service as following the 3 Steps to Giving Great Service.

---

[3]It seems likely that stonecutters probably have more technical terms for what they do than "whacking at stones".

13.3 Zingerman's 3 Steps to Giving Great Service

This is a simple recipe, and probably on the "baking" end of the spectrum (i.e., not as open to modification). But while it's simple, it's not necessarily easy. And built into it is an ongoing challenge. (Because that's how Zingerman's rolls.)

1. **Figure out what the guest wants.** Seems like we're starting out pretty slow here. Isn't this pretty obvious? But our members may come in with wants that are not on the surface. We could ask them what they want, but...

   - They may not know what they want
   - They may be embarrassed about what they don't know
   - They may ask for the wrong thing

For some folks, a makerspace may be a confusing proposition. What they want might be the object itself, so we may not be going in the right direction when we start explaining what classes they need to take. Instead, we might outline how we can find someone to make the object for them. We can also bear in mind that non-verbal clues can help us determine what they really want, and engaging in relaxed conversation, if they have time, can allow the person time to organize their thoughts and help us understand more clearly what they'd like. So, if we think we understand what the guest wants, next we need to...

2. **Get it for them.** I know, we're getting pretty complicated here! Figure out what they want and get it for them. Let's add:

   Accurately: Recall that for this interaction to be value-add for the guest, it needs to be done right the first time.

   Politely: (A bridge too far for some companies, it seems.)

   Enthusiastically! There are exceptions, though. The earliest Zingerman's business was the Deli, and bright and early one morning a customer walked into the Deli to be greeted by Cathy, a naturally effervescent individual who had been working at the Deli almost from the start. Right off the bat, she was there with a "Good morning! And how can I help you?" in her normal, enthusiastic way. The customer replied "well, the first thing you can do is to turn it the f**k down because it's too early for that." What did the customer want? They didn't want bubbly and enthusiastic—they wanted a lower energy interaction before their coffee. If you skip the step of figuring out everything the customer wants (coffee and quiet, for example), it may be hard to give them great service, even with the best of intentions.

   In order for our staff to get what the guest wants, they need the ability to get what the guest wants. That means, in most cases, our staff needs to be empowered to do what is necessary. (This is also going to be true for dealing with customer complaints.) Great customer service is not waiting while a manager is consulted, or even being passed off to a supervisor.

3. **Go the Extra Mile.** We listened, we got. Hopefully that met our guest's expectations. Now we want to exceed it. And we want to do that in each guest interaction—that's why it is in the recipe. We're going to start small. (We don't always succeed in doing that, though!) A few examples:

- If it is raining, we can shelter the guest and their project under an umbrella to their car.

- A local nonprofit was hoping to find someone to build a custom electronic timer for presentations—we built and programmed it as a shop project.

- We can send postcards after an interaction, mentioning something specific that was discussed and offering additional thoughts, or at least a thank you.

Perhaps you've already seen the challenge with extra miles—the first time you hold the umbrella, it's an extra mile. We exceeded their expectations. The next time it's raining, holding an umbrella might be an expectation. Now what's your extra mile? The good news is that we can often plan extra miles ahead of time. And if we have a great culture in place, extra miles are not going to be a stretch.

Is correcting a mistake an extra mile? Nope, it is not. It's only an extra mile after we got the item for the customer. If we didn't get it right the first time, we didn't finish step 2 (and it was also not value-add).

Now that we have a definition of what Giving Great Service is, you can follow the culture recipe to teach, recognize, and reward it. And make sure systems support your staff.

By the way, we find a nice way of opening a conversation isn't "can I help you?" (which is too easy to answer "no" to), but "what brings you in today?" They may not need your help, but in our makerspace context it's helpful for staff to know what folks are up to. Maybe there's a recent development in that area, or an opportunity we can mention ("be sure to check out the pile of free acrylic we have at the back dock" or "we just added a corner-rounding bit to the ShopBot tools").

13.4 The 5 Steps to Handling a Complaint

What complaints? All complaints, *even if they aren't anything to do with you.*

Handling complaints is rarely anyone's idea of a great time. So it's especially important to give our staff a good tool to deal with complaints. There's less guesswork of what we expect.

We often speak of "retail theater"—the idea that our staff have a role to play with respect to our guests. The 3 Steps to Giving Great Service, the 5 Steps to Handling a Complaint—all are stage directions for our staff. Each staff person is bringing a different take to the role, which is exactly what we want, but everyone is hitting each of the steps as they wend their own way through the interactions.

1. **Acknowledge the complaint.** Number one is that we hear you. "Wow", "oh no", "man, that's not good". We would never deny that something happened (even if we suspect it may not have happened exactly that way). The guest is telling us what they believe happened. And in a lot of cases, that's everything that they want—for someone to validate that (they believe) this happened to them.

2. **Sincerely apologize.** This can feel very difficult, as though we are saying we accept responsibility for every possible thing, but here's what we're asking our staff to do: to sincerely express our empathy for someone over something that just happened.

It may not be our responsibility—we are not necessarily saying this was our fault (though of course it may be!)—but regardless, we are sincerely sorry that this thing happened to you. We weren't driving their car on the way here, but we can certainly be sincere in saying we're sorry that they got a ticket.

Before we get to solving the problem, the next step, be sure that you've gone at the speed of the guest. Are they done telling you the complaint? Have they felt heard? You don't get to say "wow—I'm sorry the bandsaw is broken, here's a free soda, thanks for letting us know" and go on to the next guest.

3. **Take action to make things right.** When the guest has been heard, and you've empathized, now is the time to start to fix the issue. How do you do that? Follow the 3 steps to giving great service.

   - Find out what they want. It's okay to ask what would help make things right for them. Or, if you have an idea, you can offer it—"I'm so sorry you broke your leg and missed several weeks—could we extend your membership that many weeks?" We always tell our staff to "start small"—we probably don't want to give away equity in the business every time a drill bit breaks.

   - Get it for them. This means that staff must be empowered to—and expected to!—take reasonable actions to make things right. In turn, this means our staff should have a good idea of what things cost. For example, membership has a lower marginal cost than a class, so offering to extend a membership, if that can make a problem better, is a nice place to start.

   - Go the extra mile. Don't forget that if you feel you have arrived at a good place, is there an extra mile you can tack on? A discount to a class? Some materials? Hopefully something is specific to the guest and their work.

Note that often what people want is for this not to happen again. Making it right for many of our members is often about fixing the system, improving the SOP, etc. They accept that things happen, tools break, and they mostly want us to know so the next person or the next time they're in, the machine is back working. So, let them know that you'll get someone to fix the machine as soon as possible, for example. You'll let the shop manager know about the leak. You'll make sure to mention it at the weekly huddle to see how this problem can be solved.

4. **Thank them for letting us know.** For each complaint that we get, there are 9 that we don't ever hear. One of the ways of looking at this is to say "yay! 9 complaints I don't have to hear about!" But, this means 9 times you might have gotten feedback and improved something in your makerspace. And that something might be costing you membership renewals, new members, staff retention, etc. We appreciate that the guest stayed engaged while we tried to solve it. *The guest doesn't have to do anything.* It's not their responsibility to let us know if we messed up. The guest cared enough to say something. And the majority of the time, it will hopefully be because they want us to do better. They want to be here, they want us to be here, they want us to succeed. Tell them you appreciate the feedback.

5. **Write it up.** Complaints are an important input to continuous improvement. Write them down. We capture most of our complaints by recording them at the end of the day in our notes. During our weekly staff meeting (our huddle), we review the occurrences during the previous week. We start with the incident:

13.4. THE 5 STEPS TO HANDLING A COMPLAINT

- What happened? (Who, when, why, where)
- How was it resolved, if it was?

Then we ask how to prevent this from happening again:

- What was the cause?
- Is there an SOP that needs to be improved?
- Is there a system that failed?
- Is this likely to happen again?
- Is it something that is even under our control?

Then take action if needed. (See the section on Monkeys.) Sometimes it is something so far out there that there's no chance we'll ever see that circumstance again[4]. But, usually there's something we should do.

The above works for most of the minor complaints and incidents that tend to happen in our makerspace. But when something bigger happens, we want to document it in more detail—this is a Code Red. We'll use a Code Red form when

- there's a significant safety component
- there's been a major impact to the member or the shop (even if it has been resolved)
- the issue hasn't been resolved

What to have on your Code Red form:

1. What happened? E.g., machine failure, missing tool, no bench space, interaction with other member/staff, missing material, etc.
2. Initial guest state: happy, calm, annoyed, moderately upset, very upset, furious
3. What did the staff do to make this right? E.g., membership, materials, refund, etc.
4. Final guest state: happy, calm, annoyed, moderately upset, very upset, furious
5. What further actions (extra miles) should we take to make this right? E.g., contact from manager, etc.
6. Who was involved? Guest name, guest contact info, staff name, time, date, area of shop.

A Code Red does want to get signed by a supervisor kind of person, and may need immediately action instead of waiting for the next weekly meeting.[5]

---

[4]This alone may be the best definition of a makerspace.

[5]A Code Red documents dissatisfaction on the part of the member, but there may also be times when you will be dissatisfied with a member's action (especially around safety). If the behavior is serious enough for the staff to say "if this happens again...", then it is appropriate to document the incident in a Document of Occurrence. Record the behavior, why that isn't appropriate, and what the consequence for repeating that behavior will be. Clearly documenting the incident will allow the entire staff to be aware of the situation, rather than the knowledge resting with just a single staff person (or, more likely, a series of staff people, all unaware of the serial nature of the behavior).

13.5 Steps to Handling a Compliment

Very similar to the steps for handling a complaint, and with good reason—our members don't have to compliment us, and when they do they're giving us good feedback. Plus, if it is about our staff, it is really important to pass that along as noisily as we can.

1. Acknowledge the compliment. "I'm so happy to hear that..."

2. Describe the actions you will take. It may be letting folks know at the next meeting, or making sure that it will be recorded in the daily end of day notes. If this about a specific person, we can be clear how that person will be told, and their supervisors, too.

3. Thank them for letting us know.

4. Write it up. Even a general compliment is great to record in the daily notes. It never gets old.

We've been talking a lot about our guests or members. But who should receive great service in our organization? We will have more to say in the section on Servant Leadership, but the short answer definitely includes the staff. It also includes the FedEx person, the prospective member, the visitors from out of town (who live too far away to ever be members), even the folks from the nearby city that want to start their own makerspace. Everybody gets great service. Put another way—is there some group of people that we shouldn't give great service to?

13.6 10-4

A common service recipe, and another that Zingerman's and others teach, is the "10-4" rule. If a staff person is within 10 feet, make friendly eye contact with the customer. Within 4 feet greet them or say something friendly.

In practice, you'll often want to wave or somehow acknowledge members even if they're across the shop floor[6], and of course we don't want to interrupt someone on the table saw to say hi. And since we're more of a relational situation, vs. the transactional of a retail business, this applies to the first time you see someone that day. The usual social rules apply—you've said hello once. The next time that day you see that member, you might ask how their project is going, what wood they're using, did they come up with that design, etc.—that is, if their work and body language makes it seem like they'd welcome some interaction.

---

[6]There is no need to carry a physical tape measure. A laser or ultrasonic tape measure will do fine.

Chapter 14

Learnings from TWI for Makerspaces

Training Within Industry (TWI) was a program created by the US government during World War II. This was a voluntary program, and the trainers only came into a plant by invitation. The situation it attempted to address was the simultaneous increase in the demand for war-related production with the decrease in the number of trained, skilled personnel (who were going off to war). Add to this the fact that the workers who were available had often been denied the opportunity to be part of the manufacturing workforce before, including minorities and women.

Now, makerspaces are hopefully rarely going to be in that particular situation. There just aren't that many armed conflicts between makerspaces anymore. (Not after what happened in Spring 2015.)[1] But the solutions that TWI came up with can be very applicable today as you've already seen from How To Instruct. Why should these wartime solutions apply some 70+ years later to a makerspace? A large part of the answer is because we welcome people with a wide range of skills into our makerspaces and face the task of bringing them up to speed quickly so they're able to operate machinery safely and efficiently. There are some other useful insights we'll discuss as well.

What were the effects of TWI back in WWII? The results were impressive: by 1945, 86% of the facilities reported efficiency gains of 25% or more. Remember—this was with the war-time personnel, many of whom were women and minorities who had not had these opportunities before. *Rosie the Riveter and her coworkers were usually outproducing their pre-war counterpart, and sometimes by a great deal.*[2]

TWI was the product of experiments by a number of experts on efficiency to identify not just what skills and training was needed, but who needed it. Their answer was that it was the supervisors who should be the focus of TWI, and that they needed the following specific skills:

Knowledge of the Work. How the work gets done. The heavy lifting here is with our SOPs.
    So much so that, as we mentioned earlier, at Maker Works we tend to hire based

---

[1] Really? You were expecting the details of some fabled armed conflict between rival makerspaces? That has the potential to be pretty epic, though everyone would probably wait until the last minute to fabricate their particular weapon. Plus, all the duct tape. All the duct tape.

[2] We can't discount the fact that this was during a war with widespread public support, so motivation was high. Even so, planes are not going to fly if you don't assemble them correctly. Just being motivated is not enough.

much more on the type of customer service a person can provide (accurately, politely, enthusiastically!) and their willingness to use SOPs than their knowledge of the tools. We'll also create a plan for each staff person outlining what classes they'll take, and the path forward to a few classes they'll be expected to be able to teach. (Their "passport".)

Knowledge of the Job Responsibilities. Workplace policies and other non-production issues. These are things that will be in your staff handbook. Especially important will be policies and procedures around, as Tom sometimes says, "promoting a staff member to guest"[3]. (We haven't had to do that but once, but you want to be clear how the process works.) This is fairly generic stuff—we can't just ignore it, but on the other hand, makerspaces don't have much strange or unique going on here.

Skill in Leading ("Job Relations"). As a culture, we're not completely there yet, but we are much further along in workplace fairness than in the 1940's. Back in the time of TWI, cronyism, favoritism, prejudice, and other practices were prevalent enough to justify an entire training program, instructing supervisors how to be fair. So while we shouldn't ignore it, it's a mainstream issue and shouldn't be a surprise to anyone.

Skill in Instruction ("Job Instruction"). Covered earlier in How to Instruct.

Skill in Improving ("Job Methods"). See later as How to Improve.

The first two needs are local to a given place and must be learned for each new situation. But the last three are universal skills that can be applied regardless of the situation. And all five are necessary for effective supervision.

As makerspace operators, how do we use this information and the related training? We can begin by asking who is doing the work in a makerspace, and who is teaching? It turns out that there's a good parallel between our makerspace members and the frontline workers of TWI. Our members spend lots of time in the shop and are subject to the types of rules and policies that would apply to frontline workers in a traditional business. In this respect (and a few others, as we'll see later with open book finances), it is useful to look at the relationship we have with our members as similar to a worker relationship in terms of instruction and management[4]. If this is true, then the supervisors that TWI targeted are our frontline staff in the makerspace.

This is one of what Tom calls the Gifts of TWI: it tells us that we should focus our energy on developing the 5 necessary skills of supervisors in our front line staff. We don't know about you, but we think that's pretty cool! We serve our organization, the makerspace, best when we develop the supervisory skills of everyone on our staff. These are life-long skills that will serve them well in any situation, not just as they're working for us.

But here's a potentially embarrassing question: If TWI produced such amazing results, why did US manufacturing move away from these practices? (Awkward silence as the titans of industry look away, studying the potted plant in the corner, hoping you and your questions will just go away...)

First, the end of the war saw the return of the soldiers overseas. There wasn't the same need for high efficiency as there had been during the war. Providing jobs, especially for returning veterans, was a higher priority than raw output. And second, much of the world was recovering from a devastating war, leaving less competition for the US. In short, once

---

[3] In other words, firing them.
[4] Just to be clear, though, our members are obviously not employees in any legal sense whatsoever.

the wartime needs were over, it was too easy to slip back into the way things had been before, and TWI was largely let go. Except halfway around the world, where a desperate situation was developing at the end of WWII.

Chapter 15

Learnings from Lean for Makerspaces

We think it's worth giving the briefest of overviews of Lean. Probably 80% of the benefits of Lean for a makerspace are contained in things we've already covered, but knowing some background and some of the other areas it addresses may provide some useful insights. At the very least, the human-centered emphasis is reassuring, since it might be easy from a distance for folks to confuse the efficiency of things like SOPs and 5S-ing with rigid, dehumanizing constraints.

There's a fascinating story[1] around the car makers Toyota and General Motors (GM) and their perhaps surprising joint venture at a plant called NUMMI in the early 1980's. At the time, GM was struggling to build cars that people wanted to buy (both the type of car and the quality), while simultaneously Toyota was puzzling out how to build cars in the US with a US workforce, so the joint venture made sense to each for their own reasons.

NUMMI (New United Motor Manufacturing, Inc.) was established at GM's Fremont Assembly plant. Fremont had been one of the worst performing plants that GM had. Nearly any vice you could name could be had—not just in the parking lot, but on the assembly line itself. This is no exaggeration—prostitution, alcohol, drugs, etc. Morale among workers was about as low as you could get. Cars went down the line with obvious defects, piling up in parking lots for expensive fixing. Some workers even actively sabotaged cars, dropping items into the doors to rattle around and annoy customers.

Fremont was shut down, and when it reopened as the NUMMI joint venture, Toyota took many of those same workers to Japan and showed them a different way of building cars—one where workers were respected, and quality was valued above quantity. Within months of the joint venture NUMMI opening, it was producing vehicles with the same high quality of those built in Japan. Morale was on a completely different level. Workers looked forward to coming to work. You really should read the article—it's fascinating, especially the response of the workers to being treated with respect.

The secret ingredient, the Toyota Production System ("TPS", major elements of which are approximately synonymous with "Lean"), is now widely used and copied in whole or part across many industries, particularly the automotive industry, but it faced a great deal of

---

[1] https://www.thisamericanlife.org/561/transcript

resistance. A major concern was that this system was too based in Eastern culture—TPS would never be a good match for workers in a Western culture.

Except, a major element of TPS came from TWI. *It came from the US.*

In the later 1940's, even as TWI was starting to fade from US industry, General Douglas MacArthur was facing a problem in Japan as the effective ruler in his role as overseer of the occupation. Postwar Japan faced a lot of economic challenges, and he needed some powerful tools to aid Japanese industry and avoid an economic disaster. Here, high productivity would be extremely important. Among the tools he introduced to Japan was TWI.

Toyota Motor Corporation took TWI, added other influences[2], their own insights, and (perhaps most importantly) their own values around the development of the worker, and created the Toyota Production System. It was an excellent solution to the challenges that a small car company like Toyota faced. For example, the huge stamping machines that automobile manufacturers used to turn flat metal sheets into car body panels would normally make long runs of the same panel, stockpiling them in large piles because it took twelve or more hours to change the dies. Big US car companies felt they could afford this stockpiling, but this practice seemed *wasteful*[3] to Toyota and they worked hard to bring the changeover time from many hours to an hour and a half, and eventually to less than 10 minutes per die. This had a dramatic impact on the cost due to overproduction of parts, and meant that it was economical to produce exactly the right type and number of parts at the right time.

TPS/Lean was not instantly adopted in the US, by car makers or other industries. (A sad footnote to the NUMMI experiment is the failure of GM at the time to adopt Lean practices in a sustainable way. See the This American Life for more details.) Now many years down the road, a lot of different industries have adopted Lean practices, though not always with the other values and goals of the full TPS. [4]

---

[2]E.g., Henry Ford. This source describes Ford as the basis for TPS, with nary a mention of TWI or other influences: https://www.sixsigmadaily.com/henry-ford-lean-manufacturing/

[3]You're about 2 minutes away from our discussion of the 8 Deadly Wastes. Stay tuned!

[4]In the US, the Lean Enterprise Institute is a useful resource for bringing Lean practices to organizations. www.lean.org

15.1 A System of Systems

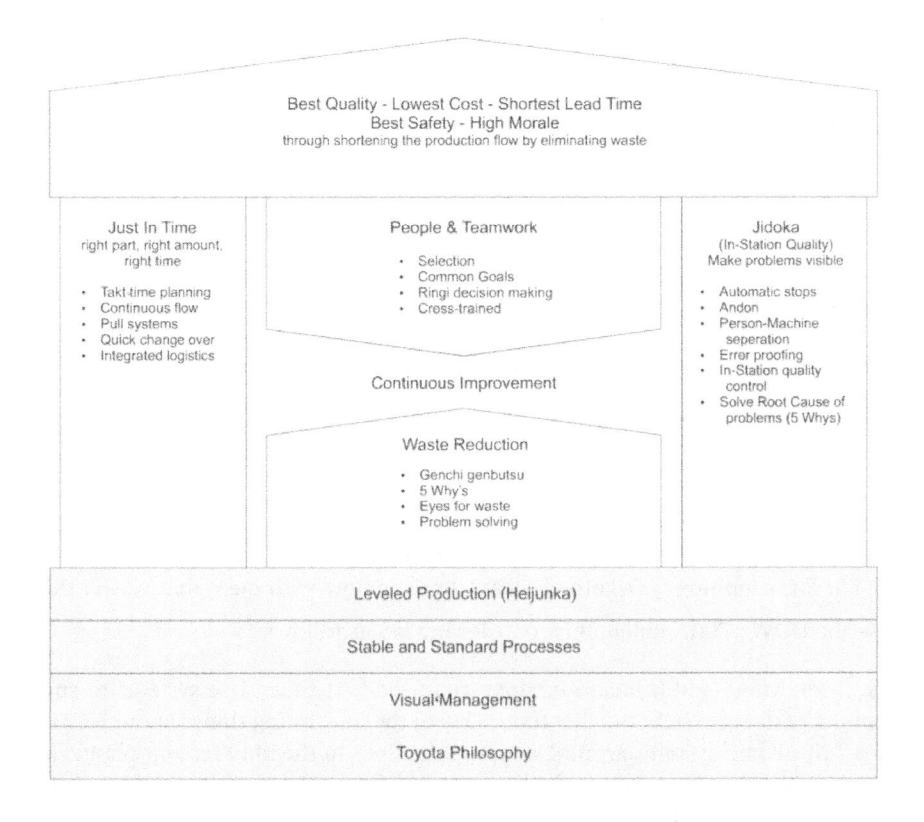

Figure 15.1: The Toyota House

TPS is a system of systems. It is sometimes represented diagrammatically as a house (the Toyota House), figure 15.1, emphasizing the interrelatedness of the systems. Just as the various systems that make up an actual house—electrical, frame, plumbing, heating/cooling, network, etc., must all be present and working for the house to be fully functional, all the systems of TPS must be present to fully realize the goals of the Toyota Production System.

This isn't a primer on Lean or TPS; we're going to pick and choose the elements of TPS that we feel have the most value for makerspace operations, so some elements are going to get short shrift. See, for example, Jeffrey Liker's The Toyota Way for more details..

The following is going to be very helpful in understanding Lean and TPS:

At the core of Lean/TPS is the idea of maximizing value to the customer while minimizing waste, and that this is a process that will never be done but is instead a journey of continuous improvement.

We thus expect Lean/TPS to give us tools around value-add activities, waste, and continuous improvement.

15.2 The Benefits of the Toyota Production System (TPS)

The TPS has the following goals: To produce the best quality, at the lowest cost, with the shortest lead time, and the best safety and morale. It promises sustainable efficiency.

15.3 The 8 Deadly Wastes

A very helpful lens in Lean is around waste reduction, and the list is known as the 8 Deadly Wastes[5]. (You may have seen this earlier in the Maker Works 5S guidelines.)

Why look at waste? Reducing waste can make it obvious what is value-add. Recall that we have the three categories of activities:

- Value-add (transformative, customer is willing to pay for, done right the first time)
- Necessary but not value-add (do them, but try to minimize)
- Not necessary and not value-add (get rid of them!)

The 8 Deadly Wastes let us trim away the things that are not necessary and hence cannot be value-add. (Waste reduction doesn't automatically lead to value-add—if we started with nothing but fat, trimming isn't going to leave us somehow with meat that wasn't there.)

We'll use the DOWNTIME mnemonic to order the list as follows:

Defects. To be value-add it has to be done right the first time. Use systems to support a culture of doing it right the first time. One of the interesting things about NUMMI was the culture and systems around stopping the line. In the old Fremont plant, stopping the line could get you fired. The line stopped for no defect, and nearly no reason. It was exactly the opposite in the joint operation with Toyota—workers were expected to signal any problems, and immediately there was an effort to fix the problem. If the line had to stop to fix it, it stopped. Defects were caught as quickly as possible—which is exactly where there's the most chance to solve the problem, at the lowest cost.[6]

Overproduction. Producing more than the customer wants is a waste. If it is a product with a limited lifetime (e.g., food), we can incur immediate loss since the product expires before we can sell it. If we can keep it in inventory, we incur the inventory losses described below. "Batching" production can all too easily lead to overproduction, and as we'll discuss in just a moment, batching is usually a response to large setup costs. Here in the shop, we just had a great experiment in practicing Lean when we went into production of face shields after our local hospitals put out the call during the COVID-19 pandemic. Instead of 3D printing (which was taking at least 30 minutes per face shield holder), we laser-cut three pieces out of ABS sheets and ultrasonically welded them together, and could produce hundreds per day with just a few people. But the temptation was strong to run the lasers as fast as we could, overproducing some parts to "get ahead" for the next day, since the laser was the slowest part of the process. This was fine except when we changed our design, and now we had a pipeline full of the old version. We'd either have to scrap the old version, or make more of an inferior design. (We were up to version 9 or so at the end, so improvements to the design happened frequently.)

---

[5]Doesn't that sound like "click-bait"? "You'll never believe what 8 deadly wastes this makerspace operator found in their makerspace."

15.3. THE 8 DEADLY WASTES

Waiting. It's time that we're not either producing or developing ourselves. But wait[7]—what about all those products (cheese, meat, alcohol, etc.) that we pay extra money for because it's been aged? Why isn't that a waste? In theory, this is time that the customer is willing to pay for—it produces a better product. If aging didn't contribute anything to the taste past a certain point, then the customer won't pay for it, and it would be waste.

Not Utilizing Talent. It turns out that if you search for the 8 Deadly Wastes, you'll often come across the "7 Deadly Wastes." Not everyone lists "not utilizing talent" as a waste. We're going to disagree. When we fail to utilize the talent of our staff, we fail them as their employer in not developing them, and we fail ourselves by not using our resources fully. "Shut up and do your job" or "I didn't hire you to think" is this waste's hallmark. Any comment of this ilk should send you running.

It may be surprising to you to hear that Toyota has replaced robotics on some of its assembly lines with human workers.[8] Why? *Robots were not improving the work.* They did the same thing over and over. On the other hand, people can analyze the work they're doing and make suggestions for improving. These improvements reduced waste and improved production time on a crankshaft production line when over 100 workspaces were changed from robots to people. And the people who replaced the robots were developing an understanding of the work and skills so when things broke, they knew what to do. It was more robust. And developed their staff.

Transportation. When we needlessly transport items, we incur transportation waste. It could be by truck across the country or by cart from one end of the shop to the other. How far did the item travel? How far does it really need to travel? (That is, how far would the customer be willing to pay to have it travel?)

Inventory. Inventory can feel like a good thing—we're not just caught up with demand, but we have breathing space. But inventory is our capital tied up in non-liquid form. It takes up space (which costs money), costs money to monitor, often degrades over time, is subject to damage, has cost us labor and materials before we really needed it, takes time to count and keep track of, and so on. This is one of the hardest, least intuitive wastes, so be particularly wary around inventory. The title of the list is "deadly" wastes, and that is particularly apropos here.

Motion Waste. This is wasteful motion on the part of the worker. Motions that are not value-add or necessary are waste.

Excess Processing. Recall that the customer has to be willing to pay for any transformation—just the fact that we're transforming something doesn't make it value-add. If we're doing more than what the customer wants, it is waste.

Yes, a lot of Lean/TPS is coming from a manufacturing point of view, so things like flow, batching, and leveling production may feel far removed from what we do to operate a makerspace. But we're going to be tempted with inventory from paper towels to end mills

---

[6]So why wouldn't Fremont have wanted to stop the line? One possibility would be if the financial incentives for individuals (supervisors, managers) were focused on cars out the door—and if the fact that these cars required rework wasn't factored in. We must always be alert to mismatches between incentives and our desired outcomes.

[7]See what we did there?

[8]https://qz.com/196200/toyota-is-becoming-more-efficient-by-replacing-robots-with-humans/ retrieved 5/5/2019

to brochures. We might put our tool crib in a handy room that ends up being far from where most of the tools are used (transportation waste)[9]. And so on.

The area of overproduction and large batch sizes is a particularly rich vein to explore. "One-piece batch size" is surprisingly applicable to so many different processes, and also well represents a core principle in Lean: We should subject our processes to evaluation and constantly look for improvements. We think for these reasons "batching" is worth examining in more detail.

Why do we "batch"? For example, instead of cooking a single cookie, we'll make 20. When we print a member handbook, we print a dozen. When we make pusher sticks for the table saw, we make 6. The reason almost always comes down to the setup costs for the process. We have to heat up the oven, which takes a while. We have to mix the batter—might as well make 20 cookies. In fact, we can't get 1/12th of an egg—we have to mix up batches big enough to use an entire egg. But is that ideal? We have to have a cookie jar (inventory costs). If you eat two cookies hot out of the oven (and why wouldn't you?), there's 18 that will be eaten that are not freshly baked. Will you eat all the cookies before they get stale? Okay, probably yes. But you can imagine other stuff might not be consumed and there would be waste. So what is the alternative?

Lean asks us to start at the other end and assume a single-piece flow, instead of always starting with a batch. If the process can produce a single piece at a time, what would we save? At a minimum

- No overproduction

- No inventory

- Fewer defects

The first two are obvious. But the fewer defects might not seem obvious at first. But here's what happens when we batch—any mistakes are magnified by the batch size and the length of the pipeline. Leave out sugar from one cookie, and you'll learn before you make any more. We get to evaluate the final product before we've made irreversible errors on the other items. Leave sugar out of a batch, and that's twenty bad cookies—we don't learn of the problem until all 20 are bad.

But how could we make cookies one at a time? Isn't turning on an oven for a single cookie wasteful of energy and would take tons of time? It is and would, so let's use a toaster oven. We can get "liquid eggs" in a container and measure out the 1/12th. We could have flour, sugar, and all the rest of the ingredients in an organized caddy so we don't have to gather them. In the end, if we're serious about making cookies one or two at a time, we can greatly reduce the setup time, and produce a superior product (fresh each time).

Lean does not say that the answer is *always* a single-piece batch. But it does ask us to ask ourselves what about the setup costs is driving us to batch, and is it worth the cost. It's the same question that Toyota asked about their stamping machine. All the big car companies in the US were stamping out huge piles of panels, building up an inventory, switching to a new die (which took 12 or more hours), stamping out another big pile, and so on. Toyota started from the ideal—what if we could change the die very fast? It completely changes the equation.

---

[9]We would never, never have done such a foolish thing.

We have a member handbook—about 60 pages, card-stock four-color cover, "saddle stitched" (i.e., stapled on the spine). One approach would be to send them out to a printer, but they'd want to print 50 or 100. That's money that's tied up, copies that are worthless if content needs to be changed, and storage that must be found. Another option would be to print them in batches internally using our color and black and white laser printers. Which is what we do now, in batches of about 5. But is that the best we can do? Why 5? It turns out that the big old guillotine paper cutter that we use is at the opposite end of the building, up in a mezzanine, and often covered in stuff. No one wants to walk the length of the building, then up and down the stairs each time a handbook is printed. For 5 copies, it seems just worth it. But is that our only option? For example, maybe we don't trim the edges—or we find a more compact paper cutter than will trim the edges. Or would the big paper cutter get used more often if we moved it closer to the front desk? (Maybe members would like to use it?) We can set up the job on a computer so with one click the cover is sent to the color printer (where a single card-stock sheet has been loaded) and the rest of the book sent to the B&W laser.

We talk about "flow" in Lean processes as the opposite of batch. A favorite example of Tom's: if we had a faucet at one end of the room and a big barrel to fill at the other, batching would be using a bucket to ferry the water from faucet to barrel; flow would be using a hose. Batching can resemble a snake eating a badger—the lump moves down the line. Ahead and behind the lump, though, there's no badger. Ahead and behind the batch of goods, we may have wasted time for our workers. Flow is our ideal because it implies a lack of waiting. There are no queues, no space needed for parts to wait between one stage and the next.

There's so much more to say about batching and flow. All we can say is that we've been there, done that, and that our intuition about batching always being the solution is almost always worthy of being examined.

15.4 Look Familiar?

At this point you can probably map a lot of the elements of the Toyota House to the concepts we've gone over.

- At the base of the Toyota house is the Toyota Philosophy, the core set of beliefs and Guiding Principles upon which the organization is built.

- 5S—visual management—is the next layer of foundation.

- And above that, stable and standard processes (SOPs).

- People and teamwork along with waste reduction (the 8 Deadly Wastes) lead to Continuous Improvement.

We'll admit that it's going to be a stretch to apply a few of the Toyota House elements to the typical makerspace—we just don't tend to have many assembly lines, for example. But before we go, we would like to draw your attention to one of the Jidoka[10] elements, error-proofing.

---

[10] Jidoka roughly means automation with human intelligence.

15.5 Error Proofing / Mistake Proofing

We introduced the concept of "make it easy to do the right thing and hard to do the wrong thing" very early in this book. In Lean, there's the formal concept of "error proofing" and "mistake proofing" ("poka-yoke" in the Toyota Production System). Mistakes will be made. It's inevitable—we're just people. But we can have as a goal to eliminate defects—that is, mistakes that make it to customers. There are a number of tools in the Lean toolbox for mistake proofing, including:

- Preventing the mistake from being made. For example, a bolt will only fit in one hole. A tool will only turn on if the cover is closed. A pre-adjusted tool holder will fit only the correct one of the two lathes.

- Providing notification that the correct operation has been made, or conversely that it is not yet completed. A status light can signal that a heater is up to temperature. LEDs show the air pressure on a tool is in the correct range (or not).

- Part of the SOP can be an inspection by the worker, using testing jigs, go/no-go gages, etc.

Worrying that someone made a mistake and cut their board 1/4" short probably isn't going to keep you up at night. The mistakes that should keep you up are the ones where someone gets hurt. That leads us to our next chapter.

Chapter 16

Safety

Safety is the product of the systems, culture, and guiding principles of the organization. Having only systems in place doesn't do it if the culture doesn't back it up. Claiming "Safety is #1!" in a big poster, hoping to create a culture of safety, is worthless without the systems that make it easy to do the right thing. And we're not spending money or energy if safety is not actually a value. (If we're not willing to do anything to realize a value, then it's really just a marketing point, or a happy delusion.)

Safety policy and information is in layers at our shop, which may be a useful way of looking at it. At the top, our shop-level "Principles of Safety" (below) are shared at the start of every class, regardless of how many times you've heard it before. It's in the member handbook, and it's on posters. This is the baseline for safety in the shop. Staff are given a laminated copy most carry with them in their lab coat. Copies are also tucked in the front of the "Train the Trainer" or teaching SOPs. Yes, nearly everything on it, from dull tooling to materials that are dangerous when machined, is in there in response to something that's come up. It's one of the charms of running a makerspace.

16.1 Maker Works Principles of Safety

- Be polite and professional in all interactions at MAKER WORKS, particularly when giving or receiving feedback about safety.
- Your Own Safety
    - Attention
        - Give the work and the tool your undivided attention.
        - One and only one person should operate a machine and must attend it while running.
        - Operate machinery with a clear mind, never while fatigued or under the influence of drugs or alcohol.
    - Attire
        - Wear ANSI Z87 safety glasses or goggles and closed footwear at all times in WOOD, METAL & JEWELRY

- Wear hearing and breathing protection as appropriate to the work environment.
- Do not operate rotating machinery while wearing long sleeves, gloves, loose jewelry, loose long hair, neckties, hoodie strings or anything else which may be caught and draw you into the machine.

○ Ask for Help

- If you are not familiar with a machine or operation.
- Handling long, large, or heavy materials.
- Seek first aid immediately for any injury.
- If at any time you feel unsure about the safety of what you are about to do.

• The Safety of All Those Around You

○ Safe Materials

- Do not bring toxic, flammable explosive, or radioactive materials.
- Do not bring materials which may become dangerous when machined or heated.

○ Sharpness of Tools

- Dull tools:
- Require excessive force.
- Can pose a fire hazard.
- Have a higher likelihood of ejecting material from the work area.

○ Startling

- Allow others to give their work their undivided attention.
- Do not tap people on the shoulder.
- Move into others' line of sight before attempting to attract their attention.
- Stay Clear of areas where others may move unexpectedly without checking for your presence.
- Give warning before making sudden loud noises.

• The Safety and Health of the Tools

○ SOPs

- Live at each machine.
- Consult machine manuals for additional information.

○ Authorization

- Use only tools you have been authorized to use through the Maker Works Checkout procedure.

○ Check and Report

- Inspect machinery before using to ensure it is in proper working order.
- Consult staff if unsure about anything.
- Immediately report if something breaks.

16.1. MAKER WORKS PRINCIPLES OF SAFETY

Signs on the doors of shops deliver area-specific safety like Personal Protective Equipment[1] requirements.

Every checkout class includes any machine-specific safety issues. These might be generic to an area (e.g., flammables in the welding area) and are repeated for each tool, but most are specific to that tool. We also emphasize safety issues that may already be in the "Principles of Safety" but are especially applicable, such as safety around rotating machinery.

Other safety related policies will involve:

- Young people. What areas are they able to tour, visit briefly, hang out, assist in, or work in? What classes can they take? What is the level of parent/guardian participation?

- Guests. Where/when are they welcome, what can they do?

- What tools can regular members use? Are there tests, required classes, required reading/videos?

- What requirements are there for using SOPs? Is SOP use required, preferred, optional?

- What are the consequences for not following shop policies, including around safety?

- What safety-related equipment is provided by the shop, and what by the user? We expect our serious members will bring their own fancier PPE, but we provide glasses and hearing protection, and have masks available for purchase.

- What is the policy around member-owned tools? We may require the user to take a brief checkout for the tools we allow.

- What is the shop policy around cleanliness where it intersects with safety? For example, around clutter and floors (slipping, tripping).

- What materials, tools, and processes are not acceptable due to safety issues? (Sometimes these will overlap with insurance, zoning, or fire department requirements.)

"Making it easy to do the right thing and hard to do the wrong thing" should be at the top of your mind when thinking about making your shop safer. Is there a different tool that does the same operation but in a safer way? How can you prevent someone from performing a dangerous (but alluring) operation?

---

[1] E.g., safety glasses, shoes, breathing, hearing protection. (This footnote was added long before the COVID-19 pandemic, so it seems charming now that we thought we had to explain what PPE means.)

Chapter 17

Management Tools

17.1 Servant Leadership

Servant Leadership is a philosophy of leadership that prioritizes the development and well-being of staff, and has the flow of service out toward the front-line staff and then to the customer (or member in our case).

Why should we invert the "normal" way of doing things? Shouldn't the leader, the person at the top, be served by those below her or him?

1. It's the right thing to do. It's consistent with our values. It reduces the difference between how we act in our personal lives and how we act in our business lives.

2. It gives us the chance to help others grow and succeed. (In our case, that's one of our bottom lines.)

3. It begets better service to the member. You can't serve two masters. Front-line staff can devote their energy to serving the member. Managers and higher direct their energy toward serving the front line staff. And everyone is modeling delivering great service.

4. It creates a more appealing workplace. What message would you want to receive from your boss—a list of things they want you to do for them, or a query if you need any help or resources?

5. Service sets the tone for the organization. Who is served? Everyone.

6. It helps you move toward what you want for yourself.

So what does Servant Leadership look like in practice?

Provide inspiring and strategically-sound vision. We've already mentioned this as a responsibility of leadership.

Give great day-to-day service to staff. This is at all levels—from things that are systematized to asking who needs a coffee from the coffeeshop. *Every moment brings an opportunity to serve.*

Manage in an ethical manner. What would Mr. Rogers do?

Learning and teaching. Learning and teaching are important opportunities for development for everyone in the organization, regardless of their level. In the larger and more formal Zingerman's organization, teaching is an expectation of everyone, but especially at the higher levels.

Help staff succeed. There is no way the organization loses when the staff succeeds. Robert Greenleaf, who gave this type of leadership the label "Servant Leadership" in 1970, described the best test of Servant Leadership as "do those served grow as persons?"[1]

Say thanks. We'll have more to say on this in Section 17.4, but making sure everyone knows you appreciate them is always the right thing.

We don't feel Servant Leadership is something that we "bolt on" to the organization, but is a natural consequence of the practices we've been discussing in this book. You can learn more in Robert Greenleaf's books and essays such as "The Servant as Leader".

17.2 Open Book Management

Open Book Management is the idea that everyone in the organization (for-profit or non-) has not only the right but the responsibility to understand the financial situation of the organization. So it is the case that, quite literally, a dishwasher will know how the restaurant's income and expenses are doing this month and how the overall profit situation looks for the year. (They will, in fact, have a particular interest in how the overall profit for the year goes.)

Why on earth would we want to not only share the financials of our organization or business with the staff, but actually spend time educating them on how to interpret the information?

- Foremost, it produces better bottom line results. When everyone is "thinking like an owner", it leads to better decisions at every level. (How do we get everyone thinking like an owner? Keep reading.)
- It is in line with our principles.
- It builds commitment.
- It shares the "weight" of financial concern among everyone affected.

And before we go any further, two issues that come up all the time:

- Is it really that important that your finances are secret? Well, maybe if there's some element there that would make staff or members unhappy. But if your finances are in line with a reasonable rate of return, sharing the finances can make it easier for staff (or even members) to understand what the situation is. And as for your competition—in reality, it's probably not that valuable of information. Zingerman's publishes recipes for many of their products, including their famous "Magic Brownies"[2]. It's going to take a lot more than just the recipe to compete. More like an entire book of recipes. (Hmm.)

---

[1] www.greenleaf.org
[2] At the time of this writing, their magic nature is entirely grandma-friendly.

- What about salaries? Two answers—first, you can group salaries into a big category, so individual salaries are not listed; second, is there a reason why people would be upset knowing what other folks in the organization are earning?

17.2.1 The SOP for Open Book Management

The SOP we'll share is short and sweet:

1. Know and teach the rules.
2. Keep score.
3. Share the winnings.

Know and Teach the Rules

Just sharing the financial figures isn't enough. Each person in the organization must be able to understand the multiple viewpoints into the financial health as reflected in the balance sheet, profit and loss, and cash flow. You can do this in stages, at each weekly meeting tackling a new subject to cover or review. In our favor is the fact that the example we can use—the finances of our own makerspace—is very motivating to the learners!

The world of accounting has its own language, often with multiple names for the same thing. Right off the bat it may not be obvious to everyone that the "P&L" is the same as a "profit and loss statement" and "income statement". So, it is useful to pick the terminology you'll use and be consistent.

Our brief outline of topics to cover would be as follows:

Accounting provides us a view of the financial health of the organization at a particular time, providing us the information to make decisions. We also keep accounts in order to satisfy the requirements of investors and taxing or regulatory government agencies (e.g., the IRS).

Accounts let us group activity into useful bins—for example, marketing expenses, or income from running events. The books of the organization are a set of balanced transactions between accounts. Every financial event in an organization produces a balanced transaction. If we pay cash for an expense, we subtract that amount from the cash account and add the same amount to the expense account. We can often choose how detailed we are with accounts. For example, we can have a single "utilities" account, or we have individual accounts for electrical, gas, phone, etc. The latter allows us insight into questions like, has our electricity bill gone down since we installed LED lights?

There are three main financial viewpoints that we can generate from the books:

- Balance Sheet: This report summarizes the total assets, liabilities, and owner's equity. The assets must equal the sum of the liabilities and owner's equity. For example, it allows us to see if, despite having cash in the bank, the overall organization is heavily in debt. It is a snapshot at a particular time, summarizing everything that's happened in the business up to that time.
    - Assets: Things like cash, land, machines, accounts receivable, and other things of value.

- Liabilities: Things the organization owes to other entities—for example, the unpaid balance on credit cards, accounts payable, etc.
- Owner's Equity: What's left over if you subtract Liabilities from Assets. If the business were sold right now, how much would the owners pocket?[3]

- Profit and Loss Statement: This report summarizes the income and expenses over a given period, often in stages that separate out expenses that are directly related to the goods or services produced (e.g., cost of materials, labor), and those expenses that are (largely) independent of how much is being produced (overhead like insurance, rent, etc.).

- Cash Flow Analysis: As we'll see in a moment, "Cash is King". Value tied up in inventory, accounts receivable, and other non-liquid assets are not available for paying wages or venders. A business can be profitable on a long time scale, but fail because they run out of cash on a shorter time scale.

Another concept to cover is that of "cash" vs. "accrual" accounting. Briefly, accrual accounting gives us the most accurate picture of our organization's finances by taking into account things we owe but have not yet paid, and amounts we're owed but have not yet received. This can range from memberships we've sold but the members haven't used yet, to spreading out expenses like insurance that get paid every 6 months or even annually. "Cash" accounting ignores these obligations, and can provide a somewhat misleading picture depending on the scale of your operation, however is much easier to do. (Because makerspaces may charge memberships in advance (e.g., month, quarter, or year-long), it's likely your accountant will have you using accrual, so your staff should understand the implications.)

We do have to say that in addition to all the jargon in accounting (which sometimes feels like it is intended to keep non-accountants out), there are many elements that, let us say delicately, diverge from reality, often due to an endless list of laws and regulations, which doesn't help to make accounting more approachable. But the important numbers, the income and expenses, are often the ones that are affected by the staff's actions, and can be shared in a fairly clear way to everyone's benefit.

Keep Score

It is not necessary—or useful—to review the complete finances of the organization at every weekly meeting. Instead, a dashboard (a high level summary of just a few measures) can provide the information needed for decisions and to keep everyone up to date. Common figures to include would be income-related figures, such as number of memberships, membership income, number of classes taught, class income, events, consulting. The dashboard is posted in a common area, and shared with whomever is interested, but always reviewed at weekly meetings.

Share the Winnings

How do we get our staff to think like owners? Owners clearly benefit from net profit, but why would a staff person care? Their hourly rate is fixed—what's in it for them?

---

[3] Those greedy bastards.

17.2. OPEN BOOK MANAGEMENT

And that is indeed a problem. There are no incentives for a staff person to increase net profit (either through increasing revenue or decreasing expenses). Except perhaps the drastic result of having a job or not.

If we instead provide an incentive, a share of the winnings, everyone's incentives are now aligned. A profit for the organization is a profit for the staff as well.[4]

17.2.2 The 10 Rules

Here are 10 rules for Open Book Management:

1. Begin with a plan. An annual business plan provides a base to measure your financial progress through the year. It is very specific, and describes what the preferred financial state of the organization at the end of the year will be, and at every point in between. In the annual cycle of an organization, it would be produced after the vision for the year, since the assumptions built into it are driven in part by the vision (and of course historical data, when available).

2. Profit is vital. The long-term survival of the organization is dependent on either profit or a continued influx of cash. (Please let us know about this unending fountain of cash, if you would. Asking for a friend.)

3. Cash is king. Profit may be vital, but if you do not have sufficient cash flow, the jig is up. You can't pay wages, utilities, rent. This is why the cash flow analysis exists, since the balance sheet may show an overall positive asset balance. But if the value of the business is tied up in inventory or accounts receivables, that's not value that's very available. The utility company is unlikely to accept a pile of steel or cases of unsold books in exchange for electricity. Cash flow has been the end of many businesses that were overall profitable.

4. Building value is essential.

5. Scorecards are #1. Dashboards or other means of continually monitoring the financial state of the organization are vital. Sometimes we'll say that more than the actual number on the board, we value more the story behind the number. Why are classes up this week over last week? There was a Girl Scout troop making bat houses. Okay, now we know that was a one-time event. If instead it's because we have a new welding instructor, now we have a longer term effect. So tell the stories, too.

6. It's gotta tie out. Make sure any stories we tell make sense. If we just had a big marketing push, do the membership numbers show any effect? Or maybe memberships are up but the membership revenue hasn't gone up—did we just give some memberships away to a robotics group?

7. A dollar today is worth more. This is the concept of the time value of money, the idea that there's more value to receiving money now than later because of the potential earning (e.g., interest) of the money during that time. It's pretty low in this list, but worth making people aware of. Over longer periods of time, depending on the interest environment, it can be significant enough to take into account.

---

[4]You might ask what Maker Works is doing along these lines. We describe ourselves as still in the "profit-seeking" mode, so profits remain hypothetical. However, it is clear to all the staff that an improvement in our finances will be shared with the staff as a high priority.

8. 80/20 rule. No, not that 80/20 rule. This is a rule to use when discussing finances. And unfortunately it runs counter to our natural inclinations. It says that in our financial discussions, we should spend 20% of our time looking at where we've been, and 80% discussing where we want to be (our financial vision). The unfortunate part is that we have excellent, nicely formatted reports of all kinds about what did happen (the past), so that's easiest to discuss. We need to acknowledge the nice printouts, and then step into the less well defined future.

9. We speak the same language. As we said before, the field of accounting is mined with special and confusing terminology. Pick your terms, define them, use them.

10. Success starts here.

For more information on the impact that open book management can make, check out the book *The Great Game of Business* by Jack Stack. For a quick read, see "Why Open book Management is an Excellent Way to Run a Business: 5 Reasons Our Dishwashers Know Our Net Operating Profit" at https://www.zingtrain.com/article/why-open-book-management-is-an-excellent-way-to-run-a-business/

17.3 Bottom Line Change

17.3.1 The Effective Change Formula

Much of the material in this chapter comes from the teachings of Zing Train. For more details, see www.zingtrain.com.

Change in an organization is inevitable. The need for change can come from internal or external forces, but it is a fact of business life that organizations must change over time to continue to deliver on their mission—regardless of whether you're for-profit or nonprofit. Learning how to manage change is an important skill for leaders and managers for the following reasons:

- It increases engagement within the organization
- It improves the effectiveness of the organization
- It is less stressful

Change is necessary, but it can be hard because people have a natural resistance to change, particularly if it is imposed on them. (Though of course, if it is our own idea, we very much like that kind of change.) This natural resistance is a good thing! If we believe in standard processes, random changes for no good reason would kill any consistency and make improvement well nigh impossible. But this natural tendency does mean that when we do want or need to make a change, we need to overcome this resistance.

At Zingerman's, they've come up with the Effective Change Formula to talk about this resistance and how to overcome it:

Change will only occur if the amount of dissatisfaction (D) times *the vision (V) of a better future* times *the existence of a reasonable first step (F) is greater than the amount of resistance to change (R).*

Or more compactly:

$$D \times V \times F > R$$

They're multiplied because if any one of the factors on the left is low, the ability to overcome resistance is also going to be low.

Zingerman's Effective Change Formula tells us that, as leaders, if we want to make a change in our makerspace, we need to address all three of these elements. This is only a statement about the necessary condition, though. What we really need is a recipe for implementing change, one that acknowledges the resistance to change reflected in the change formula.

17.3.2 Zingerman's Bottom Line Change (BLC) Recipe

The purpose of the Zingerman's Bottom Line Change recipe or SOP is, given the need for a change to be made, to

- leverage the knowledge within the organization to make the best decisions
- increase buy-in for the change
- reduce stress around change
- improve capacity for making changes in the future
- produce changes that "stick"

You'll know that your use of BLC has succeeded when you announce to your staff that some change has been implemented, and their response is, rather than gnashing of teeth or pouting, an almost puzzled "Didn't we already do that?"

The steps are as follows:

1. Create a clear and compelling purpose for change

Recall the first condition necessary for resistance to change to be overcome: dissatisfaction with the way things are. If everyone does not share your dissatisfaction, one reason could be that you're crazy, and that things are actually great the way they are. But it may also be the case that you have information or experience that other people don't, in which case in this step you'll need to organize and share this with the hope that other rational people will take in that information and likewise become dissatisfied. Not because we want to manipulate them, but because if we want the best possible decisions in our organization, we must engage everyone we can and provide them with all the information they need to participate in those decisions.

Who will have the most compelling data and experience to share? It's usually the people actually doing the affected work.

2. Create a positive vision of the future AND get leadership agreement on that vision

Here's the vision element of the Effective Change Formula. What will things be like once the change is in place?

The vision isn't just for convincing people to take the plunge, to buy into our argument for change. The vision is what will sustain them during the implementation. The reality is that for many significant changes, *it's going to be hard before it gets better.* The vision gives us hope, an optimistic and inspiring goal.

Like all visions, this vision should be inspiring, strategically sounds, documented, and communicated.

Once we have a vision, the decision-makers need to agree on that vision. (Note that what we have at this point is an agreement on the vision and not on the steps to get there, the action plan. That's a little later. However, the Effective Change Formula applies here, so a First Step may be needed at this stage.)

If decision-making is concentrated in just a few people, this stage may be easier than with a large and diverse group. The larger the group, in general, the wider the variety of concerns, and so the need for more data, a more carefully crafted vision, etc. On the other hand, a large group can bring a wider array of experience to the decision, potentially improving the quality of the decision.

Regardless of the decision-making process and who is involved, everyone involved in deciding must commit to supporting the decision. If your decision-making process doesn't require that, you may have a hard road ahead implementing the change. As we said, often big changes will mean things will get harder before they get better, and if everyone in a position of leadership isn't on board, that transition is going to be more difficult to get through.

3. Engage a microcosm to determine who needs to know about the change and how to get the information out

Change is easier if it is clearly communicated with plenty of notice. If we face resistance with change in general, change that is unexpectedly thrust at the last minute upon someone is on another level altogether. This step has us reach out to a cross section of people who may be affected and help us identify

- who needs to know
- what do they need to know
- by when
- in what way

(Sounds a bit like the training question, doesn't it?)

If you have a small staff, as useful as answering the above questions may be the fact that you're working with some folks ahead of time to get their help and, hopefully, their buy-in. At this point we have all the elements of the effective change formula ready to help in selling the change.

4. Collectively create an action plan for rolling out the change

Who likely has the most to contribute to an action plan to implement the change? The people doing the actual work. Not only are they often the most informed, if they are the ones crafting the change, resistance is naturally lower.

Note that this step talks about planning for "rolling out the change". Again, you'll know your use of BLC has been a success if the actual implementation of the change is met as "old news". Everyone has known about and had input on the change for days (or weeks, or even months). Allow time in the action plan for everyone to be bored about it. In fact, if there's still a lot of energetic talk about the change, maybe there's still some work to be done.

5. Implement the change

Follow the action plan. Realize that some big changes will involve periods of time when things are hard before they get better. If this change is spread out over time, include in your plan opportunities to celebrate success, and to periodically review not just the progress but the vision of where you are heading.

An example of this from Maker Works was our change to our online scheduling. For many years we used a particular online scheduling program for scheduling tool reservations and classes. It didn't do everything we wanted, but the "problem" was that it worked pretty well. It was the 80% or even 90% solution, and if you've ever changed software systems you can imagine we were not excited about all the work changing to a new system would entail, especially since the old system was meeting so many of our needs. For years we had a lot of resistance to changing it. (Dissatisfaction was low, there wasn't a clear vision, and we had no first-step to get anywhere.)

But Tom and some folks on staff became increasingly aware that there were some things that were actually costing us time and money. For example, we had many no-shows for our classes because we weren't able to integrate our payment processing system with the reservation system. This meant we didn't collect class fees at time of reservation. (It turns out that once people put down money for a class, they tend to show up.) They gathered the data on no-shows, and also put together a list of other things that we had worked around, but weren't ideal with the current scheduling software. Sharing it at the staff huddle allowed everyone to see the problem with the current system, which was important since not everyone interacted with the system in the same way, nor had an idea of just how bad our no-show problem was. They also offered a specific vision, a piece of software that would address the issues we had.

Who needed to know what and by when? Everyone on staff interacts on a daily basis with the system, and the majority of our members as well—basically most everyone in the shop. But for other changes, the answer might be a much more limited subset—for example, only renters, or only staff—and engaging the microcosm to identify that subset would then be important.

Nearly everyone on staff contributed to creating the roll-out plan. The front-line staff could speak to member concerns, while a smaller set of staff were more involved in the behind the scenes details. We picked a switch-flipping date and time (one weekday morning well before we opened, so usage of the system would be low), and worked backward to figure out when we'd start notifying members, when we needed to copy information over from one system to the other, and so on. Note that we said "started to notify"—members got the message about the new system multiple times, from emails, newsletters, posters, the website, etc.

There were a few hiccups, and the first weeks of using the new system were a bit rough, but we had a clear vision of what we were aiming for, and we got there. Without a lot of drama or stress.

Again, change is the only constant. This recipe can help make changes less stressful and more successful.

17.4 Appreciation

An important guiding principle is that of appreciation. There are plenty of opportunities each day to express our gratitude to the staff, members, and other people in our community. You can build appreciation into your systems[5]—our weekly huddles (and other meetings) have a closing agenda item of "Appreciations". Here are recent ones:

- Josh appreciates everyone for the Sorting!

- Kirstin appreciates Bob for being her project partner, and Dale for loaning the drill chuck.

- Josh appreciates the "sorting" going on around the shop.

- Al appreciates Dulce for helping to organize and throw away stuff.

- Bearded ladies for their beards.

- Eric for cleaning out the mezzanine!

- Dulce and Pamela for cleaning out behind the desk and loading dock.

- Pamela's work on the jewelry studio.

- Dale appreciates Eric's work on the mezzanine!

- Josh appreciates everyone getting the GMR packed up in crates!

- Je'Tone appreciates Kirstin for printing out SOPs and laser cutting items.

- Kirstin appreciates gelato.

- Josh & Al appreciate everyone's work on packing up the GMR.

- Al appreciates Pamela and Stone for making access to the compressor easier.

- Josh appreciates Kirstin for pressing for clarity on how to maintain focus.

---

[5]Like so many other things, here's a chance for there to be gaps between systems, culture, and values. If our agenda (a system for meetings) didn't include appreciations as an item, it'd make it a lot less likely to happen. Likewise, if we didn't have appreciation as a value, things are going to be a little awkward if that's an item on the agenda and we're not into it.

Some of these aren't going to make sense to anyone who wasn't there, but that's not important. In fact, the more gelato and beards, the better.

You might be concerned that frequently expressing appreciation will feel artificial to you or the recipient. We can tell you that it doesn't. You can find a genuine place of gratitude for the choice people made to be here this day, and to do the work they did. And it's good to say so in the moment, rather than in an annual review[6].

17.5 Decision-Making

Different types of decisions will likely be made by different groups of people in your makerspace. Should we take out a loan for a new addition to the building? Should we buy green or yellow Post-It notes? The structure of your organization and the way decisions are made can have a huge impact on your sustainability: Poor decisions can obviously waste resources. Slow decisions can miss opportunities. If people feel their input has not been solicited or heard, their level of interest can decline and they may exit the organization. If people do not participate in decision-making, we lose the chance to develop their skills in presenting proposals and making decisions. The ideal decision-making process would be fast, well-informed, and include the right people. Unfortunately, as with most things in life, these can be at odds.

The Centre for Teaching Excellence at the University of Waterloo breaks down decision-making methods into the following categories[7] (some have been omitted):

Decision by Authority: The (hopefully benevolent) dictator can make decisions very fast, but may not get input from others (on either the raw facts or in making the decision), and any support from the group may be due to the position of the decision-maker, versus the actual merits of the decision. Tom and Dale make some decisions this way for high-level issues, but try to have most decisions by consensus (below).

Decision by Majority: Majority-win voting. This form is familiar (e.g., Robert's Rules of Order), well-established legally (and may be required for certain types of organizational decisions), and can be efficient. However, up to 49% of the decision-makers "lose", and may feel actively ignored or rejected. This rejection, and the sometimes resulting factions, can have negative consequences over time. It may feel at times as though the process is more valued than the outcome. And there isn't necessarily an effort to gather and disseminate accurate information built into the process, so it may not generate the best decisions. Taken to extremes, the process can be abused.

Decision by Ranking: Decision-makers rank different options using a numeric scale (e.g., 1–5), and votes are tallied with the winner having the largest total. Can feel inclusive, but is also possible to "game" (i.e., some voters may not vote their actual preferences).[8]

Decision by Consensus: A decision is approved only with everyone's agreement. In most consensus systems, a single decision-maker can block a decision if they feel the decision is not in the organization's best interest, but in practice concerns and potential blocks are taken as opportunities for the proposal to improve, given the assumption

---

[6]Batching is rarely the best answer!
[7]https://uwaterloo.ca/centre-for-teaching-excellence/teaching-resources/teaching-tips/developing-assignments/group-work/group-decision-making

that everyone is acting with the best intentions for the organization. This is among the most potentially time-consuming methods, and can require skilled facilitation, but results in decisions with the best input, broadest support, and best outcome in terms of group dynamics.

It is important to make sure that the decision making at every level is consistent with your guiding principles. And to the extent that a decision-making process is unfamiliar, to provide education so it can be used effectively. (This is especially true of consensus decision making, which may not be familiar to everyone.)

The Toyota Production System places a high value on reaching a decision slowly through consensus based on all the options, then implementing that decision quickly.

Maker Works is a for-profit organized as an LLC. As we said, Tom and Dale, as the two partners, do make some higher-level decisions as a team. For example, paying bonuses. Many more decisions are made by staff in the course of their work (e.g., how can we address the inconvenience of a member who wants to use a tool that is broken), or at our weekly all-staff huddles by consensus (e.g., should we participate in a local STEAM event). If someone raises a concern, even if everyone else is in support, you'd better believe we want to hear what the nature of their concern is. What do they know that the rest of us don't?

Not everyone is able to participate in consensus decision-making effectively. If they don't agree with the mission, the guiding principles, and other guiding documents of the organization, they may view the right to block a decision as an opportunity to wield outsized influence over the group. Some level of education for both facilitator and meeting attendees is almost certainly required.

---

[8] If you want to go down a rabbit hole, there's a whole area of study around voting systems that maximize various measures.

Chapter 18

On-Boarding Members and Staff

Among the people we'll welcome to our makerspaces, members and staff will dominate our time. How we on-board them can pay enormous dividends down the road, since initial impressions and instruction will carry a lot of weight.[1]

18.1 Members

What are your goals for member on-boarding?

- Members are safe
- Members feel comfortable
- Members are efficient (know where things are and how they work)
- Members self-serve
- Members are aware of the policies and culture
- Members serve as resources to other members
- Members are ambassadors for the space
- Members know the values of the space
- Members feel they belong

The on-boarding process for members is informed by every element of the business perspective chart, from systems to values, culture, mission, and so on. It's unlikely your process will look the same as ours, but it will probably have elements such as the following:

- Staff-led in-depth tour (is it the same as the "I'm interested in seeing your shop" tour?)
- Member handbook (physical, online)

---

[1] Recall what we said earlier about providing feedback—we have a limited window in which to present information. Later on, it will be much harder to change people's behavior.

- Audio or video presentation
- Class (required or optional)
- Partner with experienced "buddy"
- "Scavenger hunt"[2]

Not everyone needs to (or wants to) know everything right off the bat, so combinations like a tour and handbook, for example, could cover most of the territory. What is that territory?

- Overview of how this makerspace works (makerspaces are new concepts to most people—bring everyone onto the same page)
- Your space's history/story (stories are compelling)
- Hours
- Types of membership
- Kids at the makerspace
- Contact information (including emergencies after hours)
- Safety rules (overall shop), including policies on what is made, what materials can used, etc.
- Rules/policies around tool use, including
    - Member's tools
    - Consumables & tooling
    - Reserving tools
    - Using tools for production or outside their normal use
    - Dealing with broken or dull tools or tooling
- Shop computers (e.g., installing new software)
- Internet, local data storage, other network policies
- List of your major tools (compatible consumables?)
- Using the space (e.g., tables, lockers, conference rooms, kitchen)
- Food in the space
- Ways of getting work done: do it yourself, hiring a consultant, hiring the work out, etc.
- Your local community of makers (e.g., meetings that happen at the shop, other local makerspaces, other local resources)
- Classes (not just "how not to kill yourself" classes)

---

[2]Yes, really. A nearby makerspace, I3 Detroit, requires applicants to complete a scavenger hunt to familiarize themselves with the shop, policies, and people. It is not trivial—the record for the fastest time is more than a day. It's really a DIY, in-depth tour, which is very much in keeping with the principles and culture of that makerspace.

18.1. MEMBERS

- Tours of the space
- Recurring and special events
- Renting (or licensing) space at the makerspace
- Teaching existing or developing new classes
- Opportunities to work (volunteer, paid) or help manage (e.g., board of directors)
- Participating in decision-making
- How to start your own makerspace (links to resources)
- Guests
- Operations not supported (e.g., production use, sanding, finishing, sandblasting, painting, chemicals, automotive, etc.)
- Privacy, photo/video
- Donating, loaning, trading, bailment[3] of tools
- Your mission
- Your vision
- Your guiding principles
- Cultural guides (e.g., Noisebridge's "Be excellent to one another"; Maker Works' "The Code")
- Agreements (e.g., membership, guest, renters, etc.)
- Applications (e.g., 24-hr membership, renting space, etc.)
- Map of buildings, neighborhood (including where to get food)

If this information is collected into a handbook of some kind, don't forget:

- Version or date of handbook (front or back cover)
- Posting (PDF) on website
- SOP for staff to order or print and bind more copies
- Periodic review to improve/update

This is a long list of things to figure out, so let us acknowledge the attitude "we'll cross that bridge when we come to it." Given all the work to set up a makerspace, there's something to be said for prioritizing the work of setting different policies. However, we'd suggest you would be well served by figuring out some of the important ones before the family of six (including a toddler) shows up at your door.

---

[3] Bailment is a formal way of loaning equipment. Definitely look into it as a way of creating clear agreements around "loaned" equipment.

18.2 Staff

You can copy and paste everything the member needs to know from above, and then we'll go from there. By the way, we've been fortunate to have most of our staff start out as members, so we already have a common language and understanding.

Our process for on-boarding staff begins with tryout shifts[4] to build familiarity and give both the new staff person and the organization an opportunity to see if this is a good fit. Our bias, as we discussed earlier, is to recruit staff that are excited about delivering great customer service; we'll give them the opportunity to pick up expertise on tools later on.

Our "passport" or new employee checklist will then lay out expectations for their first month or two with us. This will include attending classes, becoming certified to teach one or two classes, and so on. Because this is another form of the Training Compact, we do need to spell out exactly what the consequences of completing or not completing the passport are. It could be continued employment. It might be an increase in pay. It may be a title or position. But it should be clear to everyone what will happen if X or Y does or doesn't happen.

18.2.1 No Surprises

This seems like a good place for another very general principle, that of "no surprises." We have (probably) failed in our responsibilities as leaders if our staff are badly surprised by our actions. For example, if we have a staff person who isn't into using SOPs or doesn't believe in delivering great service and we need to let them go[5], it should never be a surprise to them or us. It should happen only after we have reminded them what the expectations are and, usually, provided them with an opportunity for modifying their behavior in a specific way by a specific time frame. (This should be in the form of a written agreement, just so everything is clearly spelled out.)

The new employee "passport", conveying the mission, vision, and guiding principles, and every other bit of sharing we do hopefully brings everyone on the same page and allows us to accurately convey our expectations and needs. And it's really okay if that's not a match right now for us and that staff person. Let's find it out early, and be clear from the start.

18.3 "Outside" Instructors

Non-staff instructors obviously don't need to know all the mechanics of the shop, but they do need to know our mission, vision, and values. And they have to buy into whatever systems we use, and the culture we wish to have.

We use instructors primarily for skill-development classes; our "how not to kill yourself" (checkout) classes we tend to teach using staff. (We're very concerned about the quality of checkout classes—they're often the initial experience a person has at the shop, and they form the basis for that person's use of that tool from that point onward.) Skill-development classes are optional, and usually build on the basic skills and operations we cover in the checkout class. These classes are usually supported by and related to equipment in the shop—welding, woodworking, etc. But sometimes we'll have something like paper making or leatherworking.

---

[4]They are of course paid.
[5]Euphemistically, "promote them to guest".

18.3. "OUTSIDE" INSTRUCTORS

Our instructors might have their own curriculum already, in which case they're the only one to deliver that class. Often we'll fund the development of a class, in which case the curriculum belongs to us and we can offer the class in the future should an instructor move or no longer want to teach it. We'll provide help in creating the class. Or the instructor may be stepping into a class we already have developed.

Whether or not the instructor had developed the class, we want them to go through our "How to Instruct" class, and probably sit in on some of our other classes to see how we'd like the class delivered. We'll have them deliver a test run or two to staff and friends. And we'll need to provide them with the basic information on things like how to get reimbursed for materials, how to turn in their hours to get paid, how to schedule classes, etc.

And even long after we've on-boarded an instructor, we'll ask class attendees for feedback, just like we do for all our classes.

Chapter 19

Challenges

Here are a few challenges waiting for a solution.

19.1 Checkout Classes

Let's take a tool like the traditional table saw. Even with safety features like an automatic blade stop (e.g., "SawStop"), there are plenty of ways to not use it right. So we're going to

- Pick a machine with safety features
- Add jigs and other accessories to make operations safer and easier
- Create SOPs for safe operation
- Create SOPs for how to teach the checkout class
- Check in with people to make sure they are operating safely
- And the other things we've described.

From the member's point of view, some of these are value-add (jigs, a good quality machine, safety features). The checkout class can be either value-add (we have, and you'll probably have, some members who only seem to be interested in taking the classes, not in actually making things) or "necessary but not value-add". But what about the time the member spends waiting for the class? If the member wants to create a bookshelf using the table saw, they have to either wait for a normally-scheduled table saw checkout class or, at least at our shop, they can request a class to fit their schedule. (If they are willing to have other people in it—that is, they aren't asking for a "private" class—and it is more than a few days out so we can potentially have other students, then it is the usual class price.) Either way, there's a barrier, a delay to getting what they want. Recall the first of our 3 steps for great customer service—we know what they want (to use the table saw), but they may also want to get started this afternoon. When we tell them the next class is next week, they haven't gotten what they wanted—the ability to use the table saw this afternoon.

We won't be able to get the member what they want every time. They may want a 1,000 watt laser so they can cut steel. (It's not in our budget.) But the general desire to have access to tools, quickly, does seem reasonable.

In a blog posting (now deleted), Dan Rasure wrote about how "TechShop 2.0" would be different from the original TechShop, which had just gone under. One of the points was "Training will be available everyday without waiting for a class to be scheduled."[1]

For the past year or so we've been trying to make it easy to request a class to fit the member's schedule, but the truth is that we can't offer what we really want—same-day access to tools, even if you have not used that tool before. Could we abandon having checkout classes—just have members use the SOP? That doesn't feel right, but on the other hand a lot of what we cover in class might be okay for the member to read ahead of time, or watch in a video. Could we get the amount of staff time to safely instruct a member to a much smaller amount than the 1–3 hours we do now, and be compatible with our guiding principles, systems, and culture? (Could Toyota and others get the die changing time for their stamping machines from 1–2 days down to minutes?) Suddenly, if the staff time required to verify a member can safely use a tool has dropped to 10 minutes, the whole equation has changed. (We'll still assume that somehow, the member is putting in time on a simulator, videos, reading, etc.) Quite a challenge, yes?[2]

19.2 From Checkout Class to On Their Own

Another challenge we face in our makerspace is the transition from the checkout class, where everything is standardized and laid out in an SOP, to the moment when the member is standing in front of the machine on their own, raw material in hand.

How to Instruct in a production environment can present and have the member try out the actual operation they'll be expected to do, perhaps in its entirety. In a makerspace checkout class, we're teaching the basic operations and safety issues, but typically the member's project will involve countless variations on the themes of the SOP.

How can we bridge the gap between the teacher-led checkout class, where the member does not have to plan out the sequence of operations, to the first "solo flight" where they must use the information they have and synthesize it to apply to their project? We've tried something we call "bridge projects". They are SOPs and prepared raw material that represent a well documented project. The member is encouraged to come in later on their own time (with a special 2-hour membership that is part of the class fee, for example) and use the bridge project SOP to complete the project on their own. This accomplishes two things. First, the member has used the SOP entirely on their own, without the instructor and other students there to prompt or guide. Second, the bridge project SOP, since it represents a complete project rather than the isolated operations of the typical SOP, can be a template for similar projects the member takes on.

---

[1] Dan Rasure, "Training will be available everyday without waiting for a class to be scheduled." https://www.techshop2.com/blogs/post/How-TechShop-2-0-will-be-different/ No longer available. Retrieved 12/16/2017.

[2] In July 2020 we started a project to see if we can shift some of the instruction to online learning, then have the member come in for a fairly short hands-on session. We'll let you know how it works out.

Chapter 20

Floobydust

> "Floobydust" is a contemporary term derived from archaic Latin miscellaneous, whose disputed history probably springs from Greek origins (influenced, of course, by Egyptian linguists) — meaning here "a mixed bag." — National Semiconductor Audio Handbook, 1976

Some of what follows comes from a document we wrote a number of years ago called "The N Laws of Makerspaces". (Ideally it would have been 7 Laws, but more kept getting added.) It included random observations about the reality of makerspaces that we hadn't realized when we started. To this we've added some other hints and wins.

- Everyone believes themselves an expert on how you should market, price, locate, and operate your space. They are often the people that will not show up to help paint or rip up carpeting.

- Once all the wood has been gathered for the bonfire, there will be plenty of people with lighters. The folks who helped gather the wood (the un-sexy jobs) are the ones to keep close.

- Do you have problems teaching your woodshop classes when all around you other members are making noise? (Why must woodworkers be so noisy? What's their deal? Chill out, people.) We've had some success with the instructor wearing a pilot's headset (headphones and boom microphone) with a little FM transmitter and an FM receiver (for feedback). Then each class member has an off-the-shelf WorkTunes or other FM receiving hearing protection. It doesn't solve the problem of the instructor hearing the student[1], but it makes it much nicer for everyone. (Except if the instructor has the sniffles.)

- Space is freedom to allow more activities. Keep space open. Clutter is your enemy. Members will fill all available space with their "temporary" storage. It is not "temporary," it will not be touched for years, but if you throw it out or use it, they will ask the next day where it went. Make your policies clear.

- If you can, having some flexible space is really useful. Our "conference" room is a meeting room, event room, staging area, temporary large project area, etc.

---

[1] Is this a problem, or a feature?

- There are many different types of members (business, hobbyist, artists). Each will value tools, cost, culture, environment, similar users, etc., differently. *You can not be everyone's ideal makerspace.*

- Very few people have enough time to rush.

- Time and money are great filters of people who say they want to help.

- An interesting test of a makerspace is what happens when you break a tool due to a mistake.

- How the space operates (open books, Lean, servant leadership, etc.) may be as useful a resource to members as the tools. Make these accessible.

- Measuring a process makes it more likely to improve.

- The voices you'll hear from membership are not always representative. It is easy to be swayed by the loudest voice or the most eloquent email, but these are not always a fair representation of everyone in the group. It is often useful to discount input proportional to how loud it is expressed, since they are often outliers.

- If you will have volunteers at your shop and you don't have experience coordinating volunteers, find someone at a large organization that has lots of success coordinating volunteers. It is really easy to get it wrong. Do we serve volunteers? Absolutely.

Appreciations and Acknowledgements

This book is the product of many years of being around some really wonderful people.

First, the staff and members of Maker Works are among the nicest, smartest people you'd ever hope to meet, and it is our honor to work with them each day. We're pretty darn lucky.

Steve Garran of Club Workshop in Denver generously allowed us to spend a day with him in July 2010, sharing how he operated his makespace and giving us the encouragement to start ours. We've tried to pass it along to the folks coming after us.

We deeply appreciate the work Dale Dougherty has done to bring makerspaces and making to a wider audience, and his enthusiasm and optimism. It's taken a while, but some of the stuff the three of us talked about in 2013 motivated us to start teaching the Makerspace Operations Bootcamp and eventually to compile this book.

Speaking of the Bootcamp, we've had the pleasure of talking about this content with a great group of current and prospective makerspace operators from all over the US. We took notes, and many of the improvements to this content are due to their great questions and input.

The Zingerman's Community of Businesses have been supportive and great neighbors to have. In the winter, you can see the path through the snow from our front door to the Bakehouse. Paul Saginaw, Maker Works member #0001, has always been in our corner. Maggie Bayless of ZingTrain helped us set up the first Makerspace Operation Bootcamps, sharing her experience in running many ZingTrain sessions.

Much appreciation to our families for their constant support and participation in this interesting experiment.

Thanks to the kind folks who read earlier drafts of this book and helped with great feedback, including Josh Williams, Larry Grover, Tim Huang, Daniel Grover, Becky Grover, and Pamela Cohen. Any errors you may have encountered are the authors'.

Finally, we appreciate the time you spent reading this book. Time is an incredibly valuable resource, and you just invested quite a bit in our scratchings. We hope at least some of the ideas are useful to you, whether in your local makerspace or in other areas of your life.[2]

---

[2] As a reminder, we welcome your "Liked Best and Next Time" about the book—send it to membership@makerworks.com. Thanks!

About Maker Works

Opening its doors in 2011, Maker Works is a 14,400 sq ft makerspace in Ann Arbor, Michigan. It features a full wood shop, metal shop (machining, fabricating, welding, CNC plasma cutter), powder coating, plastics, textile, jewelry, laser cutters, SLA and FMD 3D printing. It is organized as a for-profit LLC with the triple bottom lines of People, Planet, and Profit. Over 1,400 people have had paid memberships, and many hundreds of students in FIRST robotics and other activities have used the makerspace. A staff of about 10 (many part-time) serve the members and keep the space going.

Makerspace Operations Bootcamp

The Makerspace Operations Bootcamp is a week-long deep dive into the topics of this book, usually run 2-3 times each year since 2014. We hold it at Maker Works, so while there's class time, there's also actually experiencing the classes, working on machines, and in general seeing how a makerspace running with these ideas works. We even leave time on the last day for the bootcamp attendees to question a couple of staff members (Tom and Dale leave the room)—things like "Okay, they said they run the shop like this, but how does it really run?" It's a bit on the intense side (drinking from a fire hose), but in the end our criteria was what would we want to have known before we opened the shop. The 135-page course workbook was the outline for this book.

Our hope is that this book conveys some of the content of the bootcamp, but it's one thing to read about SOPs and another to use them to run a CNC router. If it's not reasonable to come to Maker Works for a week, maybe check out nearby makerspaces. Regardless of how they're run, you'll learn something about how a makerspace operates in the real world. If you already have a makerspace you're involved with, we hope we've given you enough concrete processes and ideas to try some experiments.

We're thinking about other ways of sharing the ideas of the intentional makerspace, and if there's interest in this book, we may follow up with some others. You can join our email list for notifications around makerspace operations at our website, www.maker-works.com.

Index

4 levels of competency, 117
4 levels of learning, 117
5S, 47
    area labeling, 74
    deadly wastes and, 52
    example standards, 52
    home tag, 64
    marking tool SOP, 70
    process tool SOP, 70
    red tag, 57
    SOP, 55
    tool address SOP, 61
8 Deadly Wastes, 162
    batching, 164
10-4 rule, 154
15-minute improvements, 21
43 folders, 123
80/20 Rule (Pareto Principle), 20
80/20 rule, finances, 176

A
access control, 135
accounting rules, 173
accrual accounting, 174
appreciation, 180
apprenticeship, 19
assets, 173

B
baking vs. cooking, 17
balance sheet, 173
batching, 164
Bottom Line Change, 176
    SOP, 177
bottom line(s), 78
bottom lines, 87
bridge projects, 190
business perspective chart, 77

C
cash accounting, 174
cash flow analysis, 174
cash registers
    face of earth, wiping from, 22
    interface, stupidity of, 22
    should be nervous, just saying, 22
checklist, 31
checkout classes, 189
classes, how not to kill yourself, 27
coin organizer, 21
competency, 4 levels of, 117
complaints, handling, 151
compliments, handling, 154
consensus decision-making, 181
cotton candy, 44
Cuisinart, hair by, 11
culture, 78, 137
    SOP, 137

D
Deadly Wastes, *see* 8 Deadly Wastes
decision-making, 181
diversity, 139
    is the solution, 140
DOWNTIME, *see* 8 Deadly Wastes
Drillinator 4000, 34

E
Effective Change Formula, 176
error proofing, 166
experience, 78

F
faux pas, Yuletide, 41
fix what bugs you, 21
flow (vs. batch), 165
flowchart, 32
freedom from, 15
freedom to, 15
Fremont Assembly plant, 159

G
Gantt charts, 44
gap, minding the, 140

genchi genbutsu, 128
General Motors (GM), 159
Ghanntt charts, *see* Gantt charts
Ghant charts, *see* Gantt charts
Ghantt charts, *see* Gantt charts
Google
    Drive, 134
    Sites, 133
Greenleaf, Robert, 172
guest, promoting to, 186
guiding principles, 78, 105

H
How to Improve, 127
How to Instruct, 109
    5-step plan, 111
    summary, 116

I
If the worker hasn't learned, the instructor hasn't taught., 112
Improvement Kata, 130
instructors, outside, 186
intentional, being, 20
ISO-9000, 26
items of significance, 44

J
Jefferies tube, 39
jig, 33
Job Instruction, *see* How to Instruct
Job Methods, *see* How to Improve

K
Kaizen foam, 55
Kant, Immanuel, 15
karakuri kaizen, 34
Kata in the Classroom, 132
K-Base (knowledge base), 133
key point, 30
knowledge base, 133
knowledge, threshold of, 133

L
leadership, servant, 171
Lean, 13, 159
learning vs. systems, 18
learning, 4 levels of, 117
Lego, 35
liabilities, 174
Liked Best, Next Time, 23
Liker, Jeffrey, 103

The Toyota Way, 161
local minima, trapped in, 22
lucre, filthy, 11

M
MacArthur, Gen. Douglas, 160
Maker Works
    about, 195
    corporate jets, 79
Makerspace Operations Bootcamp, 195
makerspaces
    key characteristics, 14
man, the, 15
meetings
    agenda, 126
    No-Magic Method, 127
    running effective, 125
member handbook, 165
mission, 78, 81
    creating, 85
mistake proofing, 166
monkeys, 127

N
nonprofit, 88
NUMMI, 159

O
onboarding, 183
    members, 183
    staff, 186
open book management, 13, 172
operations manual, *see* SOP
owner's equity, 174

P
pain prioritize, let the, 20
Pareto Principle (80/20 Rule), 20
perfection, enemy of good, 23
performance try-out, 114
Personal Protective Equipment (PPE), 169
pointy-haired boss (PHB), 110
poka-yoke, 166
poster, 34
profit and loss statement (P&L), 174

R
recursion
    infinite, 40
red tag, *see* 5S
reservations, 136
retail theater, 151

RFID access, 135
right thing, making it easy to do, 17
rope, pushing, 17
Rosie the Riveter, 13, 26
Rother, Mike, 131

S
safety, 167
    and reservations, 136
Safety, Principles of, 167
Saginaw, Paul, 22, 105
Savage, Adam, 44, 49
scheduling software, 136
scientific method, 131
servant leadership, 13, 171
service, giving great, 147
    3 steps, 150
    handling a complaint, 151
    why, 147
setup costs, 164
shock collar, 17, 23, 28, 110
single-piece flow, 164
SOP
    appearance, 29
    audio, 34
    cautionary lathe story, sad, 27
    cautionary rocket story, sad, 37
    checklist, 31
    clean binder, beware of SOP in, 37
    definition, 25
    exercise, 40
    flowchart, 32
    guidelines, 42
    how to write, 37
    improving, 44
    objections to, 27
    poster, 34
    SOP for writing, 37
    special purpose machine, 34
    template, jig, 33
    video, 34
Spreckley, Freer, 88
spring 2015
    causes of the war, 155
    important battles, 155
    running out of duct tape, 155
Standard Operating Procedures, see SOP
standard work, see SOP
Stereotype Threat, 139
stonecutters and the cathedral, 148
supervisors, skills required of, 155

surprises, no, 186
systems, 78
systems vs. learning, 18

T
template, 33
third place, 14
to-do lists, 44
Toyota, 159
Toyota House, 161
Toyota Production System, 13, 159
Tragedy of the Commons, 19
training compact, 16, 118
Training Within Industry, see TWI (Training Within Industry)
triple bottom lines, 87
TWI (Training Within Industry), 13, 155
    How to Improve, 127
    How to Instruct, 109
    results, 155

V
value propositions, 11
value-add, 143
    for staff, 144
values, 78, 105
    Maker, 105
vision, 78, 91
    elements, 92
    example, 102
    importance, 93
    SOP (group), 99
    SOP (solo), 96
    updating, 102

W
warp plasma distribution manifold
    cover removal, 39
Weinzweig, Ari, 92, 147
Why are you here?, 11
Willow Run, 26
wordless diagrams, 35
wrong thing, making it hard to do, 17

Z
Zingerman's, 13
    3 Steps to Giving Great Service, 150
    Bottom Line Change, 177
    Community of Businesses, 20
    Effective Change Formula, 176
    Mail Order, 20

mission, 82
training at, 97
Training Plan Questions, 111
triple bottom lines, 88
ZingTrain, 92
4 Levels of Learning, 117
The Art of Giving Great Service, 147

Selected Quotes for Makerspaces

Page numbers in parentheses.

Make it easy to do the right thing, and hard to do the wrong thing.[3] (17)

You can't push a rope. (Dale's Dad) (17)

Ask "Why are you here?" (11)

Watch for "freedom from" vs. "freedom to". (15)

It is "continuous improvement", not "continuous change". (16)

Never underestimate the ability of a motivated member to do the wrong thing if that's what they set their mind to. (18)

Is it a failure to learn on the part of the member, or a failure of a system? (18)

Consistency is a necessary condition for continuous improvement. (20)

In many cases, 80% of the effects come from just 20% of the causes. (20)

Fix what bugs you. (21)

You never run out of problems, but as you improve you get more interesting problems. (Paul Saginaw) (22)

The best is the enemy of the good. (Voltaire) (23)

In the absence of SOPs, members will take up all your staff time. (26)

An SOP that no one is allowed to improve is about as useful as a knife that no one is allowed to sharpen. (28)

The harder an SOP, jig, template, etc. is to change or modify, the more likely it is that you'll need to. (Consequence of Murphy's Law.) (33)

The non-negotiable part is that we'll have an SOP; the negotiable part is the form it takes. (Tom) (35)

Beware the SOP in a clean binder. (37)

When there's a problem, ask if there is a change to the SOPs or other systems that could prevent this from happening in the future. (18)

You don't get to claim credit for reducing the waste of an operation that isn't value-add or necessary. (47)

---

[3]Everything else is just commentary.

In the absence of 5S, you might succeed in finding a tool, but you'll never know if you put it back in the correct place. (49)

If you can't see it, you don't have it. (Adam Savage) (49)

Avoid drawers and doors! (49)

For-profit or nonprofit, it's still a business. (88)

The most costly machine you can have in your shop is a free/donated old CNC machine. (88)

It is the responsibility of leaders to make sure there is a clear, shared vision for the makerspace. (92)

In the absence of a unified vision, everyone will have their own. (94)

No one has enough time to create a mediocre vision. (96)

Your vision should surprise everyone in at least one aspect. (102)

A guiding principle is a best practice that you'll do even if it costs you. (via Paul Saginaw) (105)

You should not underestimate the ability of people to project their own viewpoint and values onto any situation. (107)

SOPs are necessary for instruction and improvement. (109)

Asking someone to learn something may not be the best solution to a situation. (109)

We get one best chance when the learner is open to learning. (111)

If the worker hasn't learned, the instructor hasn't taught. (Training Within Industry) (112)

If we expect the member to act on something, it must be in the SOP. (112)

When is the best time to correct errors of understanding? Now. "Now" is always the best time to provide feedback. (114)

In the class and on their own, using the SOP is part of the SOP for using the tool. (115)

Teaching is the ultimate level of learning. (118)

Did person X follow the SOP for Y? That's all we ask. (120)

The meeting facilitator is a servant of the group. (125)

A task without a person and a deadline is just a wish. (127)

"Genchi genbutsu"—go and see the actual situation, not just think about it at a desk. (128)

Everything from the customer point of view is either 1) value-add, 2) necessary but not value-add, or 3) neither. Do more of 1, optimize 2, and eliminate 3. (143)

Experiments allow us to expand our threshold of knowledge; the Improvement Kata uses experimentation and the scientific method to solve problems outside our current knowledge. (133)

You don't get to choose if you'll have a culture. But you can choose what culture you want to have and work to create it. (137)

Diversity is a solution, not a problem to solve. (The Diversity Project) (140)

Makerspaces tend to be relational vs. transactional operations. (135)

What complaints should you handle? All complaints, even if they don't have anything to do with you. (Zingerman's) (151)

At the core of Lean/TPS is the idea of maximizing value to the customer while minimizing waste, and that this is a process that will never be done but is instead a journey of continuous improvement. (161)

The TPS has the following goals: To produce the best quality, at the lowest cost, with the shortest lead time, and the best safety and morale. It promises sustainable efficiency. (162)

The 8 Deadly Wastes: Defects, Overproduction, Waiting, Not Utilizing Talent, Transportation, Inventory, Motion Waste, Excess Processing. (Lean) (162)

Batching is usually not the best approach. (164)

Mistakes are inevitable—we're just humans. But we can have a goal to eliminate *defects*—mistakes that make it to the customers. (Toyota Production System) (166)

Safety is the product of the systems, culture, and guiding principles of the organization. (167)

Servant leadership says our priority is the development and well-being of staff, and the flow of service is toward the front-line staff and the member. (171)

Every moment brings an opportunity to serve. (171)

Spend 20% of your meeting time on the past, and 80% on your preferred future and how to get there. (176)

Resistance to change is proportional to the amount of dissatisfaction around the issue, the presence of a vision for a better future, and the existence of a reasonable first step. (Zingermans) (176)

When there are significant changes in an organization, it may get harder before it gets better. (ZingTrain) (178)

It is indeed costly (in time and money) to train staff, and would be unfortunate if they left after we trained them. But it would be worse if we didn't train them and they stayed. (Tom) (97)

We have (probably) failed in our responsibilities as leaders if our staff are badly surprised by our actions. (186)

Everyone believes themselves an expert on how you should market, price, locate, and operate your space. They are often the people that will not show up to help paint or rip up carpeting. (191)

Space is freedom to allow more activities. Keep space open. Clutter is your enemy. (191)

You can not be everyone's ideal makerspace. (192)

Very few people have enough time to rush. (192)

Time and money are great filters of people who say they want to help. (192)

An interesting test of a makerspace is what happens when you break a tool due to a mistake. (192)

How the space operates (open books, Lean, servant leadership, etc.) may be as useful a resource to members as the tools. Make these accessible. (192)

Measuring a process makes it more likely to improve. (192)

The only mistake you can make is not following the SOP. (203)

Value delusional optimism! (1-203)

Colophon

This book was initially outlined in Scrivener. Once most of the structure was in place, the text was imported into Lyx, which provides a nice GUI for producing LaTeX for the typesetting. All software was run under Mac OSX.

The font used is Bitstream Charter.

We believe in the Oxford Comma, and as for our decision to put punctuation outside quotation marks, we apologize. But, it's intentional.

Made in the USA
Monee, IL
17 October 2023